Underwater Cultural Heritage

Underwater Cultural Heritage investigates cases of underwater cultural heritage, exploring ethical issues that have never been studied before. A vast cultural heritage lies beneath the sea, including the archaeological remains of more than three million vessels, as well as historic monuments and whole cities. In addition, climate change, population growth and current events around the world mean that new underwater cultural heritage is being created faster than ever before. It is, therefore, essential that the ethical issues related to the management of such heritage are considered now, especially as decisions made now will bestow the heritage with a value and will establish legal frameworks that could be used either to protect or harm underwater heritage in the future.

Considering a range of challenges related to underwater cultural heritage—including preservation, management, use, sustainability, valuation, politics, identity, human rights and intangible heritage—the book presents case studies that both illustrate the key ethical issues and also offer possible solutions to help navigate such challenges. The book will also explore the various legislative instruments protecting underwater cultural heritage and emphasise the importance of revising and updating legal frameworks, whilst also taking into account ethical concerns that may expose cultural heritage to more serious menaces.

Underwater Cultural Heritage draws on case studies from around the globe and, as such, should be of great interest to academics, researchers and students working in heritage studies, archaeology, history, politics and sustainability. It should also be appealing to heritage practitioners and policymakers who want to learn more about the issues surrounding not only management of underwater cultural heritage but management of cultural heritage in general.

Elena Perez-Alvaro holds a PhD in Cultural Heritage from the University of Birmingham, UK, and an LLM in Maritime and International Law from University of London, UK. She is the founder and Managing Director of the consulting firm Licit Cultural Heritage.

Routledge Studies in Heritage

www.routledge.com/Routledge-Studies-in-Heritage/book-series/RSIHER

Underwater Cultural Heritage
Ethical Concepts and Practical Challenges

Elena Perez-Alvaro

Routledge
Taylor & Francis Group

LONDON AND NEW YORK

First published 2019 by Routledge

2 Park Square, Milton Park, Abingdon, Oxon, OX14 4RN
605 Third Avenue, New York, NY 10017

Routledge is an imprint of the Taylor & Francis Group, an informa business

First issued in paperback 2020

British Library Cataloguing-in-Publication Data
A catalogue record for this book is available from the British Library

Library of Congress Cataloging-in-Publication Data
A catalog record has been requested for this book

ISBN: 978-1-138-60614-2 (hbk)
ISBN: 978-0-367-72967-7 (pbk)

Typeset in Sabon
by Newgen Publishing UK

To my Kais and my Lanis
You know who you are

Contents

Figures

Tables

Foreword

Once upon a time there was a galleon called *Heritage* that during the course of a long journey was forced into fighting unexpected battles.

The ship prepared her expedition with the hope of a safe trip. She was ready for it, trusting on the main traditional principle for the management of underwater cultural heritage: in order to be protected, *Heritage* has to be preserved. For this, she was armed with a powerful navigation tool: the 2001 UNESCO Convention on the Protection of the Underwater Cultural Heritage.

However, the ship did not expect to suffer a series of adversities: the ethical challenges. As a consequence, and since our galleon was not ready to encounter these unforeseen difficulties, *Heritage* was vanquished, sank and became a shipwreck.

This book expects to respect this shipwreck by identifying these enemies, properly evaluating them under an ethical perspective and categorising the key concepts in the field of underwater cultural heritage.

Our shipwreck, *Heritage*, will be, from her grave at the bottom of the ocean, a beam of light to learn from her misfortune, to overcome previous mistakes, to manage underwater cultural heritage and to apply this management to many other disciplines, all for the benefit of mankind.

Acknowledgements

For advice and support, I would like to thank Dr Aznar-Gómez and Dr Carman whom I found brilliant and inspirational in their ability to point me in the right direction in every state of my research.

Thanks to Dr Gonzalez-Zalba, Mr Manders and Dr Forrest for letting me include in this book part of our researches together.

Thanks to Elsevier, Cambridge University Press and Nova Science for giving me author's right to replicate some of my articles as chapters in this book. I would also like to thank Titanic Museum Branson, MO. & Pigeon Forge, TN., Climate Central and Mr Kourbaj for granting me rights to reproduce their images.

And last but not least, special and humble thanks to my friends and family who have made me who I am.

Part I

Introducing underwater cultural heritage

1 Introduction

Management efforts for the protection of underwater cultural heritage have mainly been directed to fight against treasure hunters. However, other legal, unexpected menaces threaten this heritage which can only be protected by establishing ethical debates and updating the legal instruments. These legal instruments seem to drive the heritage management process rather than to provide support for it and only by challenging them with new ethical discussions, underwater cultural heritage will be protected.

Imagination and dramatic mystery compensate for the absence of direct experience of the underwater cultural heritage (Maarleveld, 2009: 97). On the evening of 11 October 1982, this absence of direct experience changed for the general public: the hull of the shipwreck *Mary Rose*, sank in 1545, was raised from the shallow sea bed near the port and towed into Portsmouth Harbour (Fenwick and Gale, 1998). The shipwreck had previously been carefully studied and analysed and most of her objects on board retrieved and conserved by archaeologists. On the evening of the rising, over 60 million people watched the longest outside broadcast yet undertaken: the *Mary Rose* emerging (Stirland, 2013). The shipwreck, today a museum, can be seen by all: ghost shipwrecks lying at the bottom of the oceans were no longer in need of imagination. The mystery was dispelled.

However, before there was systematic archaeology and long before there was systematic underwater archaeology like the one undertaken by the archaeologists in the *Mary Rose*, there was a respected and lawful but very different cultural attitude to shipwrecks. This was the idea of salvage: a wreck was a valuable object, to be recovered if it can be, for the treasures it gives up being sold and for the salvors being rewarded for their risk-taking and success. Later, underwater cultural heritage became so valuable for archaeologists and heritage managers for three main reasons: first is that when archaeologists started researching those underwater sites they realised that they were what has been defined as 'unique time capsules' (McKee, 1982). This means that they provide an insight into the past because the remains are preserved often in a perfect condition, due to a protective covering of sediment (Hoffmann, 2006). Unlike most dry-land sites, wreck-sites are protected against humans and bacteria by the ocean sludge that guards them. As a consequence, we often find materials under water that on land would have usually disappeared a long time ago: wool, wood, bone, leather or canvas. On land, Pompeii is a famous archaeological example of the rare situation where we have intact vestiges captured and preserved from a single moment in time (Fenwick and Gale, 1998): by contrast, it is common in the case of a shipwreck, to have examples of some of these materials to study. This is why shipwrecks are so valuable and therefore their preservation and study such an important piece for heritage managers and archaeologists: the variety of the materials offered to archaeologists and historians provides them with valuable knowledge. The second reason is that shipwreck sites do not only feature the vessel itself, often a once-magnificent artefact, but also often hold cargo, personal items, tools, utensils, and human remains. This offers a complete picture of past human civilisations. The final reason is that the study of sunken vessels is essential to history because entire continents have been discovered, colonised, invaded and defended by sea: the products of all civilisations have been carried by water. As a consequence, as an effort to protect such an important source of information, archaeologists and heritage managers have directed their fight against the old attitude of salvage without archaeological record and to mitigate human damages, like treasure hunters. For Dean et al. (1996) what is not underwater archaeology is salvage, treasure hunting and souvenir collecting. However, Bederman (1999) claims that underwater cultural heritage is being managed in only one way: by the stands of only one community—archaeologists—without consideration for the interests of other users. As Coroneos (2006: 121) points out, 'bad' archaeology and treasure hunting is not the only ethical issue when managing and underwater cultural heritage and reducing the ethics in maritime archaeology to treasure hunters is to misunderstand the whole concept of ethics (Flatman, 2007b: 141). Therefore, the real threat is sticking to that old discourse of lost treasures and not to look ahead for future menaces. The prevention of these menaces can only be taken by analysing the facts, creating ethical debates and offering legal solutions. This book adopts an approach to heritage being understood as something that can be formed and negotiated challenging the general assumptions about the 'goodness' of heritage (Lixinski, 2015).

The next three sections will define the three pillars where our hypothesis stands on: underwater cultural heritage, ethics and law. The last section will examine the nine case studies that will be reviewed in this book.

Underwater cultural heritage

There is often confusion in the literature between maritime heritage, nautical heritage and underwater cultural heritage. According to the Australasian Institute for Maritime Archaeology,[1] maritime heritage includes ships and shipwrecks, maritime identities and landscapes, seascapes, wet or dry sites including ship burials, shipwrecks buried in reclaimed land, maritime infrastructure sites (such as jetties, harbours and lighthouses), indigenous fish traps or shipwreck survivor camps. It is all the material related to human interaction with the sea. Nautical heritage includes more specific heritage: just the one related with the ship. Underwater cultural heritage is the heritage located underwater, regardless of their connection to the sea: this is why it includes shipwrecks sites, but also sunken cities, refuse sites, aircraft wrecks or jettisoned objects. This book will be mainly devoted to underwater cultural heritage although sometimes it will include references to maritime heritage, such as shipwreck survivor camps or harbours.

As said, the importance of the study and protection of underwater culture heritage is undeniable since a 'vast cultural heritage lies beneath the sea' (Smith and Couper, 2003: 25). According to the 2001 UNESCO Convention on the Protection of Underwater Cultural Heritage (UNESCO, 2001), there are archaeological remains of more than three million vessels lying in the oceans around the world. There are parts of fleets such as the Spanish Armada of Philip II; there are also historic monuments now under water, such as the Lighthouse of Alexandria or whole cities such as Port Royal, Jamaica; the old Carthage, in North Africa; and the temples of Mahabalipuram and Dwarka in India. In fact, Smith and Couper (2003) state that all the material proof of human activities is evidenced on the sea bed. In addition, new events bring us new underwater cultural heritage. For instance, the protection of World War II underwater cultural heritage will have other kinds of heritage to preserve, such as aircraft carriers containing thousands of planes, helicopters or whole military bases, created before World War I and developed during and after the Second (Ireland, 2010). There will be all kinds of legacy that those wars have left for us, not only under water but air (aeroplanes, hangers or airfields), land (hospitals or camps), sea (navigation and submarine), or interfaces (ports and harbours). And new shapes of undiscovered form of heritage: for instance, Ford (2013) studies the reuse of vessels as harbour structures. The author describes how vessels lost their original function (transportation) and were transformed into barracks, prisons, hospitals, store ships or hotels. Those ships, however, were never intended to be permanent structures. They ended up sailing to other ports or being sunk and destroyed. However, the ships left in these harbours remain in existence: cans, syringes, pots and all kinds of objects that can carry archaeological interest. In opposition to shipwrecks navigating and scattering the remains of life on board around the world, these semi-permanent structures left full archaeological fields in the same spot. Shore whaling stations is another example of new heritage: these were locations where whalers set up on shore for capturing whales by shore-based boats. Then the whales were processed on shore for oil and whalebone (Prickett, 2002). The living quarters for whalers, the industrial components, the boats, the portable items such as glass or ceramics are all maritime archaeological evidence which may have mostly disappeared, but that gives an idea of a complete different culture. These two cases are what this book names as 'invisible heritage': the heritage that was once there, then disappeared but left its footprints behind.

Shipwrecks are the main focus of this study since, as Strati (1995) maintained, of all the underwater archaeological sites, shipwrecks are the most important in terms of their number, volume and variety. They also offer all kind of ethical issues for their condition of mobility and because their nationality is complex and creates ambiguities. In addition, shipwrecks are important not only for the vessel, but also for the cargo: works of art, architectural components, sarcophagi, marble blocks, minerals, amphorae and also mundane things, such as ballast or items carried by crew and passengers. O'Keefe and Nafziger (1994) list differences between various kind of underwater cultural heritage associated to shipwrecks: wreck (property loss at sea that may or may not come ashore), derelict (abandoned property at sea), flotsam (property loss at sea but afloat), jetsam (sunken goods thrown overboard to lighten or save a ship) and lagan (buoyed jetsam marked or identified and later recovery). Likewise, wrecks are not only found at sea but, due to maritime routes or sea battles, they are also left on the beds of rivers. As a consequence, their study would allow us to research all kind of material, objects, situations and circumstances. A less scientific reason attracts people to shipwrecks: they are mysterious and in fact they have raised stories and films such as *Robinson Crusoe, Titanic, The Life of Pi, Odyssey in ancient Greece* or *Poseidon* to name but a few.

There have been different periods and types of ships and ventures and in almost all of them we have preserved shipwrecks (Pickford, 1994): the Vikings, the Chinese junks, the Levantine trade, the Armada, the Spanish plate fleets, the pirates and privateers, the East Indiamen, the Age of Revolution, the Rush for Gold, the Liners or the World Wars' ships. Unimagined ships have sailed the waters: the *Vrow Maria*, for instance, was a shipwreck that sank in 1771 with several works of art from a collection in Amsterdam (Pickford, 1994). In addition, ships carried on board crew and passengers from numerous nationalities: in the *Titanic* shipwreck, people from more than 28 countries died, carrying their personal belongings. Therefore, all manner of shipwrecks can be found lying on the bottom of the ocean: from battleships (Lorenz, 2010) to passenger ships or cargo ships. Each one of the types has different objects carried aboard depending on the vessel: merchant (cargo), warship (cannon balls), passenger ships (crew, passengers, slaves) or exploration vessels (telescopes, glass, etc.) Some authors state that a ship, in fact, can be a miniature floating city (Pringle, 2013: 802). In addition, each wreck has a story (Smith and Couper, 2003). As Maarleveld (2009) defends, the ship, the goods and its complements have widespread cultural backgrounds and they are linked to different areas and communities and to their exchange.

How a ship becomes a shipwreck is, according to Gibbins and Adams (2001), driven by two motives: catastrophic shipwrecks (that are formed after a crisis event) and intentionally deposited or abandoned (which could be those that have been recycled or transformed). However, how shipwrecks are found is a mystery. Fenwick and Gale (1998) assert that some wrecks have always been known: they can be around harbours or rivers. Some of them are found from the records of ship losses that were made because the ships were of economic importance. Some others would appear on the news or on the naval court-martials; some of them are captured on paintings by artists and some wrecks are discovered by chance; and some of them appear by remote sensing surveys such as echo sounders and sidescan sonar.

The figures of sunken ships are difficult to calculate. According to the shipwreck registry,[2] only in the year 2013 there were more than one hundred ships wrecked around the world. If the amount is multiplied from the first years of navigation thousands of years ago, the number of shipwrecks is unimaginable. Gibbins and Adams (2001) state that in the Mediterranean region there are 1,189 shipwrecks catalogued dating before 1500 and according to Keith (2000), a minimum of 9,600 shipwreck sites worldwide have been discovered and reported and worldwide 10% of these discovered and reported shipwreck sites have been extracted. In fact, Dromgoole (2004) stated that it is now possible to recover material from 98% of the world's total seabed using current equipment. Consequently, shipwrecks once too deep to reach have become accessible and vulnerable to human interference. The famous *Titanic* is a good example: once lost in the vast depths of the ocean it has now been precisely located and can be routinely reached by modern deep-ocean exploration craft (Dromgoole, 2004).

However, for some authors such as Nafziger (1999), underwater sites are unnatural, since wrecked vessels do not belong *in situ* to the sea bottom but rather to their home ports and intended destinations. The author claims that the site of a wreck is fortuitous and as a consequence they do not need to be preserved nor their remains respected. This line of thought was developed before maritime archaeology existed and the sea bottom was already explored by other actors (Maarleveld, 2011: 925).

The oceans, today, are exploited by three main actors and their uses: transport and communication (including military uses), users of marine resources, and non-material users of the oceans and coasts such as underwater research, education or tourism. In this last use, the research of underwater cultural heritage (archaeological and non-archaeological) occupies an important place. Archaeology is the study of material culture to gain knowledge about human behaviour: it is the knowledge obtained from the relation between material cultural (data) and non-material human activity (interpretation) (McGimsey III, 1984). In the specific case of underwater archaeology, this study of the material is essential for its interpretation. This is because a wreck is an entity, a site (Villegas-Zamora, 2008: 20) and the position and inclination of the objects provide crucial data. In addition, inside a ship, we have cargo and contents, fixtures and fittings such as anchor or cannons, minor structures such as decks or masts and major structures such as hull and ribs. To get information from these sites, it is important to understand the pre-wreck nature of a ship, the wreck event and the subsequent salvage, if there is one (Gibbs, 2006). As a consequence, as McGimsey III (1984) remarks, the facts in archaeology are only the artefacts and the locations. The rest are hypotheses and theories: these theories convert the artefacts into heritage. This is why archaeology and heritage are concepts intrinsically linked: heritage is discovered, analysed and researched by archaeologists and heritage becomes heritage when archaeologists bestow it with a value—and the law recognises it. However, underwater—or maritime—archaeology is still a nascent discipline: it started to develop just after World War II. According to Gibbins and Adams (2001) maritime archaeology first started with divers who learned to be archaeologists and land archaeologists who learned to dive and finally academically qualified professional maritime archaeologists. But the discipline it is still facing new challenges and new threats.

Maarleveld (2011: 924) identifies four different traditions on maritime archaeology: Mediterranean or classical—more focused on the comprehensive survey—northern European or prehistoric—with more emphasis on display rather than on research and on geological and stratigraphic data—archaeology focused on cultural resource management, and archaeology focused on maritime historical exploration. The four have their own ways of thinking but all share the same ethical dilemmas. These dilemmas are even more complicated because of the fact that management of underwater cultural heritage needs to be a multidisciplinary domain: just to mention some, it comprises some of the techniques of land archaeology, it requires some knowledge of oceanography (for the chemical composition of water or the study of currents and water temperature), history (shipwrecks disclose important information on the study of maritime routes, naval architecture, battles, among others), heritage (shipwrecks are considered monuments, pieces of art, part of the heritage of a community, a country or a culture), law (the delimitation of the water or the protection of the heritage play an important role on the construction of the sense of underwater heritage) and, of course, ethics. This multidisciplinary domain is essential to understand this book: politics, identity, tourism, history, memory, colonialism, pollution, diplomacy, sustainability, sociology or human rights will be concepts continuously applied to underwater cultural heritage in these pages. Therefore, archaeology cannot be seen as an isolated discipline as different branches are in juxtaposition to archaeology when awarding a value to an object (Aplin, 2002). To overlook this juxtaposition will lead to the emergence of dilemmas which are difficult to resolve. In the specific case of underwater cultural heritage, Baker (1998: 17), for instance, highlighted the great number of interests involved in the study and valuation of a shipwreck: a technical historian will study the vessel's shape, an archaeologist will record the cargo and passengers, a salvor will look at the items which can be economically valuable and an oil company will see them as an obstruction to a proposed pipeline. In this regard, Kingsley (2011) emphasises the wide scope of industry on the sea, from the expander regime of exploration of sea resources to construction of submarine cables that the management of underwater cultural heritage cannot hog (Perez-Alvaro, 2013). However, the study of archaeological sites is important since as Werner (2013) defends human history owes a great deal to maritime activities: 'in any preindustrial society, a ship was the largest and most complex machine produced' (Muckelroy, 1998: 23). For this reason, maritime archaeology should be a primary focus of man: not for the study of objects for their own sake but for the insight they give to people (Werner, 2013). This is one of the main goals of this book, not the study of specific objects but its significance from a sociological point of view: shipwrecks were vehicles of communications and trade (Gibbins and Adams, 2001) and as a consequence they were influential in the mental ideologies of different cultures. In contrast with land archaeological sites that are more related to a national cultural identity, a ship embodies much greater diversity to the history of many countries and cultures and carries out unique cultural values (Smith and Couper, 2003). The drama of a shipwreck focuses on the even, but the conditions and consequences arising from the wreck are as relevant as the event itself. As Maarleveld (2012) asserts, underwater cultural heritage is 'international' heritage which stands out for its international significance.

Ethics

This work deals with ethical problems raised in underwater cultural heritage field but which are common to land heritage management. As Maarleveld (2011: 917) expressed 'maritime archaeology is part of the heritage field that is extremely well suited for the fine-tuning of ethical debate in archaeology'. The reason for it may be that since the field of underwater archaeology is still developing, new fresh dilemmas arise. In short, the process of awarding values to an object or a place for it to become heritage is an ethical process by which it is decided what is worth preserving for humanity to enjoy it and what can be ignored or destroyed. These decisions will shape the identity, emotions and memories of all. This book will examine new ethical concerns on the management of cultural heritage that has arisen from and in the development of the underwater cultural heritage field. Although the ethical debate has largely been discussed on land heritage, as Flatman (2007a) defends, these ethical dilemmas central to land archaeology have still not been solved by maritime archaeology such as ownership, treatment of human remains, the relative cultural significance of a site or the 'heritage offset' (acceptable levels of damage if they provide a broader social benefit). However, land heritage has also something to learn from the new debates raised from underwater heritage. In fact, ethics in archaeology face the same issues than other disciplines such as medicine, physics or education. Ethics may be complex and conflicting since, as Colwell-Chanthaphonh et al. (2008) claim, ethical dilemmas usually arise when there is a disagreement. Wylie

(2003) defines ethics as a set of standards that guides action and tells you what you should do. According to Maarleveld (2011: 918) ethics is about reflection on what is good and bad and on what is right or wrong. In this regard, for the author, respecting other views is as important as being aware of one's own position: it must not be seen as 'the way things have always been done'. Maarleveld (2011: 918) also claims that ethics aspires to solve situational dilemmas: can be implicit and unspoken and different groups can have different ethics (Manders, 2012). The main problem of ethics is that they are mutable and cultural and they cannot be negotiated. In fact, archaeology and in general all sciences, are developing and moving into new realms, with fresh debates on new dilemmas (Maarleveld, 2011: 919). Ethics in archaeology matter because they have influential decisions for the future of the heritage (Colwell-Chanthaphonh et al., 2008). However, we cannot forget that archaeology comes from collecting (Colwell-Chanthaphonh et al., 2008): there was first an *ethos* of antiquarianism, then an *ethos* of science and finally an *ethos* of scholarship. In fact, it by the mid-1950s, some agencies defined minimum standards and after the destruction by World War II it was aimed at safeguarding heritage by protocols. However, in the 1970s the illicit trade was expanded due to global networks of looters. In the 1980s there was a concern for public outreach and archaeologists had to recognise that they were but one group among multiple publics. In the 1990s, indigenous group started to have influence on the debate on human remains, grave goods, sacred objects and objects of cultural patrimony (Colwell-Chanthaphonh et al., 2008). Therefore, the ethics around archaeological objects have continuously changed.

Ethical challenges are very common when managing cultural heritage, as in the case of the sale of some paintings by Andy Warhol (sold by $81, 9 millions) (Sánchez, 2014). The seller was a governmental German bank property who used the sale to cover a financial gap: in fact, an administration member of the bank said 'a piece of art has value when is sold'. The same situation happened in Portugal when the State wanted to auction 85 Joan Miró paintings:

> [...] Christies cancelled the disputed sale of 85 paintings and other works by the 20th century Catalan master Joan Miró only hours before bidding was due to open. Tension had been building ahead of the London auction as opposition politicians and art lovers in Portugal took legal action to prevent the Lisbon government from selling off the artworks to recoup state assets sunk into the nationalisation of a failed bank.
>
> (Wise, 2014 [online])

Reyes (2014) highlights other ethical controversy: the story of an eagle that was part of the stern of the *Graf Spee*, once one of the most modern battleships in the world. It was recovered by private investors and could fetch millions of dollars at auction—was a symbol of the German Third Reich—with Uruguay being the rightful owner but the salvage company getting 50 percent of the profits if sold. The salvor said that 'this kind of controversial piece sells well'. Another ethical dilemma that will be explained later in this book is also well known: during the process of the case of Odyssey Marine Exploration against the Spanish Government in the wreck of the *Nuestra Senora de las Mercedes*, Peru and twenty-five alleged descendants demanded Spain, claiming to be the legitimate owner of the Spanish Crown's cargo, since Peru was part of Spain in 1804. However, Spain claimed that Peru was Spanish territory (Aznar-Gómez, 2010). Flatman (2009: 7) identifies other ethical concern which is involving the military-industrial organisation on underwater archaeological practices: for instance in Spain the divers from the Spanish Navy will substitute the underwater archaeologists since they affirm to have more training under water (San Claudio, 2013). However, archaeologists claim that the Navy is not prepared for carrying out archaeological research. In this line, it is also very controversial the use of sea lions to help explore wrecks as it has been suggested by divers (Macdonald, 2008: 11): this rises issues of use and experimentation of animals. Cockrell (1998: 91) explores an ethical conflict similar to the use of ancient lead for particle physics experiments: the *SS Central America* discovered in 1989 was found to have beer and soft drink cans lying on the seabed. The chief scientist thought that those cans could help to kill human cancer cells, and suggested their recover, with no interest in the heritage, but rather for humanitarian reasons. The scientific interest of pre–World War II steel from historical submarines and battleships has also transcended its historical interest to be used in medical research: 65 tons of steel from USS Indiana, scrapped in 1962, was used for shielding at an Illinois Veterans Administration hospital, and another 210 tons went into building a shielded room for *in vivo* radiation measurements at a Utah medical centre (Lynch, 2007, 2011). Steel salvaged from Scapa Flow shipwrecks were also used in low radiation detectors (Butler, 2006).

Underwater cultural heritage can also be controversial for being a threat: some shipwrecks are dangerous for the high level of munitions that they still contain since some of them may contain unexploded bombs or some jars can have material that exposes archaeologists and divers (Smith and Couper, 2003). In this regard, and according to Spalding (2014), the World War II shipwrecks account for 75% of the known sporadic or continuous leakages of oil and other hazardous materials from vessels on the seafloor: they may contain as much as 140 million barrels of oil. And these wrecks are experiencing metal fatigue, failure and collapse, resulting in leakage of oil, fuel, unexploded ordnance, and toxic chemicals. These may be solved with in-situ bio-remediation, stabilising metals by using anodes and hot tapping the ships to remove their oils and fuels. However, some of these shipwrecks are watery graves of those who died on board or some others are artificial reefs for different species of fish. Disturbing them to control the leak of oil and fuel could disturb both human remains and fish. And disturbing human remains is a constant topic of controversy when managing cultural heritage. For instance, some documentary makers recovered artefacts from a wreckage (Dougan, 2014) and the Chinese community in Australia accused them of disturbing the underwater graves. Some relatives claimed that 'it is important for the Chinese custom that the family gives a good grave to their ancestors' (Cheer, 2014). For them, the shipwreck is more than a shipwreck: it is a graveyard (Dougan, 2014).

Dunnell (1984) classifies all these ethical challenges in management of cultural heritage in three kinds: the ones that have just been raised, the ones that rose a long time ago but have not been solved and the new ones that are established in new facts. This study adds a fourth one: moral issues that only arise because of interference with the legislation. The first kind of ethical dilemmas is moral issues that have just been raised: for instance, the topic of the use of underwater cultural heritage, not for economic purposes but for experimental scientific purposes, like particle physics experimentation, for the benefit of humanity. The choice is between protecting the past and developing the future. And if we choose the latter, which kind of experiments are worth destroying underwater cultural heritage for? Only experiments for knowing about the future? Only experiments for medical research? Or should any kind of technology also benefit? But also, moral issues around the use of underwater cultural heritage for political ends, as in the South China Sea. Money laundering selling underwater cultural heritage objects is also an issue that is just raising. Secondly, there are moral issues that rose a long time ago but which have not been solved: for instance, the management of human remains and the dichotomy between the age limit for protecting underwater cultural heritage—under the 2001 UNESCO Convention, shipwrecks and human remains underwater for more than 100 years—and the respect for those recent human remains with living descendants. Why a deceased sailor's skeleton that died on board of the *Mary Rose*—which sank more than 400 years ago—is exhibited in the museum and how a sailor of the *USS Arizona*—sank around 50 years ago—is honoured every year by his family. The recovery of underwater cultural objects by treasure hunters or the return of cultural objects that were part of a cargo from colonised countries are still unsolved issues. The third kind of moral issue is that one established in new facts: the protection of underwater cultural heritage *in situ* might be the best option now but if seas are changing due to climate change and the shipwrecks are in *peril* there must be a point where we need to deal with the preservation and conservation before we lose them all. Maybe it is necessary to choose what to preserve, how to preserve it and if preservation *in situ* is still the safest and best way for the shipwreck's conservation. Migrant shipwrecks are also an old issue established in new facts: the comparison with slave ships and its new shape as illegal immigrants' boats make this moral issue a challenging ethical controversy. Finally, it is possible to differentiate moral issues that only rise because of the interference with the legislation, as in the violin of the *Titanic*, a symbolic object, not part of the archaeological site, but part of a collection, that has not been protected because it falls outside the definition of 'underwater for more than 100 years' has been sold and is in hands of a private owner.

Although both disciplines—land and underwater—are linked and share some ethical concerns, as Forrest (2003) states, underwater cultural heritage differs from terrestrial cultural heritage in a number of ways. Firstly, underwater cultural heritage is often very well preserved usually for the layers of sedimentation underwater; as said, this intact preservation is not the general rule for land heritage. Secondly, in the case of shipwrecks, the wreck and its contents have the same time reference, improving their contextual interpretation. Thirdly, the nature of the marine environment dictates the use of techniques and tools differently from those used by archaeologists in terrestrial excavation: in fact, the equipment needed for a deep-sea excavation is extremely complex and expensive and is often unaffordable by governments. This point is of highly importance because it establishes the reason why the economic value of underwater cultural heritage is more defendable than the economic value of terrestrial heritage for some groups: in addition, the chance of finding fortunes underwater is greater. Fourthly, maritime cultural heritage has the possibility of finding common stories of migration by sea, interracial and intergender ships, and cultural intermixing economies since there were many nations in just one ship. Finally, underwater archaeology is a relatively new scientific discipline and it is now developing: the basis that we will set for this discipline on our time will be the guidelines for its preservation for the future generations.

As a consequence, the risks threatening underwater cultural heritage preservation are new (Flatman, 2009: 5) and as a consequence there is a need of new approaches. As Tarlow (2006) announces, positing new cases is fundamental, but complex and controversial and although accidents are trying to be minimised (Villegas-Zamora, 2008: 21), ethics involve a continual examination. Having a code of ethical principles such as the 2001 UNESCO Convention and not reviewing it, will not solve the inevitable conflicts (Colwell-Chanthaphonh et al., 2008).

Law

Carman (1995, 1996, 2005) introduced the idea of the law as 'gatekeeper', where the material is first 'marked' worthy of legal coverage, then it is 'recategorised' and given a value under the law and final valuation awards it with a new value. As a consequence, the law becomes a tool to change the moral status of the material and to change the way in which the material is understood. In fact, Maarleveld (2012) claims that heritage is what society chooses to protect by law and administration. The law, as a consequence, should be seen as a vector by which moral changes are made to material (Carman, 1996). It is the law what shapes what is heritage by defining and protecting it and the 2001 UNESCO Convention it is the best example of this. With no laws, there can be no heritage (Carman, 2013a) since the law is important to the development of the idea of preserving material from the past. As Carman (2013a) reveals, legislation has a valuable role on the definition, identification, preservation and protection of the heritage: it gives value and meaning to archaeological remains. This contrasts with the attribution of values to define the heritage. For instance, the Last Supper Room in Jerusalem is sacred for Christians and respected—but used—by Muslims and Jews. No law protects it or preserves it but it has been a shrine for 2,000 years now. For this reason, Carducci (2006: 68) claims that the cultural specificity of an object is intrinsic while the legal specificity is not given automatically but only if the authorities deem it appropriate. As a consequence, for the author, legal protection is only granted to objects that have been already given a cultural value. On the contrary, in June 2014 archaeologists discovered a 5000-year-old pipeline in Western Iran (Holloway, 2014) but it is excluded and not considered 'underwater cultural heritage' under the 2001 UNESCO Convention because the Convention states in Article 1 that '(b) pipelines and cables placed on the seabed shall not be considered as underwater cultural heritage'. In this regard, Prott and O'Keefe (1984) had already discussed the relationship and controversies between heritage and law from a legal point of view, setting the legal principles before the heritage ones, as Carducci (2006) maintains. Lixinski (2015: 211) claims that the relationship between heritage law and heritage studies is not straightforward and that heritage studies are moving towards a rejection of law because of its 'definition' role on heritage. However, for the author, a rejection of heritage law would be a mistake since they both have the same interest: the protection of heritage. As a consequence, Lixinski claims that the two bodies have to work together. However, and as Cheek and Keel (1984: 206) remark, 'if there is a need of legal decision, the court will consider only legal issues, not cultural, religious or scientific values'.

It is not the purpose of this book to review the different legislation—national or international—in relation to underwater cultural heritage. However, this section will look at the concept of 'law' applied to heritage and will sum up the main regulations—maritime and on heritage—in order to have a general picture when the case studies identify the main gaps on the legislation that opens up the ethical discussion.

Legal protection of underwater cultural heritage is always a combination of both international and domestic regulations. Since in general national legislations on the protection of underwater cultural heritage are very limited (Aznar-Gómez, 2004), it is necessary to seek international arbitration to solve most disputes. Specifically, when a dispute arises from a foreign shipwreck found in international or national waters, international legislation plays the most important role (Aznar-Gómez, 2004: 24). As Dromgoole (1999) considers each State has different economic and cultural priorities, so the rules on the protection of the heritage vary. Only with an international regime underwater cultural heritage can be protected. However, international laws are binding only upon the States that have ratified and cannot be enforced against individuals or agencies unless they are part of national laws (Carman, 2013b) although states have the obligation of applying domestically those international agreements (Aznar-Gómez, 2004). In addition, as Dromgoole (1999) claims, international developments in law can have positive influences in national legislations: reasons for not ratifying an international legislation can be because of lack of resources, because they already have similar laws, because it challenges particular national interest, because they cannot be enforced or because there are Western approaches that cannot match other practices and beliefs. 'International law today offers a seriously deficient legal framework for the protection of maritime patrimony' (Aznar-Gómez, 2004: 23), an statement that Forrest (2002a) believes: that the pillaging and desecration of underwater cultural heritage is the absence of a single and punitive regime. However, creating a legal framework for the protection of underwater cultural heritage is a difficult task for different reasons such as the definition of the term, the decisions on what is worth preserving, the prioritisation of values and awarding a range of importance to the heritage or taking decisions for the future generation even by not knowing what future generations want.

The 2001 UNESCO Convention and the 1982 United Nations Convention on the Law of the Sea (UNCLOS, 1982) are both products of their epochs and as a consequence they pursue different goals. At the time of drafting UNCLOS, maritime archaeology was what the 1972 Convention concerning the Protection of the World Cultural and Natural Heritage (UNESCO, 1972a) called a 'nascent discipline' (UNESCO, 1972b) and as a consequence UNCLOS did not give any real importance to this heritage, although it referred to it in two articles. In addition, it was a law to protect the sea, not a law to protect the heritage and this differentiation is detrimental to the heritage: for instance, for the protection of heritage it is important to distinguish between the owners of the hull and the owners of the cargo (Pickford, 1994) but the rights and responsibilities get blurred when dealing with it because of the maritime zones defined by UNCLOS (Maarleveld, 2011). As a consequence, their goals are not related (Aznar-Gómez, 2004).

Maritime laws and law of the sea

Laws applied to the seas are not thought to preserve the heritage: sea laws have private interests and heritage law is important for its public dimension (Maarleveld, 2011). This legislation of the sea is translated into more than 60 international conventions, relating to maritime issues since 1884, dealing with rights of navigation, working conditions of sailors, shipping, the slave trade, fisheries conservation, environmental protection, and commercial exploitation of seabed resources (Elia, 2000). However, the most important tool for legislation of the sea is the 1982 United Nations Convention on the Law of the Sea (UNCLOS, 1982). Currently there are 130 parties to this Convention. The Convention divides the international waters into a number of zones with different legal regimes: territorial seas, contiguous zone, continental shelf, Exclusive Economic Zone and deep seabed (Area). According to the territorial principle every country has control over its territorial sea: it exercises sovereign immunity in its part of the sea. However, international waters are governed by the legal principle of 'freedom of the high seas' (Dromgoole, 2013). Most of the shipping lanes—and as a consequence most sunken vessels—are located in international waters, where no state can claim sovereign jurisdiction (O'Keefe, 1996). Since the territorial sea area extends only 12 nautical miles from a state's land out to sea, there is a vast area of sea beyond this boundary with a wealth of shipwrecks technically of 'no one'. International law implies that sunken state vessels—for instance, warships and vessels on government services—regardless of location, remain the property of the state owning them at the time of their sinking, unless it explicitly and formally relinquishes its ownership (Aznar-Gómez, 2010). They are like embassies: they remain their countries' ownership no matter where they are. However, on the high seas the applicable principle is the freedom of the high seas for research and recovery of shipwrecks although the cultural or historical precedence of the ship should be taken into account.

The UNCLOS Convention refers to underwater cultural heritage in only two articles: 149 and 303. The main conclusion of this agreement is that states are obliged to protect archaeological and historical objects found in the sea. However, both articles are vague and ambiguous (Forrest, 2002a) and open a legal vacuum (Aznar-Gómez, 2010). Article 149 reads:

> All objects of an archaeological and historical nature found in the area shall be preserved or disposed of for the benefit of mankind as a whole [...]

However, for Scovazzi (2006) the main problem is Article 303 that is where the 2001 UNESCO Convention faces its main obstacle:

> Article 303.1. States have the duty to protect objects of an archaeological and historical nature found at sea and shall cooperate for this purpose.
>
> Article 303.2. In order to control traffic in such objects, the coastal State may, in applying article 33, presume that their removal from the seabed in the zone referred to in that article without its approval would result in an infringement within its territory or territorial sea of the laws and regulations referred to in that article.

For Scovazzi (2006) it seems that the sanction 'removal' from the sea bed means that the object could be destroyed in the very place and would not be infracting any law. It is the case, for instance, of the case of pipelines constructors or some treasure hunters. A second problem of the article for the author is the no clarification of the regimen of the archaeological objects found on the continental shelf or the exclusive economic zone, leading to a 'first come, first served' approach.

The 2001 UNESCO Convention on the Protection of the Underwater Cultural Heritage

On 2 January 2009 the 2001 UNESCO Convention on the Protection of the Underwater Cultural Heritage came into force and at the time of writing (2018) 47 States have ratified it (UNESCO webpage[3]). Maritime power such as the United Kingdom and the United States abstained or voted against the adoption of the Convention (Aznar-Gómez, 2010) and some countries have indicated that they will apply the Annex but they will not become party to the Convention (O'Keefe, 2013). The Convention came before the discipline had the time to develop. In land archaeology, it was the other way around: the discipline developed for years and eventually a regulation to protect it was created. In the case of underwater cultural heritage there was insufficient time for that. Therefore, the legal instrument left vacuums in valuing, managing and protecting the underwater cultural heritage.

The issue of the definition of the term 'underwater cultural heritage' is the most problematic one, since, the term 'traces of human existence' has been criticised as being too broad (O'Keefe, 2002, 2013). Article 1 of the Convention reads:

> 'Underwater cultural heritage' means all traces of human existence having a cultural, historical or archaeological character which have been partially or totally under water, periodically or continuously, for at least 100 years [...]

The criteria for the definition were at the end both temporal and of significance. Although the United States proposed a definition 'of historic or archaeological significance', there was no consensus and the time-limit was finally decided (Boesten, 2002). The interest of the United States was more for recent heritage and the time-limit excluded, for instance, the remains of World War II. In fact, according to Juvelier (2016), the decision to make 100 years a cut-off date was arbitrary, and also for purposes of administration since some national legislation, as international instruments, included 100 years on defining underwater cultural heritage. For Forrest (2002a) this justification for the age depended on the use of that age by other national and international laws and conventions, like the 1972 UNESCO Convention Concerning the Protection of the World Cultural and Natural Heritage (UNESCO, 1972). Therefore, the time-limit became the main filter of the Convention. In this sense, two main issues arise: first, a definition under the term of a limit of years is focused more on the object, and not on the information we can obtain from it so this definition is more of a concept of the history of art and less of an archaeological one. Second, the time limit does not allow an interpretation on the definition and significance and as a consequence values cannot be bestowed: without a time-limit, definition could be based on values, and those being awarded by the characteristics of the site or object and/or the interest of that site or object for a community, a State or the international public. For instance, the United Kingdom does not use a minimum age of protection of the underwater cultural heritage, but it is based on an assessment on their significance, and in 2012 the Netherlands followed this practice (Manders, 2012b). Manders et al. (2012) observe that although the 2001 UNESCO Convention set the limit on 100 years, the reality and managing underwater cultural heritage is that some sites must be treated more significant than others (Manders et al., 2012). The problem, however, is that the definition gives a blank preservation (Aznar-Gómez, 2004). Maybe the solution would have added a clause on the Annex to include sites or objects of special relevance that have been submerged less than 100 years old, such as the *USS Arizona* or the violin of the *Titanic*. In fact, Forrest (2002a) proves that in the early drafts of the Convention there was an article that recognised that the State Party could designate traces of human existence as 'underwater cultural heritage' even if they had been under water for less than 100 years. However, the article was not finally included.

According to some authors, (O'Keefe, 2002; Aznar-Gómez, 2010; Forrest, 2002a) there are some more weaknesses in the Convention: the vague definition of underwater cultural heritage; issues of ownership and abandonment; question of warships and other state-owned vessels and the determination of the geographical scope of the Convention. In fact, the wording of the definition was very controversial. Forrest (2002a) claims that the terms 'under water', 'culture' and 'heritage' are susceptible to different interpretations. The author explores how the definition of 'cultural heritage' is too general and creates problems of interpretation: if the definition has been made as a list, it would narrow the items to be protected but if it was as general as it was in the 2001 UNESCO Convention, it would to be considered just a guide. As a consequence, the definition cannot determine what underwater cultural heritage is but only what is protected under the Convention. Forrest (2002a) also introduces a new idea: that the broad definition is due to the environment in which the cultural heritage is found rather that what constitutes underwater cultural heritage (Forrest, 2002a). For some authors, however, the value in the definition 'having a cultural, historical or archaeological character' tries to introduce the 'valuable' requirement so a bottle of Coke, for instance, will not be protected by the Convention (Manders, 2012b). Instead, Bederman (1999) questions the term and insists that the definition is so broad that it stretches to all underwater traces of human existence and as a consequence he maintains that the Convention is 'extravagant and unworkable' (334). He states (1999: 333) that it 'falsely equates age with historical significance'.

Another controversial conclusion of the Convention is the rejection of commercial recovery of underwater cultural heritage, since it is incompatible with its preservation. In fact, the Convention was adopted mainly for the protection of underwater cultural heritage from salvage and spoiling, which was largely neglected before on an international level. Since underwater cultural heritage was in danger of natural as well as human threats when the Convention was drafted, it established a legal system of protection to avoid specifically those menaces. As O'Keefe and Nafziger (1994) stated, the Convention was motivated to avoid further spoliation of the common heritage at sea and as a consequence, governments would defy the 2001 UNESCO Convention by working with commercial archaeologists (Kingsley, 2011). In fact, for Forrest (2002b), this rule eliminates recognition of the economic value of this heritage and the principle of co-operation between such interest groups such as scientific institutions, archaeologists and divers. The UNESCO draft was proposed by lawyers rather than archaeologists and commercial treasure salvors were not consulted and for this reason, for Fletcher-Tomenius and Forrest (2000) the 2001 UNESCO Convention did nothing to resolve the conflict between archaeologists and treasure salvage community since according to those authors treasure salvage companies also have the right to access underwater cultural heritage. For this reason, for Fletcher-Tomenius and Forrest (2000) prohibition of salvage is going to be ignored by salvage companies. The elimination of this group with interest in the underwater cultural heritage on the principle of cooperation means that UNESCO put all its egg in one basket, this is, only States can perform activities on the underwater cultural heritage (Kingsley, 2011).

Another issue of the 2001 Convention was the compatibility with other international bodies of law. For Maarleveld (2008) the Convention reconciles international sea laws with the principles of mutual respect: since heritage is of public interest, needs to be accessible and of public ownership. In fact, the 2001 UNESCO Convention does not supersede UNCLOS: Article 3 of the 2001 UNESCO Convention states that

> [...] nothing in the Convention shall prejudice the rights, jurisdiction and duties of States under international law, including the United Nations Convention on the Law of the Sea. So the Convention shall be interpreted and applied in the context of an in a manner consistent with international law including the United Nations Convention on the Law of the Sea.

However, if the 2001 UNESCO Convention acts in the shadow of UNCLOS, and both conventions conflict in some issues, it means that the UNCLOS Convention supersedes the UNESCO Convention in detriment of the underwater cultural heritage. For instance, UNCLOS Article 303(3) specifically preserves the law of salvage in the various maritime zones to which it applies. Likewise, UNCLOS lists:

Article 311. *Relation to other conventions and international agreements.* [...].

2. This Convention shall not alter the rights and obligations of States Parties which arise from other agreements compatible with this Convention and which do not affect the enjoyment by other States Parties of their rights or the performance of their obligations under this Convention. [...]

6. States Parties agree that there shall be no amendments to the basic principle relating to the common heritage of mankind set forth in article 136 and that they shall not be party to any agreement in derogation thereof.

Despite (or, as a consequence of) those two articles for Forrest (2003) it is clear that the more recent treaty (the 2001 UNESCO Convention in this case) will take precedence over the former relating the same matter. The author concludes that, accordingly, no conflict may be found between the two conventions. Although this may be true, the present commentary insists that even if the two conventions do not contravene each other, they do not complement each other either and as a consequence it opens a legal vacuum that greatly threatens the protection of underwater cultural heritage. In addition, for some authors (Fletcher-Tomenius and Williams, 1999), the 2001 UNESCO Convention contravenes the European Convention on Human Rights (European Convention on Human Rights, 1953) since every natural or legal person is entitled to the peaceful enjoyment of his possessions. They believe that the 2001 UNESCO Contention creates a presumption of abandonment of title unless the owner can rebut and this presumption of abandonment would mean that there is a transfer of ownership.

Lixinski (2015) observes that in heritage studies scholars generally do not distinguish between binding and non-binding instruments and as a consequence do not understand the difference between those who are just 'a code of practice'—such as the 2001 UNESCO Convention—and ones that are binding international law and that breaching them brings legal consequences—such as the 1982 UNCLOS Convention. However, although the 2001 UNESCO Convention on the Protection of the Underwater Cultural Heritage is a code of practice, it is not easy to change and it is naive to think so (O'Keefe, 2002): it took years to approve it. However, it is worth remembering that this Convention has an Annex that opens possibilities to improve and it does not have funding, which facilitates the possibility of updating it. The 2003 UNESCO Convention for the Safeguarding of Intangible Cultural Heritage (UNESCO, 2003), for instance, which has funding and does not have any annexes would be almost impossible to modify. The 2001 UNESCO Convention has a real possibility of more easily adapting its precepts if that benefits the preservation of underwater cultural heritage. Because, as Bederman (1999) asserts, the Convention failings are both systemic—ignoring the rights of other sea actors—and philosophical. In addition, as Kingsley (2011: 224) believes, management of underwater cultural heritage faces 'inadequate financial resource and a lack of creativity'. This book will try to tackle this lack of creativity by raising new challenges and proposing new solutions for the management of this heritage.

Chapters of this book

Valuation: the violin of the Titanic

This chapter studies common objects that have gained prestige as heritage items via a process of recognition of various values by different stakeholders: historical value by museums, emotional value by the media, and economic value—gained because of the existence of the other values—by auction houses. The chapter will focus on how objects are valued in order for them to become 'heritage' items. Issues such as the definition of 'underwater cultural heritage', management, tourism, memory, access, context and the intangibility of heritage will also be explored. The violin of the *Titanic*, an instrument that was sold at an auction house for £1.1 million, is not recognised as being part of our underwater cultural heritage under the 2001 UNESCO Convention, because it has not been underwater for more than 100 years. The law, as a consequence, has determined that it is not considered part of underwater cultural heritage. However, museums and auction markets, through their management, have given it the value of a 'heritage' item. The movie industry has also played a role in enhancing its value through harnessing emotions and planting a false popular memory.

Uses: ancient lead for dark matter experiments

Ancient lead (from shipwrecks that are more than 100 years old) is being used for experiments in dark matter detection, which is controversial for two main reasons: the uses that would have justified the destruction of this part of the heritage, and the amount of information lost depending on how carefully it is recovered. The chapter will look at the different uses of underwater cultural heritage, but also at issues such as sustainability, management, its benefit to humanity, its context, and cooperation between different users. It also posts the dilemma of using heritage for uses other than simply its value. The simple explanation is that ancient lead is considered to be part of our underwater cultural heritage but it is needed by physics laboratories and the microelectronics industry, which means that it is being retrieved either by archaeologists—after an agreement—or by salvage companies. The issue is whether any of these options are legal and if they could pose a problem for archaeologists. Using it would destroy it forever.

Preservation: climate change

Climate change will eventually create more underwater cultural heritage—as some places will be submerged by water—but it will also destroy many at the same time—due to changes in currents or chemical changes. If the seas are changing and underwater cultural heritage is in *peril*, then there must be a point where we need to deal with their preservation and conservation before we lose them forever. Perhaps it will be necessary to choose what to preserve, how to preserve it and which preservation method will be the safest and best way to do this. This chapter will look at how climate change can and will affect every material that can be found at an archaeological site, but it will also look at issues of valuation of the heritage, management, context and pollution issues. In addition, the chapter proposes the qualification of underwater cultural heritage as a natural resource for its preservation, establishing the same protection measures against climate change. Seas are changing, and climate change may affect not only the marine environment but the various items of our cultural heritage lying at the bottom of the sea.

Sustainability: preservation in situ

In the realm of archaeology, preservation *in situ* is usually the first option but it is not always the preferred or even the only option. Sustainable management will guarantee both its preservation and its accessibility to the public. Although tourism always brings an element of risk, there are some facets of tourism that can bring heritage items closer to the public without damaging them. Now would be a good time to test the '*in situ* preservation' options and offer new solutions. The chapter will focus on sustainability and management of underwater cultural heritage, but will also look at its uses, context, access and of course tourism. The reason for this preservation *in situ* is mainly because archaeological objects are better preserved under layers of mud and in saline water. However, continuous threats may challenge this option, such as climate change, and it is therefore necessary to consider different preservation options and their accessibility and availability to the public.

Intangibility: watery graves

The chapter deals with ethical issues concerning the protection of human remains contained in underwater cultural heritage sites. In this regard, it looks both at shipwrecks that still harbour human remains and those where the remains have disappeared but were once there. In addition, it deals with the definition of the term 'underwater cultural heritage' by the 2001 UNESCO Convention and the lack of recommendations by legal instruments for the treatment of these remains. This chapter will analyse issues such as intangible heritage, the politics involved in the management of this heritage, controversies with tourism, identity, human rights and access to these watery graves by the public against the wishes of the descendants of those whose remains are still resting there. The establishment of respect for the deceased or development for the future faces complicated moral questions. It creates tension between tradition and science (Teague, 2007). This chapter hopes to fill the legal and ethical gap on the topic as well as offer solutions by introducing three concepts applied for the first time to human remains depending on cultural attitudes: absent, invisible and intangible heritage.

Identity: nationless shipwrecks

Some shipwrecks that are lying at the bottom of the sea went down when the world was a very different place to what it is today. Some of those shipwrecks belong to areas that have since been colonised, states that do not exist today, or territories that are now under the sovereignty of a new country. This is the case, for instance, of Spanish galleons that sank that contained cargo from Latin American territories. This chapter will analyse the controversies around 'territorial provenance' and will look at the debate on the return of cultural objects found on board those shipwrecks. This will bring different issues for discussion such as politics, identity shaping, human rights, restitution of the material, colonialism and the use of diplomacy to solve these controversies. Shipwrecks have complicated legal status, not only because of their location but also because of issues such as diplomatic immunity, property of cargo or the possible conflicts of interest that may arise if the shipwreck and the cargo are of different nationalities. The solutions to these controversies are intricate—only returns on a case-by-case basis will lead agreements between countries.

Human rights: migrant shipwrecks

Refugee shipwrecks are on everyday news and it seems to have little or nothing to do with underwater cultural heritage. However, taking a closer look, the issue seems to be a continuation of the slave trade which also led to many shipwrecks. Not just the sea voyage, but also the overcrowded boats, the race and ethnicity of the victims, the fatalities due to shipwrecks and the human and legal neglect of the immigrants/slaves once they reach land are just some of the reasons for this comparison. This chapter will allow us to examine the concept of human rights applied to underwater cultural heritage. It will focus mainly on three aspects: human remains; refugee shipwrecks; and rescue, disembarking and cultural heritage of the shipwrecks. These interlocking concepts of cultural heritage and human rights are not easy to separate. Tensions between the values of different communities create conflicts between rights, since some attempts to preserve the human rights of some groups threatens the human rights of other groups. Underwater cultural heritage preservation may contravene the rights of those less fortunate in society, such as immigrants or slaves. Heritage professionals need to face up to heritage issues which may not be mysterious, idyllic or attractive but may help to unlock some issues that society may be facing, such as the protection of slaves' and immigrants' shipwrecks.

Politics: the South China Sea

Cultural heritage has been continuously used by political groups to shape the identities of some communities. Cultural heritage is a physical representation to intangible concepts such as sense of community or belonging (Smith, 2004). How heritage is managed or interpreted will have an impact on how that heritage will be subsequently understood by the community. That is a power that policy makers will have to use in order to reach political goals. This is the case of the cultural heritage of the South China Sea. The Chinese government has been using underwater cultural heritage to shape and adapt their history to suit their particular ambitions. As a consequence, international dilemmas have been raised by other countries whose underwater cultural heritage also lies at the bottom of the South China Sea. This use of underwater cultural heritage indicates that it is being used as a weapon to further territorial and political aims. The interpretation of this heritage rewrites history and becomes an essential tool for political and international strategies.

Other practices: treasure hunters and money laundering

Shipwrecks have always been a lucrative target for treasure hunters who sell salvaged objects in order to make a profit. This has created conflicts with archaeological policy makers who consider the archaeological benefit of underwater cultural heritage to be the overriding pre-eminent value. As a consequence, legal efforts have been directed towards refraining from commercial exploitation of this heritage, by targeting treasure-hunting companies who salvage this material without consulting archaeological records. However, the exploitation of underwater cultural heritage seems to have infiltrated illegal business activities such as money laundering or terrorism financing. This chapter will try to identify the techniques used for the transformation of underwater cultural heritage into a commodity to be bought and sold on the black markets. Underwater cultural heritage is being used as a tool to threaten international security.

Conclusions

The general debate on ethical aspects on the management of underwater cultural heritage does not offer solutions. For this reason, it is necessary to reset some terms and to build new concepts. At the end of the day, our actions towards the management of the cultural heritage will set a precedent for the future. This work is a complex task because, as Dunnell (1984: 62) observes,

> it is a presumptuous and intimidating task to write on any moral issue within archaeology […] since it is impossible to argue rightness and wrongness without offending nearly everyone almost all of the time.

However, just because these issues are not addressed in the literature, it does not mean that they do not exist. The only solution is facing them, approaching the facts and raising the debate. This book has been written in the shape of different subjects that raise issues concerning the management of underwater cultural heritage such as valuation, uses, preservation, sustainability, intangible heritage, identity, human rights, politics or other practices. The result is a series of topics intertwined but in a clear structure of subdivisions for the reader's convenience. Raising ethical dilemmas that threaten the management and preservation of underwater cultural heritage is a work in progress. New ethical dilemmas will raise, with new discussions to take and new solutions to propose. Legal instruments can help to solve the issue, but there is still a need to find answers in disciplines other than archaeology and law. Collaboration between fields of study is essential to preserve our underwater cultural heritage.

Notes

1 Australian Institute for Maritime Archaeology. Available at: www.aima-underwater.org.au/what-is-maritime-archaeology/.
2 Worldwide Shipwreck Database: International Registry of Sunken Ships. Available at: www.shipwreckregistry.com/index.htm.
3 UNESCO Convention on the Protection of the Underwater Cultural Heritage. Legal instruments. Available at: www.unesco.org/eri/la/convention.asp?KO=13520&order=alpha.

Bibliography

Aplin, G. (2002). *Heritage Identification, Conservation and Management*. Oxford: Oxford University Press.

Aznar-Gómez, M. J. (2004). *La protección internacional del patrimonio cultural subacuático con especial referencia al caso de España*. Valencia: Tirant Lo Blanch.

Aznar-Gómez, M. J. (2010). Treasure hunters, sunken state vessels and the 2001 UNESCO Convention on the Protection of Underwater Cultural Heritage. *International Journal of Marine and Coastal Law* 25(2): 209–236.

Baker, W. A. (1998). The technical importance of shipwreck archaeology. In Babits, L. E. and Van Tilburg, H. (eds.), *Maritime Archaeology: A Reader of Substantive and Theoretical Contributions*. The Plenum Series in Underwater Archaeology. New York: Springer: 17–21.

Bederman, D. J. (1999). The UNESCO draft convention on underwater cultural heritage: a critique and counter-proposal. *Journal of Maritime Law and Commerce* 30(2): 331–354.

Boesten, E. (2002). *Archaeological and/or Historical Valuable Shipwrecks in International Waters: Public International Law and What It Offers.* The Hague: T.M.C. Asser Press.

Butler, D. (2006). *Distant Victory: The Battle of Jutland and the Allied Triumph in the First World War.* Wesport, CT: Praeger Security International, 229.

Carducci, G. (2006). The growing complexity of international art law: conflict of laws, uniform law, mandatory rules, UNSC resolutions and EU regulations. In Hoffman, B. (ed.), *Art & Cultural Heritage: Law, Policy & Practice.* Cambridge: Cambridge University Press: 68–86.

Carman, J. (1995). The importance of things: archaeology and the law. In Cooper, M., Firth, A., Carman, J. and Wheatley, D. (eds.), *Managing Archaeology.* London: Routledge: 19–32.

Carman, J. (1996). *Valuing Ancient Things: Archaeology and Law.* Leicester: Leicester University Press.

Carman, J. (2005). *Against Cultural Property: Archaeology, Heritage and Ownership.* London: Duckworth Debates in Archaeology.

Carman, J. (2013a). A heritage of conflict, and conflicts of heritage. In Bergerbrant, S. and Sabatini, S. (eds.), *Counterpoint: Essays in Archaeology and Heritage Studies in Honour of Professor Kristian Kristiansen.* Oxford: Information Press: 747–753.

Carman, J. (2013b). A heritage of conflict, and conflicts of heritage. In Bergerbrant, S. and Sabatini, S. (eds.), *Counterpoint: Essays in Archaeology and Heritage Studies in Honour of Professor Kristian Kristiansen.* Oxford: Information Press: 747–753.

Cheek, A. L. and Keel, B. C. (1984). Value conflicts in osteo-archaeology. In Green, E. L. (ed.), *Ethics and Values in Archaeology.* London: Free Press: 194–207.

Cheer, L. (2014). Shipwreck that became a sunken tomb for 500 Chinese miners is discovered more than a century later off the coast of New Zealand. [online]. *Daily Mail.* 25 November 2014. Available at: www.dailymail.co.uk/news (accessed 5 March 2018).

Cockrell, W. A. (1998). Why Dr Bass couldn't convince Mr Gumbel: the trouble with treasure revisited, again. In Babits, L. E. and Van Tilburg, H. (eds.), *Maritime Archaeology. A Reader of Substantive and Theoretical Contributions.* The Plenum Series in Underwater Archaeology. New York: Springer: 85–96.

Colwell-Chanthaphonh, C., Hollowell, J. and McGill, D. (2008). *Ethics in Action: Case Studies in Archaeological Dilemmas.* Washington, DC: Society for American Archaeology Press.

Coroneos, C. (2006). The ethics and values of maritime archaeology. In Staniforth, M. and Nash, M. (eds.), *Maritime Archaeology: Australian Approaches.* New York: Springer: 111–122.

Dean, M., Ferrari, B., Oxley, I., Redknap, M. and Watson, K. (eds.) (1996). *Archaeology Underwater: The NAS Guide to Principles and Practice.* London: Archetype Publications.

Dougan, P. (2014). Outrage over "lack of respect" shown to *Ventnor* shipwreck. [online]. *The New Zealand Herald.* 24 November 2014. Available at: www.nzherald.co.nz/nz/news/article.cfm?c_id=1&objectid=11363495.

Dromgoole, S. (ed.) (1999). *Legal Protection of the Underwater Cultural Heritage: National and International Perspectives*. London: Kluwer Law International.

Dromgoole, S. (2004). Murky waters for government policy: the case of a 17th century British warship and 10 tonnes of gold coins. *Marine Policy* 28(3): 189–198.

Dromgoole, S. (2013). *Underwater Cultural Heritage and International Law*. Cambridge Studies in International and Comparative Law 101. Cambridge: Cambridge University Press.

Dunnel, R. C. (1984). The ethics of archaeological significance decisions. In Green, E. L. (ed.), *Ethics and Values in Archaeology*. London: Free Press: 62–74.

Elia, R. (2000). US protection of underwater cultural heritage beyond the territorial sea: problems and prospects. *International Journal of Nautical Archaeology* 29(1): 43–56.

European Convention on Human Rights (1953). European Court of Human Rights and Council of Europe. Available at: www.echr.coe.int/Documents/Convention_ENG.pdf (accessed 7 July 2018).

Fenwick, V. and Gale, A. (1998). *Historic Shipwrecks: Discovered, Protected and Investigated*. Gloucestershire: Tempus Publishing.

Flatman, J. (2007a). The origins and ethics of maritime archaeology – Part I. *Public Archaeology* 6(2): 77–97.

Flatman, J. (2007b). The origins and ethics of maritime archaeology – Part II. *Public Archaeology* 6(3): 141–154.

Flatman, J. (2009). Conserving marine cultural heritage: threats, risks and future priorities. Conservation and Management of Archaeological Sites 11(1): 5–8.

Fletcher-Tomenius, P. and Forrest, C. (2000). Historic wreck in international waters: conflict or consensus? *Marine Policy* 24(1): 1–10.

Fletcher-Tomenius, P. and Williams, M. (1999). The draft UNESCO/DOALOS Convention on the protection of underwater cultural heritage and conflict with the European Convention on Human Rights. *International Journal of Nautical Archaeology* 28(2): 145–153.

Ford, B. (2013). The reuse of vessels as harbor structures: a cross-cultural comparison. *Journal of Maritime Archaeology* 8(2): 197–219.

Forrest, C. (2002a). Defining 'underwater cultural heritage'. *International Journal of Nautical Archaeology* 31(1): 3–11.

Forrest, C. (2002b). A new international regime for the protection of underwater cultural heritage. *International and Comparative Law Quarterly* 51(3): 511–554.

Forrest, C. (2003). Has the application of salvage law to underwater cultural heritage become a thing of the past? *Journal of Maritime Law & Commerce* 34(2): 309–318.

Gibbins, D. and Adams, J. (2001). Shipwrecks and maritime archaeology. *World Archaeology* 32(3): 279–291.

Gibbs, M. (2006). Cultural site formation processes in maritime archaeology: disaster response, salvage and Muckelroy 30 years on. *International Journal of Nautical Archaeology* 35(1): 4–19.

Hoffman, B. T. (2006). Who owns the *Titanic*'s treasures? Protection of the underwater cultural heritage. In Hoffman, B. T. (ed.), *Art and Cultural Heritage: Law, Policy and Practice*. Cambridge: Cambridge University Press: 283–284.

Holloway, A. (2014). Archaeologists uncover 5,000-year-old water system in Iran. [online]. *Ancient Origins*. Available at: www.ancient-origins.net/news-history-archaeology/archaeologists-uncover-5000-year-old-water-system-in-iran-001727 (accessed 13 July 2018).

Ireland, B. (2010). *Aircraft Carriers*. London: Anness.

Juvelier, B. (2016). Salvaging history: underwater cultural heritage and commercial salvage. *American University International Law Review* 32(5): 1023–1045.

Keith, D. H. (2000). Going, going-gone! In Prott, L. V., Planche, E. and Roca-Hachem, R. (eds.), *Background Materials on the Protection of the Underwater Cultural Heritage*. Vol. 2. Paris: Ministere de la Culture et de la communication and UNESCO: 265–278.

Kingsley, S. (2011). Challenges of maritime archaeology: in too deep. In King, T. F. (ed.), *A Companion to Cultural Resource Management*. Chichester: Wiley-Blackwell: 223–244.

Lixinski, L. (2015). Between orthodoxy and heterodoxy: the troubled relationships between heritage studies and heritage law. *International Journal of Heritage Studies* 21(3): 201–214.

Lorenz, J. (ed.) (2010). *An Illustrated Encyclopaedia of Battleships from 1960 to the First World War*. London: Anness.

Lynch, T. (2007). A historically significant shield for in vivo measurements. *Health Physics* 93(2): S119.

Lynch, T. (2011). In vivo radiobioassay and research facility. *Health Physics* 100(2): S35.

Maarleveld, T. J. (2008). How and why will underwater cultural heritage benefit from the 2001 UNESCO Convention? *Museum International* 60(4): 50–62.

Maarleveld, T. J. (2009). Drama, place and verifiable link: underwater cultural heritage, present experience and contention. In Turgeon, L. (ed.), *Spirit of Place: Between Tangible and Intangible Heritage*. Quebec: Les Presses de l' Université Laval: 97–108.

Maarleveld, T. J. (2011). Ethics, underwater cultural heritage, and international law. In Catsambis, A., Ford, B. and Hamilton, D. L. (eds.), *The Oxford Handbook of Maritime Archaeology*. Oxford: Oxford University Press: 917–941.

Maarleveld, T. J. (2012). The maritime paradox: does international heritage exist? *International Journal of Heritage Studies* 18(4): 418–431.

Macdonald, F. (2008). *Shipwrecks: 100 Facts*. Essex: Miles Kelly.

Manders, M. (2012a). Unit 9: in situ preservation. In Manders, M. and Underwood, C. (eds.), *Training Manual for the UNESCO Foundation Course on the Protection and Management of Underwater Cultural Heritage in Asia and the Pacific*. Bangkok: UNESCO.

Manders, M. (2012b). Unit 3: management of underwater cultural heritage. In Manders, M. and Underwood, C. (eds.), *Training Manual for the UNESCO Foundation Course on the Protection and Management of Underwater Cultural Heritage in Asia and the Pacific*. Bangkok: UNESCO.

Manders, M., van Tilburg, H. K. and Staniforth, M. (2012). Unit 6: significance assessment. In Manders, M. and Underwood, C. (eds.), *Training Manual for the UNESCO Foundation Course on the Protection and Management of Underwater Cultural Heritage in Asia and the Pacific*. Bangkok: UNESCO.

McGimsey III, C. R. (1984). The value of archaeology. In Green, E. L. (ed.), *Ethics and Values in Archaeology*. London: Free Press: 171–174.

McKee, A. (1982). *How We Found the* Mary Rose. London: Souvenir Press.

Muckelroy, K. (1998). Introducing maritime archaeology. In Babits, L. E. and van Tilburg, H. (eds.), *Maritime Archaeology. A Reader of Substantive and Theoretical Contributions*. The Plenum Series in Underwater Archaeology. New York: Springer: 23–36.

Nafziger, J. A. R. (1999). The *Titanic* revisited. *Journal of Maritime Law and Commerce* 30(2): 311–329.

O'Keefe, P. (1996). Protecting the underwater cultural heritage: the International Law Association draft convention. *Marine Policy* 20(4): 297–307.

O'Keefe, P. (2002). *Shipwrecked Heritage: A Commentary on the UNESCO Convention on Underwater Cultural Heritage.* Leicester: Institute of Art and Law.

O'Keefe, P. (2013). Commercial exploitation: its prohibition in the UNESCO Convention on Protection of the Underwater Cultural Heritage 2001 and other instruments. *Art, Antiquity, and Law* 18(2): 129–148.

O'Keefe, P. and Nafziger, J. A. R. (1994). The draft convention on the protection of the Underwater Cultural Heritage. *Ocean Development and International Law* 25(4): 391–418.

Perez-Alvaro, E. (2013). Unconsidered threats to underwater cultural heritage: laying submarine cables. *Rosetta* 14: 54–70.

Pickford, N. (1994). *The Atlas of Shipwreck and Treasure.* London: Dorling Kindersley.

Prickett, N. (2002). *The Archaeology of New Zealand Shore Whaling.* Wellington: Department of Conservation.

Pringle, H. (2013). Troubled waters for ancient shipwrecks. *Science* 340(6134): 802–807.

Prott, L. V. and O'Keefe, P. J. (1984). *Law and the Cultural Heritage.* Oxford: Professional Books.

Reyes, I. (2014). What should Uruguay do with its Nazi eagle? [online]. *BBC News.* 15 December 2014. Available at: www.bbc.co.uk/news/world-latin-america-30471063 (accessed 16 August 2018).

Sánchez, R. (2014). El arte rescata a la banca. [online] *El Mundo.* 13 November 2014. Available at: www.elmundo.es/economia/2014/11/13/54647a5922601d2c5e8b4575. html (accessed 1 October 2018).

San Claudio, M. (2013). España y la arqueología subacuática. [online]. *Espejo de navegantes: blog de arqueologia naval.* 29 July 2013. Available at: http://abcblogs. abc.es/espejo-de-navegantes/2013/07/29/espana-y-la-arqueologia-subacuatica/ (accessed 1 May 2018).

Scovazzi, T. (2006). The 2001 UNESCO Convention on the Protection of the Underwater Cultural Heritage. In Hoffman, B. T. (eds.), *Art and Cultural Heritage: Law, Policy and Practice.* Cambridge: Cambridge University Press: 285–292.

Smith, L. (2004). *Archaeological Theory and the Politics of Cultural Heritage.* London: Routledge.

Smith, H. D. and Couper, A. D. (2003). The management of the underwater cultural heritage. *Journal of Cultural Heritage* 4(1): 25–33.

Spalding, M. (2014). Underwater cultural heritage as a potential environmental time bomb. [online]. *National Geographic: Changing Planet.* 6 October 2014. Available at: https://blog.nationalgeographic.org/2014/10/06/underwater-cultural-heritage-as-a-potential-environmental-time-bomb/ (accessed 2 June 2018).

Stirland, A. (2013). *The Men of the* Mary Rose: *Raising the Dead.* Gloucestershire: History Press.

Strati, A. (1995). *The Protection of the Underwater Cultural Heritage: An Emerging Objective of the Contemporary Law of the Sea.* Leiden: Martinus Nijhoff.

Tarlow, S. (2006). Archaeological ethics and the people of the past. In Scarre, C. and Scarre, G. (eds.), *The Ethics of Archaeology: Philosophical Perspectives on Archaeological Practice.* Cambridge: Cambridge University Press: 199–217.

Teague, L. S. (2007). Respect for the dead, respect for the living. In Cassman, V., Odegaard, N. and Powell, J. (eds.), *Human Remains: A Guide for Museums and Academic Institutions*. Oxford: Oxford AltaMira Press: 245–260.

UNCLOS (1982). United Nations Convention on the Law of the Sea. Available at: www.un.org/depts/los/convention_agreements/texts/unclos/unclos_e.pdf (accessed 4 October 2018).

UNESCO (1972a). Convention Concerning the Protection of the World Cultural and Natural Heritage. Paris, 16 November 1972. Available at: http://whc.unesco.org/en/conventiontext/ (accessed 16 October 2018).

UNESCO (1972b). *Underwater Archaeology: A Nascent Discipline*. Paris: UNESCO.

UNESCO (2001). Convention on the Protection of the Underwater Cultural Heritage. Paris, 2 November 2001. Available at: http://unesdoc.unesco.org/images/0012/001260/126065e.pdf (accessed 28 October 2018).

Villegas-Zamora, T. (2008). The impact of commercial exploitation on the preservation of underwater cultural heritage. *Museum International* 60(4): 18–30.

Werner, D. (2013). Piracy in the courtroom: how to salvage $500 million in sunken treasure without making a cent. *University of Miami Law Review* 67(105): 1005–1038.

Wise, P. (2014). Christie's pulls Miró auction after Portuguese protests. [online]. *Ft Com*. 4 February 2014. Available at: www.ft.com/cms/s/0/277c59a8-8dce-11e3-ba55-00144feab7de.html#axzz3KB9rK48K (accessed 1 February 2018).

Wylie, A. (2003). On ethics. In Zimmerman, L. J., Vitelli, K. D. and Hollowell-Zimmer, J. (eds.), *Ethical Issues in Archaeology*. Oxford: AltaMira Press: 3–16.

2   Key concepts

The major difference between the violin rescued from the *Titanic* and the most expensive violins, the *Stradivarius*, is that the first is an inexpensive factory-made violin with not a special quality sound. However, it became economically and culturally valued because it is the last sound of music heard by many of the people who died on board the *Titanic* and as a consequence it has, as part of the story, gained mythical status. This example shows how values are attributed to an object and it is this process of attributing the values that turns the object into heritage. However, definition and attribution of values to archaeological and cultural material have changed throughout history and although all values are legitimate, individuals and organisations emphasise some more than others depending on their needs and goals. As a consequence, in heritage management nothing is fixed and everything can change. This is also due to the fact that heritage has many uses but also multiple producers (Graham and Howard, 2008: 4), each one of them with multiple objectives and values. According to Carman (1996, 2002) and based on the Venice Charter (Venice Charter, 1964), this heritage management can be defined by four basic principles: heritage is finite and non-renewable, heritage is of public interest, heritage is governed by legislation and all the components of the heritage require testing for significance. For Aplin (2002) there are some criteria to establish significances on heritage: scale (local, regional, state, international), importance (how important and why) and uniqueness or representativeness. For the *World Heritage List* to become heritage, the material should represent a masterpiece of human creative genius, interchange human values, be an exceptional testimony of cultural civilisation, be an outstanding example of technological development or be directly or tangibly associated with traditions, ideas or beliefs (Carman, 2002). For the 2001 UNESCO Convention on the Protection of the Underwater Cultural Heritage (UNESCO, 2001) the criteria is not just 'of special significance' but also includes a definition according to the age. For the Sofia Charter of ICOMOS (Sofia Charter, 1996) the benchmarks includes rare aspects, yield information, demonstrating principal characteristics of a class, high degree of achievement, association to a cultural group or the life or works of persons. In any case, all the common criteria for the significance of the heritage are based on values. However, to understand this valuation of heritage, it is first necessary to understand the concept of 'heritage', which has different points of view and which has experimented a quick expansion of its definition in the last decades (Harrison, 2013).

Heritage as material

This is the oldest approach. In fact, the idea of heritage as 'things' is exemplified by the UNESCO World Heritage List that in 2018 included 1073 properties:[1] therefore 'heritage' is defined as 'properties'. In this regard, Howard (2003) defines heritage as *what* people want to save, collect or conserve and it is recognised or designated. The 1972 UNESCO Convention Concerning the Protection of the World Cultural and Natural Heritage (UNESCO, 1972) claims that judgement on the importance of a site to be listed needs to be made scientifically or objectively but Graham and Howard (2008) believe that this selection in a list excludes others equally important but undiscovered from being heritage. In addition, Smith (2006) understands that this misunderstood concept of heritage as 'things' are only useful for making and interpreting stories and ideas tangible but not for its protection.

Heritage as ideas

For Aplin (2002) heritage is not only material but mainly ideas: groups vary not only in terms of the parts of the story but also the symbols for telling them (Pitchford, 2008). However, the closer these stories are to the present, the harder they are to tell, since each group has its own perception of what is important in heritage term besides the perceptions of each individual in those groups (Aplin, 2002). It depends on a person's background, life experiences and personality, along with the local, historical, social and cultural circumstances of the group to which the individual is ascribed. Lenihan (1989) agrees and argues that people see the same event in a different way, according to their psychology and experiences. Heritage, he claims, is therefore a laboratory for analysing society's myths, symbols and images.

Heritage as data

For Smith and Waterton (2009: 42) archaeology is the basis of heritage management and heritage and archaeological data have a synergy that makes heritage 'knowable'; heritage is data for archaeologists and this creates problems for communities, for whom heritage has an emotive dimension.

Heritage as a process

There has been a recent trend towards defining heritage as a 'process' rather than as a concept. Smith (2006: 1), for instance, defines it as 'heritage work': a cultural and social process of renewing memories, which is not only about the past or material things but a 'process of engagement, an act of communication and an act of forming meaning in and for the present'. The process, as a consequence, consists of the activities undertaken around those things, a process that identify them as symbols and give them a value and a meaning, sometimes even an identity. English Heritage (2008) explains this process as the 'Heritage Cycle': if people understand the history of heritage places, they value them, they care for them, they enjoy them and they will understand them more. However, the precept they use as a basis is already misunderstood; for people to understand the history of heritage places, those places have to be pre-defined as heritage; if not, visitors will not go to see them. Other authors have attempted to define heritage and although they have not used the word 'process', they still include the concept. For instance Lipe (1984) had already established this idea of heritage as a process when in 1984 he claimed that all cultural materials are potentially cultural resources but because not all of them can be preserved or studied: we must make choices based on evaluation and re-evaluation according to the needs and fashion of the period. And as Carman (2013) defends, only recognition of cultural heritage transforms archaeological deposits into cultural heritage: this evaluation of the material, this process is what makes them heritage, therefore, heritage only exists if it is managed. Ashworth (2007: 8) supports this concept of heritage as a process which defines as 'a medium of communication, a means of transmission of ideas and values in order to satisfy various contemporary needs'. Maarleveld (2009) more specifically defines heritage as the way it is experienced through this process. Graham and Howard (2008: 2) identify heritage as 'the way in which very selective past material artefacts, natural landscapes, mythologies, memories and traditions become cultural, political and economic resources for the present' and they point out that it involves not so much the study of the past but more 'the contents, interpretations and representations of the heritage selected according to the demands of the present'. The authors claim that the process of 'selection' of heritage is the key that shapes the meaning and importance of the heritage: this selection excludes those who do not subscribe to the meaning awarded to that heritage. All heritage, Smith (2006: 2) concludes, is intangible; in fact, 'there is no such thing as heritage'.

In this task of defining heritage, authors have linked the concept to other ideas:

Identity

'Identity' seems a concept intrinsically linked to the concept of heritage. According to Graham and Howard (2008: 6), the interrelationships between heritage and identity are 'both spatially and temporally variable', since they are defined by the consumer: identity is the process of inclusion and exclusion that defines communities and this process is led by heritage (Graham and Howard, 2008: 5). For Ashworth (2007) heritage is a need of the individual and of society to reinforce a socio-cultural identity: it is a contemporary commodity. In fact, Low (2004: 400) highlights that people need to be represented by their heritage, since 'treating everyone as a visitor' neglects a sense of identity. The seven volumes of *Les Lieux de Memoire* (Nora, 1996–1998) analyse the way an object of heritage can become an evocative symbol of identification that acts as a trigger for emotions and narratives. In this regard, Ashworth (1994) mentions the concept of 'national identity' that can be shaped through a few selected points of heritage and supporting mythologies. According to Pitchford (2008) museums and other attractions, and the law, are political and powerful resources for the construction of national identities and in fact, for Firth (2002) the role of archaeology is being applied to be a soothing balm of nationalism, an idea likened to identity. This identification with the site may be more difficult to reach with some underwater cultural sites since for instance a ship embodies much greater diversity for the history of many countries, not only one (Smith and Couper, 2003).

Emotion

This identification of a person with a place or an object is established because the person recognises itself with the place—or object—and feels something related to it. In this regard, Smith (2006) concludes that the 'real sense of heritage is when our emotions and sense of self are truly engaged'. In fact, this is precisely the point developed in Chapter 3, namely, how a common and cheap object becomes valuable heritage through the emotions it has created in people: the emotional value of heritage is felt and it is reinforced through experiences and re-experiences that create a sense of nostalgia (Smith and Waterton, 2009). For these authors, nostalgia is an important issue and the heritage industry sanitise inauthentic versions to create this nostalgia. According to Russell (2010) heritage is a mixture of intellectual and emotional reasons to a material. Holtorf (2010) claims the same thing: heritage is not valued for the specific information it contains but for the notions it evokes among people.

Memories

Memories, as emotions, are not spontaneous but they need to be actively remembered (Smith and Waterton, 2009): they need a root in a concrete object or site and need to be maintained. As a consequence, memory is negotiated (Stachel, 2006) since it deals with the past but takes place in the present. As Viejo-Rose (2011) argues, cultural heritage is intrinsically political and symbolic, used *in lieu* of description to evoke memories or emotions; and it is highly selective. In this regard, there is a new concept related to the creation of new memories: it is the concept of prosthetic memory, which will be extensively exemplified in Chapter 3. The term 'prosthetic memory' was introduced by Alison Landsberg in 1995 to explain the influence of the media on peoples' memories: it is the process of a media-identification (Landsberg, 1995: 175). As a consequence, the media user feels and remembers scenes of films or television programmes as scenes lived by them, creating new memories.

Politics

Ashworth (1994) and Aplin (2002) claim that heritage contains a political component and that political actions mixed with heritage can be either extremely hurtful or extremely positive. Lipe (1984) also defends that humans attach names, myths and affective values to things that become cultural resource and every state develops its policy concerning heritage on the basis of what is worth preserving (Viejo-Rose, 2011). This political action is what results in the creation of law (Carman, 1996), an idea that will be analysed below. In this regard, some authors have expressed that all selection of heritage—terrestrial or underwater—is a political decision translated by the law. This concept will be extensively applied to underwater cultural heritage in Chapter 10.

Ownership

A vast amount of literature has been written about the ownership of heritage. In fact, Carman (2005) published a whole volume on this aspect where he presents a range of perspectives on issues relating to the ownership and preservation of archaeology outside of private property. The author defines archaeology as property and argues in favour of archaeology as common property and as an open-access resource. Scarre and Scarre (2006) also approach the concept in their edited volume where some authors discuss the issue of archaeologists as guardians of heritage, introducing a concept of 'stewards' instead of owners since the main idea of ownership is that if you own something you can do whatever you want with it, even destroy it. Some authors defend heritage as owned by the public. For Ready and Navrud (2002), culture is non-excludible (enjoyed by all) and has non-rivals in consumption (two different people can enjoy it at the same time without interfering). They maintain that the decision-making of making the heritage a public good will be based on a sense of duty and moral purposes, on ethics. For other authors, there are different owners of the heritage. Young (2006), for instance, identifies four candidates to own heritage: individuals, cultures, nations or all humanity although his hypothesis is that heritage belongs to cultures since a culture is a family resemblance concept. Gillman (2010) defends that the heritage belongs to a particular people and place and then to all humankind. Leaman (2006) admits heritage can be privately owned but he identifies three precepts: (1) legal ownership means possession;

(2) legal ownership is never absolute since it belongs to a wider community; (3) human relics are a special category and should not be treated like everything else. In this regard, Maarleveld (2012) expresses differences between the feeling of ownership (which can be disrespectful in large immigration societies, for instance) or the exclusive ownership. Prott and O'Keefe (1984) also remind that some states assert ownership of heritage and some exert control without doing so. However, states usually claim right of ownerships from the moment of discovery (Carman, 2013b): this nationalisation rides over private rights. The author identifies other alternatives such as regulation by allowing private ownership or having use of the land with limitations or control of use. However, in this regard, Maarleveld (2009) states that ownership does not have to be identified before taking any action on management of cultural heritage, since meaning comes first.

Culture

The idea of heritage as 'culture' have been widely discussed in the literature. For Aplin (2002) heritage understood as 'culture' has the power to locate the present lives both geographically and historically: heritage implies a cultural gift for future generations. Lipe (1984) argues that 'our lives are made meaningful by culture' and that culture is a symbol and a mean of communication. They are a symbol of the common human interest and of the continuity of past, present and future. A heritage object matters because as Bator (1981) states, the preservation of culture constitutes the humanity's fundamental goal: culture elevates and civilises. And the community trusts the archaeologists to manage and safeguard these nation's cultural assets (Holtorf, 2005). As a consequence, some authors maintain that the engagement should not be with the past, but with the future and the present (Colwell-Chanthaphonh et al., 2008). And in order to manage these pieces of culture, the heritage objects are awarded with a value, a value that transform a normal object into a piece of heritage that is worth preserving.

Values

Heritage becomes heritage when it is managed and various values are awarded to the material. By assigning values to it, its importance grows. However, this process of assigning values is not that simple. The process has been largely discussed as Wessex Archaeology (2006) reviews: according to Darvil (1995), archaeological material already had a monetary value in medieval times—as a treasure—but it also raised curiosity as legend and folklore: it was later, in the Renaissance, when the archaeological remains of other periods created an aesthetic curiosity but were also a proof of historical progress acquiring historic value. In the 20th century, more values—apart from the monetary, the folklore and the historical—started to be created and the categorisation became more complicated (Darvil, 1995). 'Values are learned and depend on cultural, intellectual, historical and psychological frames of reference' (Lipe, 1984: 2), therefore valuation is held individually but shared by communities, Darvil (1995) concludes. Lipe (1984) determines that values are defined by specific qualities such as authenticity, human cognition and context. For him, the process that converts a material into heritage includes a cultural resource base, which are potential heritage; a context, awarded by the economy, aesthetic standards, tradition or common knowledge; an evaluation of this material to be considered as resource; and the preservation of those cultural resources through governmental policies or material such as books or museums. For Nafziger (1999), criteria to valuate heritage are based on preservation or recovery of that heritage and depend only on significance, urgency and viability. Dunnell (1984) simplifies the classification and for him, there are two sets of values: humanistic (symbolic) and scientific (information) but the humanistic are essentially political and subject to change and it is difficult to evaluate its significance. Manders et al. (2012) define the significance of a place according to the value for past, present or future generations. However, they recognise that assessing sites is highly subjective and often determined by comparing the place against others. They also value a place for its memory value; when applied to wrecks, collective memory is on a wider scale. The aesthetic value, however, is difficult to apply to submerged heritage due to water visibility. Lastly, they remark the economic value, which for them should not determine the significance of the material but it is still important. They assess the significance by intrinsic value (importance, sensitivity, potential, information about the past, historical significance, scientific significance, aesthetic significance, social or spiritual significance, experience significance, provenance, representativeness, rarity or uniqueness, condition and interpretative potential) or by understanding how the objects change their value (dynamics of chance, processes, outcomes, significance of the change, magnitude, risk, uncertainty, significance of effects, sustainability of change, limits of acceptable change, regulation and management or indicators and monitoring). According to Okamura (2010), archaeologists have influences on awarding values to heritage for their abilities to research and educate and in fact, Clark (2010) states that every time archaeologists or other stewardship protect a site, they are making a judgment that something is of value. And since selection and prioritisation of values is subjective each user of the heritage prioritises the values according to their needs or wishes (Manders, 2012): an archaeologist will value more the information data, a treasure hunter the economic value or a physicist department the use value. For Okamura (2010), the value of the objects of the past is just immeasurable since it carries a different value for different people. However, for some authors, the decisions on awarding values are mainly bureaucratic since values are not an engagement with the past but an interpretation according to the demands of the present and of the imagined future (Graham and Howard, 2008; McDowell, 2008). Heritage has little intrinsic worth, but the values placed upon the objects are seen by different lenses (Graham and Howard, 2008). The problem of awarding values is that the objects are selected and the values are created through consumption; they change from one culture to another. For this reason, Howard (2003) claims that heritage is a problem as soon as different people attach values to it. In addition, values attributed to land archaeological differ to some extent to values attributed to underwater archaeological material because of the later development of underwater archaeology. In particular, Maarleveld (2011) remarks the different needs that underwater cultural heritage users have in relation to the ones that land cultural heritage users have, for instance because of the fact that the heritage is less accessible. However, for Bator (1981) visibility and accessibility can be postponed but if heritage objects are destroyed they are gone forever: for the author, the belief that art serves best when it is more visible is a vulgar one and he rejects the value of the heritage of being available for all, if this availability destroys it. In addition, in land, the bases are old concepts and the demands of the society and the economic market of heritage have changed (Maarleveld, 2011: 932). These new needs are especially noticeable on underwater cultural heritage management since given it is a relatively new discipline, still faces the problem of finding its own way, its own definition, its own values and its own problems and therefore problems to be solved, continuously encountering new challenges. Moreover, the development of underwater technology raises a continual change in all these perceived values. And because of these many values, constantly in state of flux, all these significances of underwater cultural heritage have created conflicts between groups with divergent goals: many items recovered are undoubtedly of archaeological importance (Fletcher-Tomenius and Forrest (2000) but some of these retrieved artefacts may also have a high economic value, both intrinsic (such as gold coins) and attributed (such as a unique anchor). Ready and Navrud (2002: 7) define the economic value of a cultural heritage as the value that the consumer is willing to pay, not its price. And it may also have aesthetic and expressive value, from both a national and universal perspective, like watery graves are a reminder of a national or universal tragedy. Therefore, there is a juxtaposition of different value systems in underwater cultural heritage management (Firth, 2002): one underwater cultural heritage site may have different values (Forrest, 2003). However, Dromgoole (2004) claims that the juxtaposition of commercial and cultural values does not exist in the rest of the archaeological world, only in maritime archaeology.

Conclusions

The concepts reviewed by this chapter will be used in the next pages: all of them are ideas related to the management of underwater cultural heritage and all of them can be applied to each one of the nine case studies examined by this book.

Note

1 UNESCO World Heritage Centre: World Heritage List. Available at: http://whc.unesco.org/en/list/.

Bibliography

Aplin, G. (2002). *Heritage Identification, Conservation and Management*. Oxford: Oxford University Press.

Ashworth, G. J (1994). From history to heritage – from heritage to identity: in search of concepts and models. In Ashworth, G. J. and Larkham, P. J. (eds.), *Building a New Heritage: Tourism, Culture and Identity in the New Europe*. London: Routledge: 13–30.

Ashworth, G. J. (2007). 'On townscapes, heritages and identities' (conference presentation). At: Regions and regionalism in and beyond Europe (session: 'Urban-rural: flows and boundaries'). Lancaster: Lancaster University (9–10 January 2007).

Bator, P. M. (1981). *The International Trade in Art*. London: University of Chicago Press.

Carman, J. (1996). *Valuing Ancient Things: Archaeology and Law*. Leicester: Leicester University Press.

Carman, J. (2002). *Archaeology and Heritage: An Introduction*. London: Continuum Press.

Carman, J. (2005). *Against Cultural Property: Archaeology, Heritage and Ownership*. London: Duckworth Debates in Archaeology.

Carman, J. (2013a). Legislation in archaeology: overview and introduction. In Smith, C. (ed.), *Encyclopaedia of Global Archaeology*. New York: Springer: 4469–4485.

Carman, J. (2013b). A heritage of conflict, and conflicts of heritage. In S. Bergerbrant, S. and Sabatini, S. (eds.), *Counterpoint: Essays in Archaeology and Heritage Studies in Honour of Professor Kristian Kristiansen*. Oxford: Information Press: 747–753.

Clark, K. (2010). Values in cultural resource management. In Smith, G. S., Messenger, P. M. and Soderland, H. A. (eds.), *Heritage Values in Contemporary Society*. California: Left Coast Press: 89–100.

Colwell-Chanthaphonh, C., Hollowell, J. and McGill, D. (2008). *Ethics in Action: Case Studies in Archaeological Dilemmas*. Washington, DC: Society for American Archaeology, SAA Press.

Darvil, T. (1995). Value systems in archaeology. In Cooper, M., Firth, A., Carman, J. and Wheatley, D. (eds.), *Managing Archaeology*. London: Routledge: 40–50.

Dromgoole, S. (2004). Murky waters for government policy: the case of a 17th century British warship and 10 tonnes of gold coins. *Marine Policy* 28(3): 189–198.

Dunnell, R. C. (1984). The ethics of archaeological significance decisions. In Green, E. L. (ed.), *Ethics and Values in Archaeology*. London: Free Press: 62–74.

English Heritage (2008). *SHAPE 2008: A Strategic Framework for Historic Environment Activities and Programmes in English Heritage*. Available at: www.english-heritage.org.uk/content/publications/docs/shapeamended02062009.pdf (15 March 2019).

Firth, A. (2002). *Managing Archaeology Underwater: A Theoretical, Historical and Comparative Perspective on Society and Its Submerged Past*. BAR International 1055. Oxford: Archaeopress.

Fletcher-Tomenius, P. and Forrest, C. (2000). Historic wreck in international waters: conflict or consensus? *Marine Policy* 24(1): 1–10.

Forrest, C. (2003). Has the application of salvage law to underwater cultural heritage become a thing of the past? *Journal of Maritime Law & Commerce* 34(2): 309–318.

Gillman, D. (2010). *The Idea of Cultural Heritage*. Cambridge: Cambridge University Press.

Graham, B. J. and Howard, P. (eds.) (2008). *The Ashgate Research Companion to Heritage and Identity*. Cornwall: Ashgate: 1–17.

Harrison, R. (2013). *Heritage: Critical Approaches*. New York: Routledge.

Holtorf, C. (2005). Beyond crusades: how (not) to engage with alternative archaeologies. *World Archaeology* 37(4): 544–551.

Holtorf, C. (2010). Heritage values in contemporary popular culture. In Smith, G. S., Messenger, P. M. and Soderland, H. A. (eds.), *Heritage Values in Contemporary Society*. Walnut Creek, CA: Left Coast Press: 43–54.

Howard, P. (2003). *Heritage: Management, Interpretation, Identity*. London: Continuum.

Landsberg, A. (1995). Prosthetic memory: *Total Recall* and *Blade Runner*. In Featherstone, M. and Burrows, R. (eds.), *Cyberspace/Cyberbodies/Cyberpunk: Cultures of Technological Embodiment*. London: Sage: 175–190.

Leaman, O. (2006). Who guards the guardians? In Scarre, C. and Scarre, G. (eds.), *The Ethics of Archaeology: Philosophical Perspectives on Archaeological Practice*. Cambridge: Cambridge University Press: 32–45.

Lenihan, D. J. (1989). *Submerged Cultural Resources Study: USS Arizona Memorial and Pearl Harbor National Historic Landmark*. Santa Fe, NM: Southwest Cultural Resources Centre Professional Papers.

Lipe, W. D. (1984). Value and meaning in cultural resources. In Cleere, H. (ed.), *Approaches to the Archaeological Heritage*. Cambridge: Cambridge University Press: 1–11.

Low, S. M. (2004). Social sustainability: people, history and values. In Teutonic, J. (ed.), *Managing Change: Sustainable Approaches to the Conservation of the Built Environment*. Los Angeles: Getty Conservation Institute.

Maarleveld, T. J. (2009). Drama, place and verifiable link: underwater cultural heritage, present experience and contention. In Turgeon, L. (ed.), *Spirit of Place: Between Tangible and Intangible Heritage*. Quebec: Les Presses de l' Université Laval: 97–108.

Maarleveld, T. J. (2011). Ethics, underwater cultural heritage, and international law. In Catsambis, A., Ford, B. and Hamilton, D. L. (eds.), *The Oxford Handbook of Maritime Archaeology*. Oxford: Oxford University Press: 917–941.

Maarleveld, T. J. (2012). The maritime paradox: does international heritage exist? *International Journal of Heritage Studies* 18(4): 418–431.

Manders, M. (2012). Unit 9: in situ preservation. In Manders, M. and Underwood, C. (eds.), *Training Manual for the UNESCO Foundation Course on the Protection and Management of Underwater Cultural Heritage in Asia and the Pacific*. Bangkok: UNESCO.

Manders, M., van Tilburg, K. H. and Staniforth, M. (2012). Unit 6: significance assessment. In Manders, M. and Underwood, C. (eds.) *Training Manual for the UNESCO Foundation Course on the Protection and Management of Underwater Cultural Heritage in Asia and the Pacific*. Bangkok: UNESCO.

McDowell, S. (2008). Heritage, memory and identity. In Graham, B. and Howard, P. (eds.), *The Ashgate Research Companion to Heritage and Identity*. Cornwall: Ashgate: 37–54.

Nafziger, J. A. R. (1999). The *Titanic* revisited. *Journal of Maritime Law and Commerce* 30(2): 311–329.

Nora, P. (1996–1998). *Realms of Memory I–III*. New York: Columbia University Press.

Okamura, K. (2010). A consideration of heritage values in contemporary society. In Smith, G. S., Messenger, P. M. and Soderland, H. A. (eds.), *Heritage Values in Contemporary Society*. Walnut Creek, CA: Left Coast Press: 43–54.

Pitchford, S. (2008). *Identity Tourism: Imaging and Imagining the Nation*. Tourism Social Science Series 10. Bingley: Emerald.

Prott, L. V. and O'Keefe, P. J. (1984). *Law and the Cultural Heritage*. Oxford: Professional Books.

Ready, R. C. and Navrud, S. (2002). *Valuing Cultural Heritage: Environmental Standards*. Cheltenham: Edward Elgar.

Russell, I. (2010). Heritage, identities and roots: a critique of arborescent models of heritage and identity. In Smith, G. S., Messenger, P. M. and Soderland, H. A. (eds.), *Heritage Values in Contemporary Society*. Walnut Creek, CA: Left Coast Press: 43–54.

Scarre, C. and Scarre, G. (2006). *The Ethics of Archaeology: Philosophical Perspectives on Archaeological Practice*. Cambridge: Cambridge University Press: 1–14.

Smith, H. D. and Couper, A. D. (2003). The management of the underwater cultural heritage. *Journal of Cultural Heritage* 4(1): 25–33.

Smith, L. (2006). *Uses of Heritage*. London: Routledge.

Smith, L. and Waterton, E. (2009). *Heritage, Communities and Archaeology*. Wiltshire: Duckworth Debates in Archaeology.

Sofia Charter (1996). Charter on the protection and management of underwater cultural heritage. *ICOMOS*. Available at: www.international.icomos.org/charters/underwater_e.pdf (3 August 2017).

Stachel, P. (2006). On music and memory: some noncommittal reflections. [online]. *Spaces of Identity* 6(3). Available at: www.yorku.ca/soi/_Vol_6_3/_HTML/safflefest_stachel.html (20 December 2016).

UNESCO (1972). Convention concerning the Protection of the World Cultural and Natural Heritage. Paris, 16 November 1972. Available at: http://whc.unesco.org/en/conventiontext/ (6 October 2018).

UNESCO (2001). Convention on the Protection of the Underwater Cultural Heritage. Paris, 2 November 2001. Available at: http://unesdoc.unesco.org/images/0012/001260/126065e.pdf (4 July 2018).

Venice Charter (1964). International Charter for the Conservation and Restoration of Monuments and Sites. *ICOMOS*. Available at: www.icomos.org/en/charters-and-texts (5 June 2018).

Viejo-Rose, D. (2011). *Reconstructing Spain: Cultural Heritage and Memory after Civil War*. Sussex: Sussex Academic Press.

Wessex Archaeology (2006). *On the Importance of Shipwrecks: Legal Report*. Aggregates Levy Sustainability Fund: Marine aggregates and the historic environment. Southampton: Wessex Archaeology.

Young, J. O. (2006). Cultures and the ownership of archaeological finds. In Scarre, C. and Scarre, G. (eds.), *The Ethics of Archaeology: Philosophical Perspectives on Archaeological Practice*. Cambridge: Cambridge University Press: 15–31.

Part II
Case studies

3 Valuation

The violin of the *Titanic*[1]

This chapter is aimed at asking questions about the significance of this violin and the way it should be treated as part of a universal history and it will consider the ethics around the preservation, conservation and transformation of the violin from a musical instrument into a relic: if the effect of hearing the sound of the violin would be more beneficial than only being able to see the violin since its sound can be in this case part of a collective memory. In this regard, Smith (2006) states that the real sense of heritage is when our emotions and sense of self are truly engaged and often, when we hear something, it triggers our feeling and thinking. In this specific case it might be difficult to identify the sound of the violin but just by knowing that the sound is that from the violin that played on in the moments of distress, i.e. the sinking of the ship, could change the way it is felt and the emotional attachment with that sound may become more intense. This attachment with the story could give the spectator a feel of sense of identification with the object and the connected part of the history.

Introduction

The story of the *Titanic* is well known: the White Star Line vessel RMS *Titanic* collided with an iceberg on the night of 14–15 April 1912 in the North Atlantic Ocean; 1,500 persons perished (Aznar-Gómez and Varmer, 2012). Wallace Hartley was one of the victims. He was an English violinist assigned as a bandmaster of the *Titanic* in 1912 (Walter, 1995).

According to some sources, Wallace Hartley played his violin—the violin—to help calm passengers while the *Titanic* was sinking:

> One famous tale of stoic heroism on board the *Titanic* was that the ship's band did not abandon their instruments and take to the rafts but rather, recognising the importance of music in maintaining an air of calm, continued playing even as the water lapped over the bow.
>
> (Willis, 2008: 112)

Wallace played with his eight members band. After playing, he placed the violin into a leather case and strapped it to his back. The violin was still strapped to him when his body was recovered as number 224 on 25 April 1912, days after the sinking (Henry Aldridge & Son, n.d.). Figure 3.1 shows the current preservation of the violin and the case.

It was his fiancée, Maria Robinson, who gave him the violin as a gift and engraved 'For Wallace on the occasion of our engagement, from Maria' on a silver dedication on the tailpiece of the violin. After the sinking and rescue, she requested its return because of the emotional connection. It was 2006 when it was discovered in an attic: after the sinking, the violin was indeed returned to Hartley's fiancée. After she died, her sister gave it to the Bridlington Salvation Army, who then gave the violin to a local music and violin teacher. He got married to a woman, who was the mother of the last owner of the violin before it was sold (Telegraph Reporter, 2013). Through all these private owners the violin could not be played, since the instrument

Figure 3.1 The violin of the *Titanic*.

© [Titanic Museum Branson, MO & Pigeon Forge, TN]. Reproduced by permission of Titanic Attraction. Permission to reuse must be obtained from the rights holder.

still today has two long cracks from the water moisture—which would not allow it to be played—and only two original strings of the four.

Issue

One of the most expensive violins in history, the *Lady Tennant Stradivarius*, was sold by its private owner through Christie's New York in April 2005 for US $2.03 million. Its main quality was its sound. *Stradivarius* violins are known for their brilliant sound quality: they produce both expressive sound and high volume. Its sound is usually the main value that is ascribed to a violin; sound spreads emotions. Other values, such as an aesthetic quality or scientific significance, are not what violinists are looking for when playing a violin, although it is highly appreciated. As a consequence, the economic value attached to those instruments appears to be mainly based on their sound: the fact that they are old, rare and have a name also bestows them a value, but the economic value would not be so high if they could not be played. In fact, not many *Stradivarius* violins are kept in museums, and those that are, can be borrowed by renowned violinists. In this regard, the violins belong to private organisations but it is their sound that is shared for the benefit of humankind.

The *Titanic* violin was sold for $1.7 million on the 19th October 2013 in an auction in Wiltshire, England hosted by the auction house *Henry Aldridge & Son*. The price was almost as high as the above mentioned, the *Lady Tennant Stradivarius*. However, the difference between the *Stradivarius* and the *Titanic violin* is that the latter is an inexpensive c1800's Maggiani German factory-made violin possibly in Markneukirchen or Klingenthal according to dealer Andrew Hooker (The Strad, 2013) which would not have had a high special quality sound, the main feature of an expensive violin. It reached such a high price because of the story about it playing the last piece of music, heard by many of the people on board the *Titanic* gave it a mythical status: through its management and interpretation, the object has become heritage.

State of knowledge

The wreck of the *Titanic* was discovered in 1985 by a joint French–US expedition led by Jean-Louis Michel of the French Research Institute for Exploration of the Sea (IFREMER) and Robert Ballard of the Woods Hole Oceanographic Institution. In 1987, Titanic Ventures Inc. and IFREMER returned to the site and salvaged some artefacts. It has been estimated that less than 1% of the total number of artefacts at the site have been recovered (Aznar-Gómez and Varmer, 2012). However, the salvors of the *Titanic* are forbidden by law to sell anything.

The *Titanic* and its cargo technically fall under the umbrella of the 2001 UNESCO Convention on the Protection of the Underwater Cultural

Heritage (UNESCO, 2001), since they have been underwater for at least 100 years. Even more, the wreck has become a symbol of the Convention (Guerin, 2012). Not only the site, but also the objects are considered underwater cultural heritage. However, the violin remains a different case since it was recovered only ten days after the ship sunk (Henry Aldridge & Son, n.d.). As a consequence, it has not been under water for more than 100 years and furthermore was not illegally salvaged. Being 100 years under water is what the rules of the 2001 UNESCO Convention demands for inclusion, even if the ship to which it is related has been under water for that long. Therefore, even if the violin could be considered *cultural heritage* strongly attached to an underwater cultural heritage site, from a number of different perspectives which will be discussed below, it is not *underwater cultural heritage*, according to the definition of the 2001 UNESCO Convention and as a consequence it can remain private property and being sold. The question is how necessary or appropriate would be being transferred to a public entity.

When the *Titanic* sank, a significant amount of flotsam and jetsam covered an area of the loss, and bodies including Hartley's as well as other were recovered along with material. Those materials have entered public museums through donation or sales and some have remained private property. Although they may be, according to the poll by the *Marist College and Sea Research Foundation* (Marist Poll and Sea Research Foundation, 2013) six in ten Americans (60%) think that artefacts taken from the *Titanic* should not be allowed to be auctioned.

Ethical dilemmas: valuation

This main section of the chapter is aimed at examining how it was possible for the violin to transform from being an object without much value to a piece of heritage of enormous an economic value and also what the implications of this transformation. The change from a simple to a valuable object is not exceptional. However, the specific process in which it happened with Hartley's violin is. As Smith (Smith, 2006) observes, heritage is about the negotiation of values. In fact, the values of the violin have changed before, during and after the sinking. This has all to do with the original context of the violin and the given context—contextualisation—through time.

Hartley's violin is often recognised as the main symbol of the *Titanic*'s tragedy. Auctioneer Alan Aldridge described the violin as the 'rarest and most iconic' piece of *Titanic* memorabilia (Kennedy, 2013). Its meaning is so strong that some survivors affirmed having heard the music being played while they tried to stay alive (Howells, 1999: 128). Thus, some of the value ascribed to the violin comes from its uniqueness, representativeness and historical significance, and were the initial reasons for having the violin exhibited at *the Titanic Branson* and *Titanic Pigeon Forge* in the United States and after that at the *Titanic Belfast Museum*. Other values ascribed to the violin are being a symbol of faith and survival enhanced by the media and the cinema, as it will be seen below. However, and as a consequence of these previous values, it is the economic value that may have been paramount in the sale of the violin to an anonymous private British buyer: the guide price for the violin was $500,000 and finally reached $1.7 million (Henry Aldridge & Son, n.d.). This economic value would have not been so high if the media and the museums had not enhanced the other values of the violin.

Hooper-Greenhill (Hooper-Greenhill, 1992) affirms that in the same way advertisements select and manipulate images, heritage can be manipulated to create relationships and associations and create identities. Indeed, heritage can be created. The economic value of the violin has been subjected to this creation as an historical and emotional symbol. The success of *Titanic*'s public media attention can be correlated with the value of its salvaged objects, and specifically Hartley's violin. As said, the wreck of the *Titanic* was discovered in 1985, which created a renewed interest in the wreck and its history. When some objects were retrieved this not only continued the interest but may have even intensified it, since these were accessible items. Cameron's film of the *Titanic* was released in 1997 (Cameron, 1997), which did spread the story of the *Titanic* over the world and romanticised it, making it attractive for a whole new group of people. The violin—basically a symbol of this same story—was sold by an auction house in 2014.

As a consequence, and in this process, it is possible to distinguish three stakeholders that have subjected the violin to interpretation and as a consequence provided context to the object and enhanced different values to it (Figure 3.2): (1) museum curators, that work for the public benefit of the heritage, (2) the film industry and the media that has given a prosthetic value to the violin, and (3) auction managers taking advantage of the valuation of the violin by the museums and the media, giving it an economic value and selling it to a private owner for the highest price.

Museum curators: values for the benefit of all

The *Titanic* has become an icon all around the world due to its proximity to mankind through emotions. The fact that the public has been able to understand the pre-wreck nature of the ship, as well as behaviour during the sinking and the subsequent salvage has been crucial for the emotional association with the shipwreck. However, although often done and even in some cases institutionalised (KNA, 2015) emotions are a dangerous measuring stick with which to award an object with a cultural heritage value (Smith, 2006). But the fact that the *Titanic* became a symbol for the UNESCO Convention even before it passed the 100-year mark for lying underwater shows the power of other than archaeological significance in the valuing of shipwrecks. On the other hand, it also may represent the most important value of an object and thus an important reason to transfer the object to the next generation by conserving it. Connected to these emotions is for

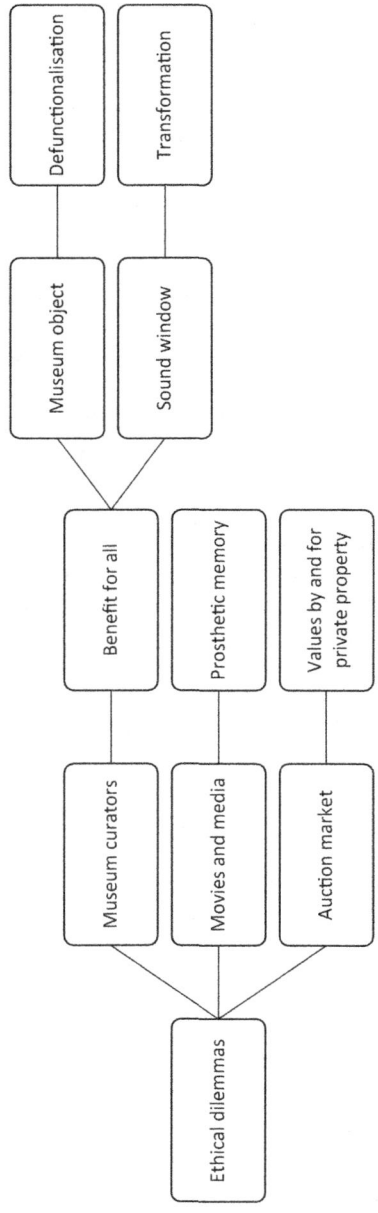

Figure 3.2 Organisation of the ethical dilemmas.

example the heroic role of the band of the *Titanic*, which played on while the ship sank. The violin and the sound of the violin are prominent symbols. However, if it is decided that it is the violin *per se* (physical object) that needs to be preserved, the violin will suffer a process of defunctionalisation, to be considered an untouched museum object and not a violin whose main feature is to be played; but if it is the music played by the violin (sound window) that would generate the emotions and the attachment on the spectator, the violin needs to suffer a process of transformation, since its current condition does not allow it to be played.

A museum object: defunctionalisation

The violin is *not* an archaeological object and it does not provide information about the archaeological context. It does not add any new facts about the archaeological site since it was never part of the site on the seabed. However, although not part of the archaeological context, the violin is part of the overall *Titanic* collection and a visual window to the past. To preserve it, from an aesthetic history of art point of view, as a museum object, it should remain as it is. The violin may have already 'suffered' (minor) stabilisation treatment to enable it to be sold in an auction and may therefore have been transformed from its original state into that of conservation—this is the state in which it was when it was found again in 2006. However, the usual policies on standards of conservation tend to leave the object as authentic and untouched as possible (Viduka, 2012: 3). The violin would be preserved as a window to the past: look and remember, but do not touch (Manders et al., 2012). And although it is beyond the scope of this chapter to fully engage in a discussion of authenticity and the attempts made to understand it over the years, and agreeing with Howard (2003) there are different kinds of authenticity: for instance of creator, material, function, concept, history, ensemble, context, experience and style. In this regard the violin would always stand as 'authentic', for one reason or the other.

McLean (McLean, 2008: 283) believes that museums are the most fertile heritage areas in which to undertake valuation work since the display is represented and interpreted and the heritage is negotiated through the exhibition itself. The difference between treating an object as a museum object or a funerary object—both possible for the violin—will change the way the spectator feels when getting closer to the object (Hooper-Greenhill, 1992). It will manipulate the spectators' approach to the object because of changing it from an historical educational interest towards a commemoration of an event. In fact, a key point in asserting value is the concept of tragedy: the concept of *memento mori*. If the violin is treated as a funerary object, the public will identify themselves with the history and story of the object and it becomes memorabilia. The context of the object would be Harley's body: he was found by Mackay Bennett ten days after the wreck, tagged as body 224, identified by the Coroner in Halifax and sent to England (Pendle Borough

Council, n.d.). As a consequence of this closeness with the death, the funerary value of the violin will not only have an effect on the price when sold, but this treatment will also be appealing at the emotional side of the spectator. In fact, the *Titanic* site has been defined by Delgado (Delgado, 2009) as a 'graveyard, made all the more powerful by the nature of the tragic event'. The violin preserves a sense of immediacy to tragedy: when played again it could be seen as a sacrilege. When treated as a museum (or a gallery) object, the visitor will look at it aesthetically, as a symbolic piece of art.

The violin would be defunctionalised. It may be acting anymore as a generator of sound but would be re-evaluated and assigned as an aesthetic object. However, a violin is not just an object and it is not just an artefact: it is a musical instrument, the function of which is generating music. Barclay (2005) states that not playing a musical instrument can be seen as denying the pleasure and emotion of playing since their main value is intangible and symbolic: the sound. If the object is defunctionalised by not playing and just exhibiting it, it may lose meaning, significance and, as a consequence, an important part of its value. If, as Delgado (Delgado, 2009) states, the story has to be kept alive, playing the violin would make it ever present.

A sound window: transformation

Of all artefacts preserved, musical instruments incur the hardest feelings if they are kept silent. Playing them is the touchstone to sensations that transcend its material being (Barclay, 2004).

Musical instruments may be the only items found by archaeologists that can help us understand the sounds of the past. For Hooper-Greenhill (2000) knowledge of an object includes handling, smelling, hearing and seeing. However, hearing is one of the five senses—sight, hearing, taste, smell and touch—rarely experienced in archaeology. When we have it is rare and unique: for instance, a sixteen-century trumpet was excavated from the *Scheurrak SO1* wreck in the Netherlands. A replica has been made which gave scientists the opportunity to investigate its sound and the different tones produced by the several mouth pieces discovered (Van der Heide, 1994). Only a few other violins or parts of violins have been found in shipwrecks: two (and a bow) on the *Mary Rose* (1545), four on the *Kronan* (1676) and three on the *Maple Leaf* (1864) (Montagu, 2005; Yllana, 2013). However, these instruments, in their present state, cannot be played. They are considered to be beyond repairing and only reconstruction could bring the spectator close to the original sound.

The issue is that if the violin is considered to have a sonority value, then the object may have to be played, and as a consequence must pass through severe *luthier*—a craftsman who makes and repairs stringed instruments modifications—which may require an almost entire reconstruction, such as changing the strings, the pegs, refinishing the wood and possibly changing the tailpiece where the fiancées' inscription is located. As Figure 3.3 illustrates,

Figure 3.3 Current state of preservation of the violin of the *Titanic*.
© [Titanic Museum Branson, MO & Pigeon Forge, TN]. Reproduced by permission of Titanic Attraction. Permission to reuse must be obtained from the rights holder.

some strings are missing, there is no bridge and two cracks are visible on the sound box. On the other hand, any modification of the violin, even the small bridge that holds the strings, would create a change of sound (Yano and Minato, 1992). However, Barclay (2004) reminds that interaction with objects means subject them to wear and damage and eventually servicing and adjustment are required; yet the object still remains 'the real thing'.

Restoring the object would emphasise its value through sound, which is rare in a cultural object. Sound can play a role in individual memory. It can inspire past situations, atmospheres and emotions. But it also can inspire a feeling of collective identity (Stachel, 2006). Being able to be played could be a tribute to the victims of the shipwreck. If there were survivors, which is not the case anymore, listening again to the same sound from the same violin would have generated countless emotions. Knowing the authenticity of the violin, knowing that the violin is the one that played on board of the *Titanic*, would it change the level of emotion? And would it change the economic value? The basic question is if this would justify the severe modification that the violin would require to be played again. The public benefit would have to be considered.

Barclay (2006) explores a protocol of the use of historic musical instruments. For the author, the potential for active function of historic instruments can only be considered on a case-by-case basis. He assigns three specific aspects of historic objects—rarity, fragility and state—and ascribe gradations to them using a rating system using stars. Under this rating, the violin of the *Titanic*, being a rare object—one of a few examples of its type, associated with a particular historic event, being high fragile—may be damaged by being played and its use has a level of unpredictability, and being used, with traces or repair and maintenance and some parts original, would score 11 stars. This means that it is a very significant object. As a consequence, the object may be demonstrated or used but familiarity with the object is necessary for the demonstrator/user. This protocol would also guarantee that the instrument would not be explored or exposed to risk of excess or inappropriate usage.

Interpretation of the object as a musical instrument or as a piece of art, or as a funerary object can distort the information. The curator or owner of an object can manipulate the public connection with the violin: heritage gains meaning through interpretation and there is more than one possible interpretation (Aplin, 2002). Those who interpret the object are responsible for the message they spread, the content of that message and how it is presented (Aplin, 2007). This process of interpretation includes bestowing the object with a value and a meaning. However, it still does not necessarily make the violin an expensive auction object. More is needed.

Movies and media: prosthetic memory

Other sinking such as the three British cruisers *Aboukir, Hogue and Cressi* (1914), *Lusitania* (1915) or the *Andrea Doria* (1956) also resulted in the death of passengers in similar circumstances but their stories have not been so well known (Howard, 2003). The reason is that although there are no witnesses to the sinking, as they are all dead: Lillian Asplund claimed to be the last eye witness died in 2006 (Brown, 2006), the *Titanic* has still had a power of attraction to those who have lived the event through the media and the cinema. The traumatic event of the *Titanic* has been lived by a large amount of people through various films and especially Cameron's film in 1997 (Cameron, 1997) which has added new context to the violin. In fact, in October 2014 the jacket that Di Caprio was wearing during the famous the scene at the bow of the ship with the actress Kate Winslet was auctioned for $70,000 (Scarpellini, 2014). This shows that this contextualisation—true or false—leads to growth of economic value.

It is what has been referred to as prosthetic memory which Robert Burgoyne defines as 'the way mass cultural technologies of memory enable individuals to experience, as if they were memories, even though which they themselves did not live' (Burgoyne, 1997). Landsberg (1995) has largely studied the term 'prosthetic memory' applied to the media and adds that prosthetic memory 'derives from a person's mass-mediated experience of a traumatic event of the past'. And, although 'prosthetic' memories complicate the distinction between memory and history, it is also, in the opinion of the authors, an emotional link to the past, a form of identification, a way to embrace the past as yours, which is what cultural heritage is about. Landsberg (1995: 175) explains that prosthetic memories are those that do not come from a 'lived experience' in a strict sense: they are implanted. The mass media is a privileged arena for the creation of prosthetic memories. The film *Titanic* has been able to create prosthetic memories of the event for perhaps three main reasons: (1) The film itself is appealing and tells the tragedy through a love story which drew an enormous number of visitors to the cinemas, (2) the appealing—and virtually unknown—world of shipwrecks and sunken treasures (3) is part of a history that shocked the world.

The sound and melody people have heard and are familiar with through various *Titanic* films, especially the music during the scene of the sinking of the ship, generate emotions (Stachel, 2006) as a symbol of not only the sinking but also of the generosity of the human spirit in moments of crisis, as the violinist, knowing he was going to die, kept playing to calm the rest of the passengers. It has not been confirmed what music was being played before and during the sinking of the ship (Walter, 1995) but the media, through a prosthetic memory, has instilled in the public some melodies which are now both a symbol of faith and also a symbol of helplessness. They represent that there was nothing else that can be done but wait to die. Obviously this experience is different from that of the survivors of the *Titanic* disaster but just as genuine. The viewer of the violin would again identify himself with the tragedy through the media and remember the event as one actually lived through (Landsberg, 1995). And this identification creates a raise in the value of the violin. The question is whether we should hear that music from the original violin or if the sound of the violin is enough for us, not matter the melody played.

Auction market: values by and for private property

The consequences of contemporary classical collecting have been largely discussed (Chippindale and Gill, 2000; Gill and Chippindale, 2007; Kaiser, 1993). Auction houses also play a crucial role in world art. They are the driving force of a market which daily moves millions of pounds (Watson, 1997).

Nowadays, auction is a sales technique which has a special magnetism. As Learmount (1985: 18), stated, this is because no fixed price structure exists and the seller can think he can obtain a high price and the buyer thinks he is going to acquire a bargain. As a result of this, Kaiser (1993: 347) identified the species of 'loot-consumer', the *acquisitor*, whose interest in antiquities is not in the object itself but rather in the profits of speculating in the market, this is the economic value of the object. Money is the primary driver for an auction house. It collects objects and sells them in order to make a profit. Heritage or historical and archaeological values are only interesting if this would drive up the price and consequently the profit. For this reason, they should not be in the position to award historical or archaeological values to objects because they are motivated by economic gain.

The violin was found strapped to the back of Wallace Hartley. The reasons why he had done so may be many: he wanted to be rescued with the violin so that he could play it again, he wanted to die with it since it was a gift from his fiancée, he hoped his body would be saved with it so both his body and the violin could be returned to his fiancée, he did not want the violin to be lost in the depths of the ocean—there is an emotional link of a violinist to his instrument—it was his most precious and valuable possession (Yllana, 2013), he could trust on being better seen for rescue or he thought about using it to float on since the wooden item and the case would help his buoyancy in the water (Telegraph Reporter, 2013). These are all possibilities, but we will never know the real reason: the possibility that prevails in our minds depends on the degree of emotion and drama we want to place on the object and its story. But this would have an effect on how we treat the object in the present. If Wallace Hartley thought of the ocean as his grave, he may have wanted the object to remain with him. If his body was saved and reburied, the violin could have been reburied with him. Similarities can be drawn with Egyptian burials—where the deceased would be buried with their most precious belongings—or the flutes in the graves at *Jiahu*—the oldest playable instruments found (Zhang et al., 1999).

For this reason, as a private object that has always been transferred through private hands and sold from private owner to private owner, the violin stands between the idea of public property and private ownership. It also challenges the concept of *property*. Property of heritage according to law has been largely discussed (for instance, see Carman, 2005). As Forrest (2002) observes, it has to be important to humankind, rather than be of value. However, the term 'property' has been criticised since in the common law system it has a politico-philosophical weight and it is fundamental to protect the rights of the owner such as to have exclusive rights to alienate, to exploit, to exclude others and even to destroy it (Forrest, 2002). As a consequence, the private owner may have the right to exploit and even destroy the violin. But if the violin may also be considered of 'public interest' and public importance, it should be visible and enjoyable for all.

It should be said that the instrument today is part of an itinerant exhibition by Titanic Museum Attractions, which recognises the value of the violin as heritage and important element of a story that needs to be told (Titanic Pigeon Forge, n.d.).

Proposal: changes in the status

The dilemma of awarding values to the violin by the various stakeholders has resulted in the violin changing from an inexpensive violin to an expensive piece of heritage. What seems clear in this chapter is that due to its uniqueness the violin should be enjoyed by all. However, it is unclear if the violin should be returned to the public domain or remain private owned (Figure 3.4).

Possible changes if the violin is considered to be public cultural heritage

The first option would be claiming the violin for its importance, not for the time it was under water: the violin belongs to the ship RMS *Titanic*, which is underwater cultural heritage according to the 2001 UNESCO Convention. However, the violin was taken out of the water only 10 days after the sinking of the ship and is not, as a consequence, underwater cultural heritage. However, the violin of the *Titanic* may not be considered underwater cultural heritage under the scope of the 2001 UNESCO Convention but it is clearly cultural heritage of considerable importance, representativeness and uniqueness (Aplin, 2002). Following the idea by Carman (1996) of the law as 'gatekeeper', the violin, for not being 'marked' worthy of legal coverage,

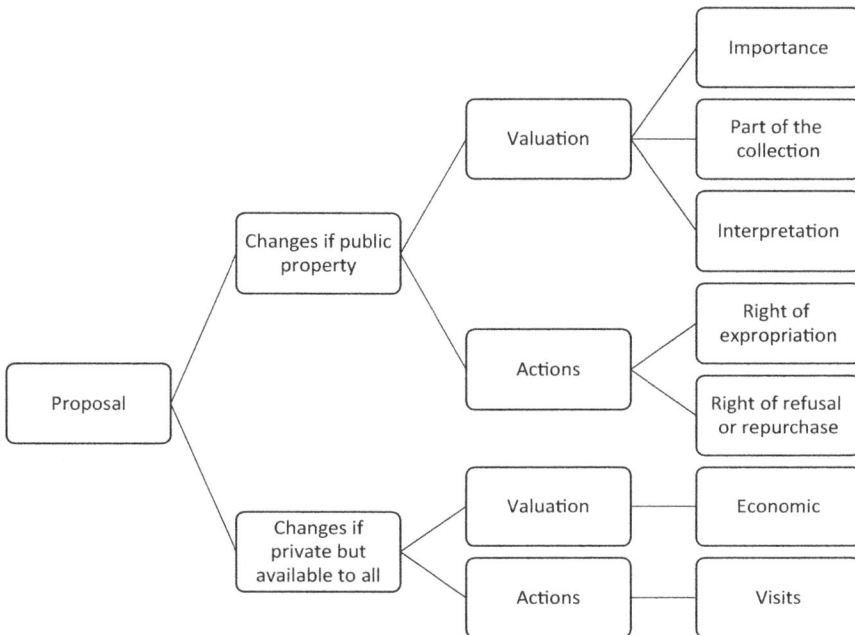

Figure 3.4 Proposal for management of the violin of the *Titanic*.

has been recategorised and revalued as an 'economic piece of heritage' since it has been sold in an auction house. The law has changed the moral status of the violin—symbolic, historical—and it has changed how it is understood. Other option would be claiming the violin as part of the collection and establishing its protection due to the reassembly of the collection: since it is not included within the scope of the 2001 UNESCO Convention, it can be separated—depending on the interpretation of 'collection'—from the main collection. It was even sold to a private buyer although it was possibly the most iconic item of memorabilia within the sunken vessel (Kennedy, 2013). A final option is that the violin could be claimed to have different interpretation of values, choosing that most applicable: the violin can be interpreted, transformed or manipulated to reach the audience by (1) leaving the violin as much as possible in an untouched state complying with the conservation and preservation rules, defunctionalising the object and granting the violin with an aesthetic value (2) awarding the violin with a memorial—and funerary—value even it has been decontextualised or (3) transforming the object to enable it to be played, stressing it as a symbolic object and underlining the emotional value of sound and the power of prosthetic memory, even if it means transforming the object. The question is what value of the violin should be the pre-dominant one for its most accurate interpretation.

Two actions could be taken depending on what the violin is claimed to be. If it is finally decided that the violin should be public cultural heritage, the states could obtain ownership exercising the right of expropriation: in all legal systems, the rights of the individual have been limited in favour of the public interest if the property is of great importance (Forrest, 2002). According to Osborn's Concise Law Dictionary (Woodley, 2009) *expropriation* is defined as 'compulsorily depriving a person of his property by the state—perhaps without compensation' for a purpose deemed to be in the public interest. The *Titanic* was a British vessel that sank beyond the jurisdiction of even the nearest coastal state, Canada (Nafziger, 1999). There are only four states—Canada, France, the United Kingdom, and the United States— with a *clear, indisputable link with the* Titanic, *its crew and appurtenances, and the passengers aboard* (Aznar-Gómez and Varmer, 2012). If the four countries with an interest in the *Titanic* decide that the violin has a high importance as a collection and as such, it should be of public benefit they could expropriate it from private property and make it available to all.[2] In fact, some countries have the right to acquire property—'nationalisation' of cultural heritage—that according to Carman (2013) has advantages like the full control over the fate of the property, but it 'rides roughshod' over private rights. However, if this right of expropriation seems excessive, 'the right of first refusal' and 'the right of repurchase' could be applied: by 'the right of first refusal', if a property of national interest is on the market, the authorities have the right to be notified of the sale and its terms, and to acquire that property before any other interested party. This could be applied to the next sale of the violin. However, if there is no notification of the sale, or if the terms are different to the market sale, the authorities have 'the right of repurchase'. It means that authorities can buy the property on the original terms even if it has already been sold, which would be the current case of the violin if the states interested in the *Titanic* would sign an agreement of protection of the objects with retrospective scope. Applying these two rights, the violin could be for the benefit of all. Thanks to 'the right of first refusal' and 'the right of repurchase' the State could have priority in acquiring the object if it so wanted.

Possible changes if the violin is considered to be private property, but available to all

The violin became common cultural heritage from the moment the *Titanic* was discovered, researched and consequently gained an interest in society (Carman, 2013). And it has been this recognition of the object as cultural heritage what has awarded it with an economic value. This economic value has to be respected because it means that the other values are acknowledged. As a result, conditions for visits could be arranged. Prott and O'Keefe (1984: 190) specify that to regulate the protection of an object it is not necessary to own it. On this basis, an alternative to expropriation of the object could be to keep the right to own private property but with some obligations by the owner, for instance allowing the study by researchers or allowing visits by the general public. The option of categorising the violin as 'of interest' would benefit the owner, in the sense that the violin could be included in national or world heritage lists. This prestige would revaluate the violin and its economic value would increase in a future sale. This would be in benefit of the owner, which could be more open to a condition of visits under this premise.

The violin of the *Titanic* is now in the hands of an anonymous collector who may or may not be a private individual or a museum, who must decide whether to exhibit it, not exhibit it or maybe even restore it to functional order. However, the violin being in private ownership challenges the issue of public property because of its importance (Ashworth, 2007.) Given its importance this valuable object should not be excluded from the public domain by a private owner. The violin of the *Titanic*, if adjudged to be of 'international interest' or 'historical interest' could be subjected to rights visits, making it available to all.

Conclusions

The chapter has explored the process of transformation of the object from an inexpensive violin to expensive heritage. Depending on who assigns the values, the violin will be managed differently. The interpretation of these values will change the way the audience will see the violin and how they will feel around the violin. It has been seen that the violin has moved from an inexpensive violin to a violin with high economic values: this economic value has been reached because of the other values that were awarded by mainly the museums and the media and cinema. Figure 3.5 illustrates the process from an inexpensive violin to an expensive piece of heritage by bestowing a series of values as a consequence of its specific circumstances; from the tragedy, to the discovery of the shipwreck and through the media and the auction market. The different values have accumulated the economic value.

The violin can be considered either a personal object—a funerary item taken by Wallace Hartley into his grave, the ocean—or an object with a value of a much larger story, a symbol and a historical document of the tragedy of the *Titanic*. However, it is interesting considering whether these values are real or have been manufactured by the cinema through prosthetic memories: an emotional and historical connection with the story that the cinema has told, not with the real one.

The chapter has also discussed the issue of public or private property: the violin is in private hands and is private property. This chapter has shown is that the violin, from first being of no importance, is now considered an object 'with universal value'. This has been achieved through a complex process of contextualisation and validation and now we cannot deny its heritage value. Acknowledgement of this power is what might make the violin being protected and possibly even available to all. The issue of private property and public property raise various controversies: the violin was a private property object that belonged to the violinist, then to the fiancée and then to all the proprietors that have been buying the object. As a consequence, its auction has been just the logical step in this path. However, if the violin is found to be a piece that should benefit everyone, seen by all and enjoyed by all, the violin should be either public property or private property establishing certain responsibilities for the owner and certain rights for the visitor. This may happen with many other pieces other than the violin. Finally, the chapter has examined if the violin should be preserved as a museum object or as an instrument. As said, for Smith (2006) the real sense of heritage is in the act of passing on and receiving memories, emotions and knowledge: the heritage user wants to experience sensations, feelings and emotions. The emotions of the user need to be challenged: moments of joy, sadness, anger or fear are necessary for a closer experience with the heritage (Robinson, 2012: 22). These emotions, memories and knowledge are engaged when the various stakeholders change, influence and manipulate the applicable values for example by adding new context. If listening to the violin, those emotions, memories and knowledge offer the public a stronger connection with this heritage, the violin should suffer a process of restoration in order to be played again. It is the sound of the *Titanic* violin that can part of a collective -or a prosthetic memory- inherited through story-telling and continuous communal interest. Preservation of the violin as a museum object or as a sound window will highlight different values. Table 3.1 summarises the different values that a piece of heritage has according to the

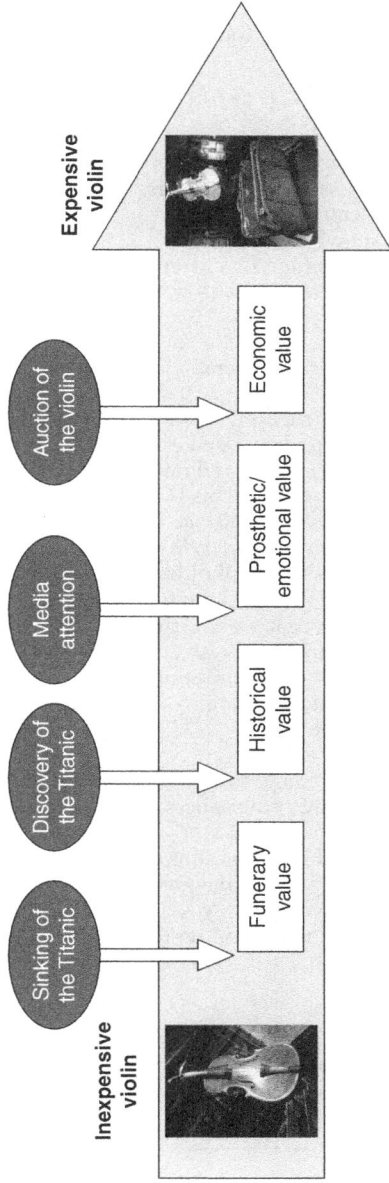

Figure 3.5 Process of moving from an inexpensive violin to expensive heritage.

Table 3.1 Comparison of values as a sound window or as a visual window

Values	Sound window	Museum object
Yield important information about the past, including archaeological	It would bring information on how the violin sounded	Its construction, provenance of the materials, any modifications, etc. All the tests of provenance have been done, it is difficult it offers any more information[a]
Historical significance	Its music [or sound?] has importance on an event in cultural history	The object *per se* has importance on an event in cultural history
Scientific significance	Its sound could provide information on current *Luthiers*	It has been researched already with Scanning Electron Microscope and X-ray Microprobe. No more tests are expected[b]
Aesthetic significance	It could lose its actual aesthetic in the reconstruction. However, it being played makes it a violin again, and not just an object. This is also aesthetic significance	As an object in a museum
Social or spiritual significance	As a funerary object. But also as a symbol of being played during sinking	It loses the emotional answer to the music from the touristic point of view
Experience significance	Listening to it would trigger the stories [collective memory and emotions] around the *Titanic*	Seeing it would trigger the stories around the *Titanic*
Economic significance	Invaluable	$1.7 millions
Provenance	Violins coming from different provenances sound different	Would be the same one
Representativeness	Its sound from the sunken. As a trigger of memories	As a violin recovered from the *Titanic*
Rarity/uniqueness	The only one that was played that night on the *Titanic*	Historical instruments are relatively rare, but not unique. An early 20th C German factory violin is not rare. However, this is the only one from the *Titanic*
Condition	Can be played	Can be exhibited
Interpretative potential	Can emotionally bring a story	Can tell a story

Notes
a In this regard, as we have seen, it has been suggested that new techniques in the future can bring to old objects of collections new information revealed.
b Some authors (Manders, 2012) establish that it is the questions you ask that give you the answers. So, there might always be new questions to ask as long as the evidences are not destroyed.

Training Manual for the UNESCO Foundation Course. All the values will be analysed establishing a comparison between preserving the violin as a sound window and preserving it as a museum object.

Issues of valuation of the cultural heritage, the importance of the context and the challenges of the management of underwater/cultural heritage have been examined. In fact, and since the 2001 UNESCO Convention set 100 years as the limit for the protection of the underwater cultural heritage, the violin has been excluded from this protection. As a consequence, it has been the law that has decided upon what is and what is not heritage and what should or should not be protected. An object that may be a unique piece of heritage may not be protected under the 2001 UNESCO Convention. However, the previous assertion assumes that that object is heritage and not a product of interpretation by the museum curators, the media and the auction market. A sense of prosthetic memory can confuse the heritage with a feeling of heritage. The fine line between these two possibilities is blurred and it needs to be well defined.

The shipwreck of the *Titanic* is waiting for an agreement to come into force between the four countries interested on her protection and management. The UK ratified the agreement in 2003 and the United States in 2004 (Varmer, 2006). It is worth remarking that in the agreement, project authorisations are necessary for entry into the hull so human remains are not disturbed and any activity aimed at the artefacts outside the hull are also regulated (Varmer, 2006). At least two countries had to ratify the Agreement for it to take effect (Agreement, 2000). Article 2 of the Agreement states that:

RMS Titanic shall be recognised as:

(a) a memorial to those men, women and children who perished and whose remains should be given appropriate respect, in accordance with this Agreement; and
(b) an underwater historical wreck of exceptional international importance having a unique symbolic value.

However, the Agreement only applies to:

[...] all artefacts recovered from *RMS Titanic* after entry into force of this Agreement [...] (Article 3)

Despite this article which gives the Agreement a non-retrospective character, this chapter poses the dilemma of if the violin, due to the fact that it is (a) a memorial to those who perished which deserves appropriate respect and (b) may have the highest symbolic value of all the items associated with the *Titanic*, should have been preserved as an exception under the Agreement, even though the collection of artefacts rescued in the first excavation have already been dispersed to various museums and private collectors.

This chapter has explored issues of contexts, management and valuation of cultural heritage, but it also has looked at the importance of the law for the definition of this cultural heritage, the weight of history and memory on the preservation of an object and the influence of external factors—such as the media—for the valuation of the object. These constant ethical challenges will continue to be explored in other chapters of this book.

Notes

1 Reproduced from Perez-Alvaro, E. and Manders, M. R. (2016). Playing the values: sound and vision of the violin of the *Titanic. Journal of Cultural Heritage* 21: 869–875. Copyright © 2016, published by Elsevier Masson SAS. All rights reserved.

2 It is worth mentioning that, in this regard, the four interested countries also consider the reassembly of collections in their legislation: (1) US Federal Regulation states than an artifact collection 'should not be subdivided and stored at more than a single repository' (36 Code of Federal Regulations 79.6 (b) (2)) Available at: www.ecfr.gov/cgi-bin/ECFR?page=browse; (2) The Guide to the Management of Movable Heritage Assets in Canada, Government of Canada (Guide to the Management of Movable Heritage Assets. Available at: www.tbs-sct.gc.ca/pol/doc-eng.aspx?section=text&id=13872 emphasises the need to 'keep heritage items in their original place and context whenever possible or, if this is not possible, keep the items in managed collections'; (3) France is also a country with an interest in the shipwreck, since the Liner called at Cherbourg (France). Under French legislation, there is no age criterion in the definition, but includes 'all assets of prehistoric, archaeological or historic interest' (Law No. 89–874 of 1 December relating to maritime cultural assets (*Journal official de la Republique Française*, 5 December 1989, 15033–15034). Available at: www.un.org/depts/los/LEGISLATIONANDTREATIES/STATEFILES/FRA. However, a court decision (*Tribunal correctionnel*, Brest, 25 October 1994, *Ministere public*, p. 10, unreported) defined maritime cultural assets as 'remains of a glorious and tragic event in the history of our country'. In this sense, the violin of the *Titanic* would fall into the terms of this legislation; (4) In the UK, Southampton was the departure point of the *Titanic*, the Protection of Wrecks Act 1973 (c. 33) includes any objects contained or formerly contained in [a vessel of historical, archaeological or artistic importance]. The violin was formerly contained and as a consequence, falls within the scope of this legislation. Members at the International Congress of Maritime Museums in 1993, including the National Maritime Museum, Greenwich, agreed that 'artefacts from underwater sites are integral parts of an archaeological finds complex which should stay together for research and display' (Hosty, 1995).

Bibliography

Agreement (2000). Agreement concerning the shipwrecked vessel RMS Titanic, 5 January 2000. [online]. Available at: www.gc.noaa.gov/documents/titanic-agreement.pdf (2 July 2018).

Aplin, G. (2002). *Heritage Identification, Conservation and Management*. Oxford: Oxford University Press.

Aplin, G. (2007). World heritage cultural landscapes. *International Journal of Heritage Studies* 13(6): 427–446.

Ashworth, G. J. (2007). On townscapes, heritages and identities. Paper presented at the Institute for Advanced Studies Colloquium on Urban-Rural: Flows and Boundaries, Lancaster University.

Aznar-Gómez, M. and Varmer, O. (2012). The *Titanic* as underwater cultural heritage: challenges to its international legal protection. *Ocean Development & International Law* 44(1): 96–112.

Barclay, R. (2004). A decision-making protocol for the use of historic musical instruments. *Journal of the Canadian Association for Conservation* 29(2004) 3–7.

Barclay, R. (2005). *The Preservation and Use of Historic Musical Instruments: Display Case and Concert Hall.* London: Earthscan.

Barclay, R. (2006). *The Stradivarius and the DC-3.* Providence, RI: American Institute for Conservation.

Brown, D. (2006). *The Last Witness. The Washington Post*: www.washingtonpost.com/wp-dyn/content/article/2006/07/26/AR2006072601280.html (2 July 2018).

Burgoyne, R. (1997). *Film Nation: Hollywood Looks at U.S. History.* Minneapolis: University of Minnesota Press.

Cameron, J. (Director) (1997). *Titanic* [Motion Picture]. USA: Paramount Pictures.

Carman, J. (1996). *Valuing Ancient Things: Archaeology and Law.* Leicester: Leicester University Press.

Carman, J. (2005). *Against Cultural Property: Archaeology, Heritage and Ownership.* London: Duckworth Debates in Archaeology.

Carman, J. (2013). Legislation in archaeology: overview and introduction. In Smith, C. (ed.), *Encyclopaedia of Global Archaeology.* New York: Springer: 4469–4485.

Chippindale, C. and Gill, D. (2000). Material consequences of contemporary classical collecting. *American Journal of Archaeology* 104(3): 43–51.

Convention on the Protection of the Underwater Cultural Heritage, UNESCO, 2 November 2001.

Delgado, J. (2009). *Adventures of a Sea Hunter: In Search of Famous Shipwrecks.* Vancouver: Douglas & McIntyre.

Forrest, C. (2002). Defining 'underwater cultural heritage'. *International Journal of Nautical Archaeology* 31(1): 3–11.

Gill, D. and Chippindale, C. (2007). The illicit antiquities scandal: what it has done to classical archaeology collections. *American Journal of Archaeology* 111(3): 571–574.

Guerin, U. (2012). *The Protection Accorded to the* Titanic *by the UNESCO Convention on the Protection of the Underwater Cultural Heritage.* Paris: UNESCO.

Henry Aldridge & Son (n.d.). Titanic & Iconic Memorabilia. Available at: www.henry-aldridge.co.uk/.

Hooper-Greenhill, E. (1992). *Museums and the Shaping of Knowledge.* London: Routledge.

Hooper-Greenhill, E. (2000). *Museums and the Interpretation of Visual Culture.* London: Routledge.

Hosty, K. (1995). A matter of ethics: shipwrecks, salvage, archaeology and museums. *Bulletin of the Australian Institute for Maritime Archaeology* 19(1): 33–36.

Howard, P. (2003). *Heritage: Management, Interpretation, Identity.* London: Library of Congress.

Howells, R. (1999). *The Myth of the* Titanic. London: Palgrave Macmillan.

Kaiser, T. (1993). The antiquities market. *Journal of Field Archaeology* 20(3): 347–355.

Kennedy, D. (2013). *Titanic* violin fetches £900,000 record price. [online]. *BBC News*. 19 October 2013. Available at: www.bbc.co.uk/news/uk-england-wiltshire-24582739.

KNA (2015). *Quality Standard for Dutch Archaeology.* Available at: www.sikb.nl (accessed 1 June 2017).

Landsberg, A. (1995). Prosthetic memory: total recall and blade runner. In Burrows, M. F. (ed.), *Cyberspace/Cyberbodies/Cyberpunk: Cultures of Technological Embodiment.* London: Sage: 175–190.

Learmount, B. (1985). *A History of the Auction.* Indianapolis, IN: Barnard & Learmount.

Manders, M. (2012). Unit 9: in situ preservation. In Manders, M. and Underwood, C. (eds.), *Training Manual for the UNESCO Foundation Course on the Protection and Management of Underwater Cultural Heritage in Asia and the Pacific.* Bangkok: UNESCO.

Manders, M., Van Tilburg, H. and Staniforth, M. (2012). Unit 6: significance assessment. In Manders, M. and Underwood, M. M. (eds.), *Training Manual for the UNESCO Foundation Course on the Protection and Management of Underwater Cultural Heritage in Asia and the Pacific.* Bangkok: UNESCO.

Marist Poll and Sea Research Foundation. (2013, March). The legacy of the *Titanic*: over a century later. Available at: www.searesearch.org (accessed 3 July 2017).

McLean, F. (2008). Museums and the representation of identity. In Howard, B. G. (ed.), *The Ashgate Research Companion to Heritage and Identity.* Cornwall: Ashgate: 283–297.

Montagu, J. (2005). Dance and skylark: musical instruments. Music on board the *Mary Rose*. In Gardiner, J. (ed.), *Before the Mast: Life and Death Aboard the* Mary Rose. Portsmouth: Mary Rose Trust: 226–249.

Nafziger, J. A. R. (1999). The *Titanic* revisited. *Journal of Maritime Law and Commerce* 30(2): 311–329.

Pendle Borough Council (n.d.). Bereavement services. Available at: www.pendle.gov. uk/info/20089/bereavement_services/54/bereavement_services/6 (3 May 2018).

Protection of Wrecks Act (1973). Legislation UK government. Available at: www. legislation.gov.uk/ukpga/1973/33 (21 May 2018).

Prott, L. V. and O'Keefe, P. J. (1984). *Law and the Cultural Heritage.* Oxford: Professional Books.

Robinson, M. (2012). The emotional tourist. In Robinson, D. P. (ed.), *Emotion in Motion: Tourism, Affect and Transformation.* Surrey: Ashgate: 21–39.

Scarpellini, P. (2014). La ropa que mojo Dicaprio en *Titanic*, a subasta. [online.] *El Mundo.* 2 October 2014. Available at: www.elmundo.es/cultura/2014/10/02/542c672722601d2c038b4594.html.

Smith, L. (2006). *Uses of Heritage.* London: Routledge.

Stachel, P. (2006). On music and memory: some noncommittal reflections. *Spaces of Identity* 6(3).

The Strad (2013). Violin said to have been played as *Titanic* sank to be auctioned. [online]. *The Strad*. 15 March 2013. Available at: www.thestrad.com/violin-said-to-have-been-played-as-titanic-sank-to-be-auctioned/5890.article.

Telegraph Reporter (2013). Violin played on *Titanic* revealed for the first time. [online]. *The Telegraph*. 14 March 2013. Available at: www.telegraph.co.uk/history/9929996/Violin-played-on-Titanic-revealed-for-first-time.html.

Titanic Pigeon Forge (n.d.). See the *Titanic* violin. Available at: www.titanicpigeonforge.com/ (3 June 2018).

Van der Heide, G. (1994). Reconstructie van een bijzondere Italiaanse trompet van de vindplaat Scheurrak S01. In Bierma, R. R. (ed.), *Vis en Visvangst: Inleidingen gehouden tijdens het xevende Glavimans symposion*. Amersfoort: Glavimans Stichting: 107–114.

Varmer, O. (2006). RMS *Titanic*. In Grenier, R., Nutley, D. and Cochran, I. (eds.), *Heritage at Risk Special Edition. Underwater Cultural Heritage at Risk: Managing Natural and Human Impacts*. Charenton-le-Pont: International Council on Monuments and Sites (ICOMOS): 14–17.

Viduka, A. J. (2012). Unit 11: conservation and finds handling. In Manders, M. and Underwood, M. M. (eds.), *Training Manual for the UNESCO Foundation Course on the Protection and Management of Underwater Cultural Heritage in Asia and the Pacific*. Bangkok: UNESCO.

Walter, L. (1995). *A Night to Remember*. New York: Henry Holt.

Watson, P. (1997). *Sotheby's: Inside Story*. London: Bloomsbury Press.

Willis, S. (2008). *Shipwrecks: A History of Disasters at Sea*. London: Quercus.

Woodley, M. (ed.) (2009). *Osborn's Concise Law Dictionary*. London: Sweet & Maxwell.

Yano, H. and Minato, K. (1992). Improvement of the acoustic and hygroscopic properties of wood by a chemical treatment and application to the violin parts. *Acoustical Society of America* 92(3): 1222–1227.

Yllana, A. (2013). *Contribucion de la arqueologia subacuatica al conocimiento de la evolucion de la guitarra*. Madrid: Universidad Complutense de Madrid.

Zhang, J., Harbottle, G., Wang, C. and Kong, Z. (1999). Oldest playable instruments found at Jiahu early Neolithic site in China. *Nature* 401: 366–368.

4 Uses
Ancient lead for dark matter experiments[1]

Although underwater cultural heritage is under threat from various menaces such as natural deterioration or illegal salvage (Manders, 2004; Aznar-Gómez, 2010), it also faces what we call 'legal threats', such as 'clean' energy provided by wind, wave solar and other 'renewable' energy facilities and their construction (Flatman, 2007: 86). The laying of submarine cables and pipelines (Perez-Alvaro, 2013b) that has been largely forgotten by literature and legislation is another threat, since

> Thousands of kilometres of submarine cables lie on or under the seabed carrying telephone calls and internet data (only 1% of telecommunications are established via satellite). In 2013, 283 cables are active with 29 new routes planned.
>
> (Perez-Alvaro, 2013b: 56)

The dilemma is what would happen if one of the routes for laying cables were planned to go through an underwater cultural heritage site since there is a no legal regulation for protecting those submerged places. The quandary is if the protection of these sites should require diverting these routes with resulting in a longer and more expensive route since some underwater cultural heritage sites can have large areas such as the submerged part of the village of Port Royal, in Jamaica with an area of 13 hectares (28.6 acres) (Hamilton, 2006). Other 'legal threats' include the construction of ports and developments in harbours or fishing since as Dromgoole (2013) mentions, some types of fishing, especially bottom trawling, could cause damages to possible underwater cultural heritage lying at the bottom of the ocean.

The case of the use of ancient lead and underwater cultural heritage opens a new window not only for the realm of physics, but especially and mostly for the realm of underwater cultural heritage management. If this interchange is licit and beneficial both for the dark matter discoveries and for the preservation of underwater cultural heritage it is a matter, again, of prioritising values and not a matter of eradicating one of the values. It is possible that of all the competing values inherent in cultural heritage, the archaeological and historical evidence derived can take preference, which is not to say that the others should be ignored. However, the case of the use of lead for particle physics experiments is only one of the various examples of how laboratories in different industries deal with the recovery and use of the lead.

Introduction

A 2,000-year-old shipwreck's cargo is planned to be used for experiments related to research of dark matter (Nosengo, 2010). Italy's new neutrino detector, CUORE (Cryogenic Underground Observatory for Rare Events), at the Italian National Institute of Nuclear Physics, received from the National Archaeological Museum of Cagliari 120 archaeological lead ingots proceeding from a shipwreck recovered from the sea 20 years ago at the coast of Sardinia. The so-called 'ancient lead'—both Greek and Roman— will be used as a shield for the dark matter detectors because over the past 2,000 years the lead has lost its intrinsic radioactivity due to natural radioactive decay to levels approximately 100,000 times lower than freshly mined lead. 'The use of these objects as stock for experimentation had never been an issue before, but now it is beginning to be deemed ethically questionable' (Perez-Alvaro, 2013a). Roman lead proceeding from a shipwreck under water for 2,000 years is underwater cultural heritage and it is protected under the umbrella of the 2001 UNESCO Convention on the Protection of the Underwater Cultural Heritage (UNESCO, 2001) for being traces of human existence having a historical character which have been underwater for more than 100 years (UNESCO, 2001).

However, it is not only the use of this heritage that presents a concern, but also its recovery and documentation. In the CUORE case the excavations and documentation of the underwater cultural heritage were done by archaeologists under archaeological standards (INFN, 2010). However, in the case of other laboratories the ancient lead is bought from private companies whose end is a profitable recovery where the archaeological standards are unlikely to be accomplished (Throckmorton, 1998):

> The CDMS team — Cryogenic Dark Matter Search — had to find old lead [...]. An Italian colleague mentioned that he had been using lead taken from two-thousand-year-old Roman ships that had sunk off the Italian coast. The CDMS team located a company that was selling lead salvaged from a ship that had sunk off the coast of France in the eighteenth century. Unaware that they were doing anything illegal, the researchers bought the lead. The company, however, got in trouble with French customs for selling archaeological material. Illegal or not, the lead worked.
>
> (Ananthaswamy, 2010)

The issue introduces a new consideration on the treatment and the protection of underwater cultural heritage and its use for non-commercial/scientific experiments. The fact that underwater cultural heritage recovered for experiments that will benefit mankind—although it will be modified or even destroyed by those experiments—introduces a new ethical dilemma for the management and the protection of underwater cultural heritage (Perez-Alvaro, 2013a). However, the use of this material is also becoming popular in different scientific fields such as microelectronics (Ho-Ming Tong, 2013) and low background detectors (ORTEC). The dilemma, which was raised by Perez-Alvaro (2013a), created curiosity in the press and in archaeological and physicists communities (Pringle, 2013b; Moskowitz, 2013, 2014; Gwynne, 2013). However, the debate is complex and requires a sound understanding of all the issues before reaching any conclusions. The quandary is not the use of ancient lead for dark matter experiments alone, it is the growing extended use of this material for other kinds of experiments, from medicine to microelectronics. The question raises the necessity to set boundaries and protocols for the use of the underwater cultural heritage.

Issue

The research on dark matter detection aims to underpin some of the most fundamental properties of the universe. It has been demonstrated experimentally that ordinary matter, i.e. elements of the periodic table, constitute only 17% of the total matter of the universe whilst the remainder is attributed to dark matter (Komatsu et al., 2011). The understanding of the origin of the remaining 83% of the matter present in the universe remains one of the most fundamental open questions to humankind (Perez-Alvaro and Gonzalez-Zalba, 2014: 56).

It basically aims to shed light on one of the most fundamental questions that modern astronomy, in particular, and humanity, in general, can ask: what is our universe made of? A deeper understanding of the properties of dark matter could clarify the origin of the universe and the impact these new particles will have on its evolution. However, direct observation of its existence has remained elusive so far due to its particular properties, as it does not emit radiation and only interacts weakly with ordinary matter. Nowadays, direct detection requires extremely low levels of background signals to distinguish a particular dark matter event from collisions produced by cosmic rays (fast-moving particles that continuously shower the Earth from deep space) or by the intrinsic radioactivity of the environmental materials (Perez-Alvaro and Gonzalez-Zalba, 2014). Particle physicists have to shield dark matter detectors from unwanted sources of spurious signals so experiments are conducted a few kilometres deep underground. These laboratories adopt a combination of shielding materials of which one must be a high-density element (Lang and Seidel, 2009). Among high-density elements that could provide a suitable shield we find precious metals such as platinum, palladium, iridium and rhodium which approach the market price of gold $18010/lb (a suitable candidate as well) and rare and toxic metals such as osmium. None of these elements offer a viable solution due to cost or availability knowing that state-of-the-art dark matter detectors, such as CUORE, require around 4 tonnes of material. Only tungsten ($21/lb), with the potential to achieve extremely low levels of intrinsic radioactivity (Danevich et al., 2003; Bernabei et al., 2013), could be a sensible element for shielding cryogenic detectors underground. However, this is still 20 times more expensive than freshly mined lead, the most commonly used shielding material in radiation rich environments.

Lead is the material par excellence in radiation rich environments as a shielding for damaging radiation. It can be found in nuclear power plants but also in more common environments such as hospital X-ray chambers (Smith et al., 2008). Lead's properties, independently of its origin, of its large atomic number, low intrinsic radioactivity, good mechanical properties and reasonable cost make it an excellent shielding material. In short, it efficiently absorbs unwanted background radiation that could generate spurious signals in the detector. However, freshly mined and processed lead has a finite level of intrinsic radioactivity. This level of radioactivity is unsuitable for state-of-the art dark matter searches and therefore methods to reduce it are necessary. The most problematic radioactive impurity present in lead is one of its unstable isotopes, lead-210 (^{210}Pb), which decays into the stable isotope lead-206 (^{206}Pb) through a series of radioactive transitions. The presence of ^{210}Pb can severely affect the sensitivity of experiments searching for dark matter candidates (Lang and Seidel, 2009).

Low-alpha lead can be currently obtained from a number of sources. The first source is 'cold' ores, since lead is mainly obtained from galena ores. Low-activity 'ores' can provide a reasonable high quality lead that combined with optimised process production can yield alpha emission rates as low as 260 mBq/kg (Johnson&Mathey's) (Alessandrello et al., 1993). The second source is microelectronics grade lead: a commercially available solution to low-alpha lead is currently provided by different suppliers. The production is based on laser isotope separation, a technique that selectively ionises the target material making it separable and removable. However this technology is expensive and currently limited in capacity. Finally, the ancient lead. A Roman yearly production of lead has been estimated at 80.000 tonnes a year (Callataÿ, 2005) providing an important source of non-renewable low-alpha lead. In that sense, 2,000-year old Roman lead recovered from the Mediterranean Sea has been studied in detail (Alessandrello et al., 1998) which has demonstrated extremely low levels of intrinsic radioactive emissions. This type of lead with unprecedented low levels of intrinsic radioactivity is planned to be used at the CUORE experiment. Another prime example is 2,400-year-old Greek from silver lead ores on Mount Lavrion (Attica) and recovered from the bottom of the Black Sea. The reasons behind the extremely low 210Pb content in salvaged ancient lead are due of a combination of natural radioactive decay, ancient ore refining and preservation under water. As a rule of thumb, the longer since the lead was originally processed the lower its intrinsic radioactivity. In addition, and although seawater does not purify lead, it helps in the decay process. First of all, the overburden of water prevents the chemical contamination of lead by for example radioactive elements present in the atmosphere such as radon. Moreover, the cosmic ray flux that showers the earth continuously is greatly reduced at these depths. Cosmic rays can activate stable lead into radioactive elements reducing the rate of decay.

To sum up, the low level of emission of ancient lead cannot be achieved by current lead manufacturing capabilities which are currently expensive and limited in capacity. Although there are artificial techniques available to reduce the radiation content of modern lead to the same level as that has been in seawater for centuries, it cannot achieve the level of purity of ancient lead samples (Alessandrello et al., 1993). Only tungsten could provide an alternative solution. Each sample of salvaged ancient lead should be analysed and benchmarked against the commercial grade ultra-low-alpha lead. Only if it is demonstrated that the level of purity required by each individual experiment is lower than what commercial sources can provide, ancient lead should be considered for use.

State of knowledge

In order to establish a fair comparative debate in the following this chapter will aim to list the main core arguments in favour and against the use of the ancient ingots from a point of view of the cultural heritage preservation.

Criteria in favour of the use of underwater cultural heritage items on experiments comprise for instance the importance of the experiments: the research on dark matter aims to shed light on one of the most fundamental questions that modern astronomy, in particular, and humanity, in general, is facing: what is our Universe made of? A deeper understanding of the properties of dark matter could clarify the origin of the Universe and the impact these new particles will have on its evolution. Another reason is what some authors have named as 'trade goods': replicated elements of cultural artefacts under considerations such as age, rarity and condition (Stemm, 2000). For these authors, these trade goods may be sold or traded, but only with appropriate record and documentation complying with archaeological standards. In this regard, if, of a 1,000-ingot shipwreck cargo carefully studied and documented, 300 are transferred for other uses such as dark matter experiments, there would not mean a significant loss of heritage. Another reason for the use of lead on experiments is that this lead is a 'half product', 'since the site of metal production was often far from areas of manufacturing or consumption, metals, once refined, were rendered into a convenient form for transport such as ingots' (Gale, 2011). Some of them were used as ballasts but most of them were half products, intermediate products (Manders, 2013). Its original function was to be transformed into something else. As a consequence, their use recovers their functionality. A last but very important reason for the use of this heritage is the funding for excavations: a new approach to finance underwater archaeological research is the exchange of ancient lead in order to fund an archaeological intervention on the site. In this sense, the reasons of the Museum of Cagliari for transferring the ingots to the laboratory open two scenarios. First, the material might have been too accessible for treasure hunters or private companies and the museum decided to preserve it *ex situ*. Looking for funding for the excavation they found the laboratory's willingness to establish an agreement—this is for archaeological ends. Or second, the museum might have known that the laboratory was looking for ancient lead and having a record in its archives of the existence of this specific shipwreck, decided to reach an agreement with the laboratory. In exchange of a number of ingots the Museum of Cagliari received the necessary funding for the excavation—this is for commercial ends (INFN, 2010).

Criteria in favour of the preservation of underwater cultural heritage items includes the importance of the heritage: 'where does it all stop, if we accept that evidence of our past can be converted into something that people can buy and take home?' (Pringle, 2013a). But also, in the future archaeological methods may developed allowing to obtain additional information from the ingots. This could facilitate the reconstruction of the historical context through processes such as trade or ancient commercial routes. Once the objects are processed and melted for experimentation the historical information is lost. In addition, if the lead is not used, there is still alternative materials: current lead manufacturing capabilities cannot reach the level of intrinsic radioactivity for state-of-the art dark matter searches but with further technological development this might become a competitive solution. On the other hand, tungsten can be purified to similar levels of intrinsic radioactivity than ancient lead and could provide an alternative shielding material (Danevich et al., 2003; Bernabei et al., 2013). Currently low-radiation tungsten is not commercially available and production costs are undetermined. However, if the price is the only issue, it raises concerns about the commercial exploitation of the underwater cultural heritage. Another reason for the preservation of the ancient lead is the decision on the excavations: selecting sites for commercial reasons is a sliding scale. Excavating sites should be done either because the sites are being threatened and the only way to protect is ex situ or because the scientific questions are important enough to justify this excavation. Excavating sites because it is of interest for scientific experiments eventually leads to selecting areas only for this reason and ends up with a monotone research of the same kind of sites that we already know a lot about. Finally, the size of the collection decreases if the lead is destroyed: there may be a difference between seeing an exhibition of 1,000 ingots instead of seeing only 700 (Yorke, 2013).

Ethical dilemmas: uses

The law needs to catch up with new developments (Trubek, 1972). Underwater cultural heritage is a field which has evolved mainly in the last 20 years. The general 'demand' for historic shipwrecks has grown, increasing their economic value (Kaoru and Hoagland, 1994) and the conflict between different users. However, the 2001 UNESCO Convention for the Protection of the Underwater Cultural Heritage was drafted more than 15 years ago, and, as a consequence, the use of cultural heritage for purposes other than archaeological knowledge has not still being contemplated by legislation. The law needs to adapt to new changes, either by the implementation of new agreements or the creation of new annexes.

The most important conclusions of the 2001 UNESCO Convention are (1) preservation of underwater cultural heritage for the benefit of humanity, (2) *in situ* preservation of underwater cultural heritage and (3) prohibition of commercial exploitation of underwater cultural heritage. And although experiments of particle physics or other kind of experiments are not expressly mentioned or regulated by the 2001 UNESCO Convention, some aspects mentioned in various articles can be interpreted on this direction. However, its interpretation can open the legal vacuums where the ethical controversies are born.

For the benefit of humanity: which benefit?

Article 2.3. States Parties shall preserve underwater cultural heritage for the benefit of humanity in conformity with the provisions of this Convention.

Benefit of humanity is a term that has traditionally been applied to the exploration of the Antarctic and the exploration of outer space, including the Moon. It was also applied under the United Nations Convention on the Law of the Sea (UNCLOS, 1982) for using the sea bed resources in the interests of mankind (Churchill and Lowe, 1999). The concept is usually assigned to vulnerable sites to make them available to all and property of no one, and to preserve them for future generations (Tenenbaum, 1990). In Article 2.3 of the UNESCO Convention no definition of the term benefit of humanity has been given and it leaves unclear what 'benefit' means: economic, emotional, educational or cultural benefit. In this sense, the dilemma is that its preservation benefits humanity, but also its use for experiments on dark matter searches following UNESCO recommendations.

Fundamental research is the expression of human curiosity: of the need to understand the structure of matter, life, the structure and evolution of the Universe, which are the main subject of fundamental research, so that we can decode our past and predict our future.

(Revol, 2007)

This leads us to the dilemma: the deposition should not prejudice the 'scientific interest' of the material (Dromgoole, 2013). Rule 2 of the 2001 Convention Annex says:

[...] (b) deposition of underwater cultural heritage should not prejudice the scientific or cultural interest or integrity of the recovered material [...]

Dark matter experiments and their promise to shed light on the constituencies of the Universe are of scientific interest—as well as the archaeological information revealed by the ingots—and hence fulfil the recommendations of the UNESCO 2001 Convention. However, the preservation of underwater cultural heritage is thought to be for 'the knowledge of future generations'. The quandary is which scientific interest should prevail. In fact, opening the door for the use of underwater cultural heritage to all those that need it, only to some or even to none, is an important ethical dilemma to consider:

No uses allowed

For some authors, giving away any underwater cultural heritage in favour of scientific experimentation of any kind would open a window to a market difficult to regulate: this is, as a consequence, a matter of valuation of this heritage. If it is decided that underwater cultural heritage should not be used under any circumstances, then the possibility of using underwater cultural heritage for experimentation in science should also be rule out. However, not all decisions are black or white as we shall proceed to assess.

Only justified uses allowed

Research on dark matter aims to answer one of the most important questions that modern astronomy, and humanity, is facing: what is our universe made of? This question is expected to be answered by understanding the properties of dark matter. However it is not only this science that needs ancient lead to build a shield against radiation. Perez-Alvaro and Gonzalez-Zalba (2014) explain that the scientific interest in pre–World War II steel from historical submarines and battleships has transcended its historical interest to be used in other domains. For example, medical research: 65 tonnes of steel from *USS Indiana*, scrapped in 1962, was used for shielding at an Illinois Veterans Administration hospital, and another 210 tonnes went into building a shielded room for in vivo radiation measurements at a Utah medical centre (Lynch, 2007, 2011). Equally, steel salvaged from Scapa Flow shipwrecks has been used in low-radiation detectors (Butler, 2006). These shipwrecks and shipwrecks from the World War II are still not underwater cultural heritage for not being under water more than 100 years: they will become so in 2039. In addition, they are tombs of deceased sailors. However, the quandary is if it is more important to preserve those shipwrecks and show respect to the deceased than developing medical technologies that could help to save lives in the future.

The debate of archaeologists as 'owners' of underwater cultural heritage has been largely discussed (Scarre and Scarre, 2006; Carman, 2002). The Society for American Archaeology recognises archaeologists as 'stewards' of the cultural heritage (SAA, 1990: 11):

> Principle No. 1: Stewardship. The archaeological record, that is, *in situ* archaeological material and sites, archaeological collections, records and reports, is irreplaceable. It is the responsibility of all archaeologists to work for the long-term conservation and protection of the archaeological record by practicing and promoting stewardship of the archaeological record. Stewards are both caretakers of and advocates for the archaeological record for the benefit of all people; as they investigate and interpret the record, they should use the specialized knowledge they gain to promote public understanding and support for its long-term preservation.

Therefore, archaeologists have a responsibility to use their influence and specialised knowledge to protect heritage as stewards of the heritage. In this regard, it is worth comparing the situation with politicians. If politicians are 'stewards' of a country, and theoretically they are prepared academically, professionally and by experience to be so it would be unimaginable that this task were going to be taken by an unqualified plumber or an unqualified writer. Heritage, following this example, should be managed by experts in the field and this should not lead to problems of ownership of this heritage. However, it is necessary not to confuse 'stewards' with 'owners'. There is a good example in the case of the Human Genome experiments that have proprietary rights to the researchers but are intrinsic to every human being and as a consequence should be seen as Common Heritage of Humankind (Sturges, 1998). The Human Genome faces, as well, the same problem as underwater cultural heritage: it cannot be researched if it does not attract investors and allow them to make a profit. The crossroad is research with funding or survival without it. The Human Genome has chosen the first option: being funded, allowing a profit, but being for the benefit of humanity (Sturges, 1998: 223). Researchers are only stewards of the human genome as archaeologists are on the heritage.

All uses allowed

As said, the use of ancient lead is becoming popular not only in dark matter experimentation but in other scientific fields such as microelectronics (Tong et al., 2013) and low background detectors (Perez-Alvaro and Gonzalez-Zalba, 2014). Although dark matter laboratories may produce an economic benefit at the end of their research (sponsorships, scholarships or publishing) their primarily goal is not motivated by profit but by knowledge. However, other industries in search of ancient lead, such as the microelectronics industries (Perez-Alvaro and Gonzalez-Zalba, 2014), being private, aspire to gain an economic profit: their knowledge will not necessarily be for the benefit of humanity. It is necessary to evaluate and weigh the loss (of humanity) against the gain (of knowledge). If the balance in some industries will not gain enough knowledge to justify the loss, ancient lead should not be used.

In situ *preservation of underwater cultural heritage*

Article 2.5. The preservation *in situ* of underwater cultural heritage shall be considered as the first option before allowing or engaging in any activities directed at this heritage.

Preservation *in situ* is the first option for the preservation of underwater cultural heritage, but not the only option (Manders, 2008; Maarleveld et al., 2013). Preservation *in situ* is the first option since it slows down degradation (Manders, 2004, 2008). As a consequence, the recovery of underwater cultural heritage would not be contravening this article of the Convention and the recovery of the ingots for the experiments is not penalised. However, study and documentation of the shipwreck site is essential for the recovery of information (Villegas Zamora, 2008). The archaeological practice is a process that reconstruct the puzzle of history, for instance, the position of the objects sheds light on the wreck circumstances. For this reason 'heritage agencies throughout Europe are increasingly seeking to preserve archaeological sites and their associated artefacts *in situ* through legal protection and minimization of excavation' (Caple, 2008). The deal between the Museum of Cagliari and the laboratory opens a new window not only for the realm of physics, but especially and mostly for the realm of underwater cultural heritage management. If this interchange is licit and beneficial both for the dark matter discoveries and for the preservation of underwater cultural heritage it is a matter, again, of prioritising values. Maybe, it is not a matter of eradicating one of the values. It is possible that of all the competing values inherent in cultural heritage, the archaeological and historical evidence derived can take preference, which is not to say that the others should be ignored. In this regard, also the integrity of the material should be weighted. The melting of ingots is an irreparable loss of underwater cultural heritage.

Rule 2. Annex. [...] (b) the deposition of underwater cultural heritage [...] provided such deposition does not prejudice the scientific or cultural interest or integrity of the recovered material [...]

Ingots are of great value for study to archaeologists as a manifestation of ancient Rome's manufacturing and trading powers. In the case of the agreement between the Museum of Cagliari and the laboratory, before melting the ingots, the inscriptions on each one of the ingots were removed and sent back to the museum for conservation and exhibition (the trademarks contain the names of various firms that extracted and traded lead). In addition, and after being recovered, small samples of the ingots were analysed and recorded by the laboratory (Alessandrello et al., 1998). As a consequence, although the object is destroyed, most of the information is preserved. A different situation would arise in the case of the recovery of ingots by private companies where no trademarks are preserved.

Commercial exploitation: is it commercial exploitation?

There is a danger of focusing the debate just around the cultural objects, this is, the ancient ingots. As said, the real concerns on the issue are both the salvage method used to recover the material and the extended application of this material on other industries. The arguments against its use are not the necessity of retaining the objects, but the consequences of not preserving them. As said, study and documentation of the shipwreck site are essential for the recovery of information (Villegas Zamora, 2008: 20). As a consequence, the archaeological context is essential for obtaining information. Only the adequate process of study, analysis and excavation guarantees the correct interpretation of the objects. And even if the procedure is followed, recovering and destroying the object (even if due record is kept) still eliminates evidence of our past that new technology in the future could re-interpret or re-discover. The vessel used for the experiments in Grand Sasso was found by a scuba diver in 1991 30 metres deep. It was a *navis oneraria magna,* built between the year 80 and 50 BC. The vessel came from Cartagena (Spain) and it was heading to Rome. Besides the ingots of ancient lead, other artefacts were found, like amphorae and anchors. Every ingot had an inscription: *Carulius Hispalius,* corresponding to an Italian family that exploited mines in Spain (M.R.E., 2010). This information has been obtained because the shipwreck has been properly studied and recorded by archaeologists and objects on board have been recovered and analysed. However, when the cargo from the shipwreck was discovered, the Museum of Cagliari did not have enough funds to research the archaeological site, so it was thought that Italy's National Institute of Nuclear Physics (INFN) contributed 300 million lira (US$210,000) to the operation. In exchange, a proportion of the recovered lead (a 20%) would become available for the physicists' experiments (Nosengo, 2010). However financing underwater archaeological research in exchange for material recovered was controversial (INFN, 2010).

However, funding archaeological research is not the main issue. Archaeological research is a largely commercialised practice and the source of income has passed from governments to the private sector (Aitchison, 2009). The problem is that even if the archaeological record is perfectly executed, the exchange results in the loss of ingots (underwater cultural heritage objects). Commercial exploitation of cultural heritage can be done in different forms. Treasure hunting is just one practice. But also tourism is, as well as merchandising, paid exhibitions, and sale of reproductions (Dromgoole, 2013). But not all the procedures are so straightforward. It is the reasons and the goals underlying those actions what converts those uses into commercial exploitation. This chapter proposes three points of analysis for future debate in relation to commercial exploitation of ancient lead:

Trade of ancient lead ingots in exchange for funding for excavations

Commercial exploitation using methods that do not involve the sale of underwater cultural heritage—or other exchange—are not an infringement, unless they result in the dispersal of the material (Dromgoole, 2013). Rule 2 of the Annex says:

> Underwater cultural heritage shall not be traded, sold, bought or bartered as commercial goods[.]

Exchanging the ingots as a *quid pro quo* for the transaction is not allowed under the 2001 Convention (Maarleveld et al., 2013):

> All archaeological activity can be governed by commercial principles, as long as the activities are authorized in conformity with the Convention, and as long as the finds that belong to the site are not part of the commercial equation.

Economic profit for the laboratories

Archaeologists and museums are expected to act under policies that offer part of the heritage only for experiments beneficial for the humanity (dark matter detection) and not for the benefit of companies like semiconductor industries (Lee, 2000). Intending to profit a few at the expense of many is incompatible with the protection of the underwater cultural heritage. It could be arguable that particle physics laboratories could obtain an economical benefit from patenting secondary technology developed for the successful outcome of the experiments. It could be arguable that if that a component of that technology were ancient lead this would contravene the UNESCO 2001 Convention. However, the primary use of ancient lead on particle physics experiments is aimed to perform basic research, not motivated by profit and hence does not form part of a commercial equation. Microelectronics industries, on the other hand, aim to achieve a commercial gain. And even if those laboratories would achieve an economic profit, it has to be evaluated if that profit is incompatible with the knowledge for the benefit of humanity.

Private trade and market of ancient lead

Legally, or illegally, there is a market for ancient lead: one the third low-alpha lead is obtained through sea salvage companies, for instance Aloveo and Sea Recovery Ltd. (Lee, 2000). It has been also known that Odyssey Marine Exploration (Channel, 2009) operates on the same business. These companies have identified or located about 600 tonnes of Roman lead.

The use of these objects triggers more salvage: just by a quick search on Google with the words 'low-alpha lead' it is possible to find some forums of sale and buy of ancient lead. This market is becoming more appealing for more groups and industries and it is generating big controversies (Pringle, 2013b). Other sources range from lead obtained from water pipes in ancient Roman cities or lead on the roof of old churches. In fact, AFAIR, is a company that offers to re-roof old churches free if they can keep the old lead they remove. However, private companies looking for an economic benefit speed their recovery, paying little or no attention to archaeological record, and try to obtain a profit selling the objects to any company despite their ultimate goals (UNESCO, 2001).

Proposal: animals' protocol

This study proposes an implementation of a protocol establishing certain rules for the use of underwater cultural heritage for scientific purposes. There is a danger of uncontrolled activities on shipwrecks to extract ancient lead for particle physics experiments. Even if the problems can be resolved by adopting a case-by-case evaluation, there is a possibility of an increase in the use of the material for other kinds of experiments. As a consequence, a jurisdiction should regulate it so the extraction and use of the heritage could be conducted in a regulated form, in the same way that the use of animals is controlled for biological experiments. Our proposal will be to apply a similar protocol to that on experimentation with animals. The European Union established the *Council Directive 2010/63/EU Act* (Directive, 2010) to protect animals used for experimental or scientific purposes by ensuring that they are adequately treated and that no unnecessary pain or suffering is inflicted. The reason for choosing the protocol on animals is because it is applicable to our purpose, because in both scenarios the elements will be used for scientific experimentation. The final aim of these activities is the search for new knowledge. Ultimately the animal or the underwater cultural heritage object is lost during the process. In addition, like scientific experimentation with animals, dark matter is a new frontier that may result in beneficial knowledge for humankind. The search for knowledge and new discoveries advance more rapidly than the ethical protocols or the laws regulating them. Finally, there is a need to comply with the intent of international collaboration. Establishing a protocol assures that every nation is contributing to science and heritage likewise.

Four main articles of this Protocol for the protection of animals could be applied in the case of the underwater cultural heritage:
Purposes of uses:

Article 5. Purposes of procedures.
Procedures may be carried out for the following purposes only:

(a) basic research;
(b) translational or applied research with any of the following aims:
   (i) the avoidance, prevention, diagnosis or treatment of disease, ill-health or other abnormality or their effects in human beings, animals or plants;
   (ii) the assessment, detection, regulation or modification of physiological conditions in human beings, animals or plants; or [...]
(c) for any of the aims in point (b) in the development, manufacture or testing of the quality, effectiveness and safety of drugs, foodstuffs and feed-stuffs and other substances or products;
(d) protection of the natural environment in the interests of the health or welfare of human beings or animals;
(e) research aimed at preservation of the species;
(f) higher education, or training for the acquisition, maintenance or improvement of vocational skills;
(g) forensic inquiries.

The animals' protocol clearly establishes the purposes where the use of animals is allowed. In the same way, a protocol for uses of underwater cultural heritage should list the specific cases where its utilisation is allowed, such as treatment of diseases, dark matter experimentation or research aimed at preservation of other underwater cultural heritage.
Competence of professionals:

Article 23. Competence of personnel
[...] 2. The staff shall be adequately educated and trained before they perform any of the following functions:

(a) carrying out procedures in animals
(b) designing procedures and projects;
(c) taking care of animals
(d) killing animals

Persons carrying out the functions referred to in point (b) shall have received instruction in a scientific discipline relevant to the work being undertaken and shall have species-specific knowledge. Staff carrying out functions referred to in points (a), (c) or (d) shall be supervised in the performance of their tasks until they have demonstrated the requisite competence.

[...] 3. Member States shall publish, on the basis of the elements set out in Annex V, minimum requirements with regard to education and training and the requirements for obtaining, maintaining and demonstrating requisite competence for the functions set out in paragraph 2.

Personnel managing underwater cultural heritage should be educated and trained before investigating and rescuing any underwater remain. In addition, any archaeological excavation should be authorised and decided by the State administration. In all cases the use and preservation of shipwrecks as a source for experiments shall be monitored by a competent authority to prevent avoidable damage or destruction.

Complete release of information about the experiments:

Article 13. Choice of methods:

[...] 2. In choosing between procedures, those which to the greatest extent meet the following requirements shall be selected:

(a) use the minimum number of animals;
(b) involve animals with the lowest capacity to experience pain, suffering, distress or lasting harm;
(c) cause the least pain, suffering, distress or lasting harm; and are most likely to provide satisfactory results. [...]

Experiments should be regulated and the amount of material necessary for the experiments should be reported to authorities. In addition, information stating the specific shipwreck to be researched, the kind of cargo carried and the team of experts that are going to carry out the excavations should be declared. Archaeologists, on the other hand, shall only provide the material if the shipwreck has been archaeologically studied, recorded and excavated.

Grace of necessity of the material (only if absolutely necessary):

Article 4. Principle of replacement, reduction and refinement

1. Member States shall ensure that, wherever possible, a scientifically satisfactory method or testing strategy, not entailing the use of live animals, shall be used instead of a procedure.
2. Member States shall ensure that the number of animals used in projects is reduced to a minimum without compromising the objectives of the project. [..]

Underwater cultural heritage should only be used if there is evidence that the activity is absolutely necessary and there is no other way of obtaining the same scientific results. Experiments must only take place if there is no alternative method that does not entail the use of underwater cultural heritage or if the alternative method is proved to be well out of the laboratories' reach.

Conclusions

Ancient lead can reach unprecedented levels of low intrinsic radioactivity necessary for dark matter researches. A combination of natural radioactive decay, ancient ore refining and preservation under water have reduced the 210^{Pb} intrinsic radioactivity by a factor of 100,000 when compared to freshly mined lead. For a given initial level of purity and preservation conditions, the more time that has passed since it was originally processed, the lower its intrinsic radioactivity. Current manufacturing capabilities cannot achieve comparable radioactivity levels but approach the required experimental limits. This chapter has aimed to raise awareness on the use of ancient lead for particle physics experiments in particular but also for other sciences in general and its consequences from a particle physics and from a cultural heritage perspective. The state of the dilemma lies in the fact that although the use of underwater cultural heritage on scientific experiments is an irreversible process, some of the uses may not be contravening any Convention. As a consequence, two main concepts have been highlighted as the main ethical conflicts on the issue:

Use

It is necessary to set boundaries and to decide which science 'deserves' a part of the past. It might be decided that underwater cultural heritage is not a stock for any kind of experiment or that only experiments aimed to cure diseases will be allowed. It might instead be decided that if the experiments offer answers for the knowledge of mankind are justified, or that it is worth widening the range of experiments to include businesses such as microelectronics. And this would entail the risk of allowing any kind of industry to use underwater cultural heritage (Perez-Alvaro and Gonzalez-Zalba, 2014). In addition, it has proved that some of these experiments on dark matter detection are executed in laboratories that do not obtain a direct economic profit from the use of ancient lead in experiments. And, as a consequence, a new concept should be considered: the non-commercial exploitation of underwater cultural heritage. If ancient lead is obtained through a legal agreement between archaeologists and museums, cultural objects cannot be considered as being used as commercial goods.

Recovery

It needs to be carried out under archaeological standards: archaeology fundamentally obtains information about the history of humankind. Only archaeological methods and techniques for analysing and excavating an archaeological site will guarantee as full as possible an interpretation of the objects recovered. Even if accepted procedures are followed by archaeologists and experts, the fact that the ingots have to be melted and lost in order to conduct particle physics experiments destroys evidence. Technological advances in the future could produce more information from these items. As a consequence, following the archaeological procedures on the recovery of the ancient ingots mitigates the damage, but there is still damage. On these grounds, the use of ancient lead bricks from underwater cultural heritage sites to perform experiments that require lead to be melted and destroyed, may result in the loss of knowledge in two different ways:

Current loss of information, which is avoidable

If laboratories obtain ancient lead from private companies whose protocol is getting the lead without keeping an appropriate archaeological record, knowledge about our past and about our history is being lost. For those companies, the more time spent on a site, the less the profit: it is 'the dollar over the data' (Coroneos, 2006: 120), and as a consequence they pay no attention to archaeological data or to gathering information. Once the objects are decontextualised, the information, which is non-renewable, is lost (Gerstenblith, 2007). If the laboratories, instead of looking for private companies, were to reach an agreement with a team of archaeologists, at least this process of gathering information and understanding the context of the pieces would follow the archaeological process.

Loss of information for the future

It is necessary to keep it up to a minimum. Even if the archaeological process is followed, the lead ingots are melted by the laboratory. In the future, with more information, more scientific development and more archaeological data, new theories, knowledge and interpretations can arise from the analysis of ancient lead from shipwrecks, such as commercial trade routes. However, if this material is destroyed, we will lose the chance to obtain that information.

The ethics around the issue become blurred when talking about 'right' or 'wrong' ownership or stewardship, or commercialisation or scientific study of the underwater cultural heritage. If the international community allows corporations or private laboratories to make decisions regarding the use of underwater cultural heritage as a source of experiments, the decision of these institutions would be based on economic principles. Only under the umbrella of the States or the international community would the use of the material be purely for knowledge. The scientific community in need of ancient lead also has to have their efforts directed to create new materials with the same properties. Ancient lead is a non-renewable source. However, renewed mass-production techniques or alternative materials, such as tung-sten, could be explored if these activities were to expand. However, sometimes it is necessary to admit that the heritage may suffer some loss to the benefit of another kind of knowledge. It is what has been called 'offset' heritage. However, its use, also acceptable, has to be regulated. The establishment of a protocol on ethically accepted scientific experiments using underwater cultural heritage would represent an effort to begin discussions. The worldwide community can then proceed to make decisions about a balance between heritage and science in relation to its collective ethical beliefs. Our proposal is to configure those moral concerns in a legal protocol to limit the use of underwater cultural heritage for scientific purposes and, when used, to manage it under archaeological standards, with archaeologists as stewards.

Underwater cultural heritage faces a new controversy: it can assist particle physics to obtain more knowledge about dark matter. However, if their characteristics are of benefit to other fields, such as microelectronics or medicine, their use will be more demanded each time by actors whose only end is not the economic profit. In land archaeology, several parts of the heritage are sacrificed *in pro* to the development of other disciplines or commodities: villages are moved for construction or motorways or reservoirs. This is the case of the Spanish village of *Mequinenza*, in the north of Spain, that was moved in order to build a reservoir: the bell of the old church can still be seen coming out from the water when the reservoir is low. The question is why this kind of public work has allowed the destruction of cultural heritage and the destruction of heritage in favour of researching particle physics is still a source of controversy. It is necessary to set boundaries and to decide which science 'deserve' a part of the past. It might be decided that underwater cultural heritage is not a stock for any kind of experiment or that only experiments aimed to cure diseases will be allowed. It might instead be decided that if the experiments offer answers for the knowledge of the human being are justified, or that it is worth to open the range of experiments to include businesses such as microelectronics. And this would entail the risk to allow any kind of industry to use the underwater cultural heritage. A protocol has to be established. Ancient lead is a non-renewable source and refined mass-production techniques or alternative materials, could be explored if these activities were to expand. Tungsten with the potential to achieve an emission rate well within the thresholds required by dark matter searches could provide an alternative solution. In addition, if those laboratories do not have the opportunity to buy a lead that has already been analysed and recorded by an archaeological institution they will need to buy it from private companies that offer the lead. The archaeological community should not adopt a position that is a denial of the reality and existence of other fields that may use the heritage but a position of triggering the conversations and offering solutions. In any case, sacrificing underwater cultural heritage has to be evaluated and weighted. Even if the dilemma could be resolved by adopting a case-by-case evaluation, there is a risk of a growth on the use of ancient lead for other kind of experiments motivated by market expectations and not by knowledge. Its use should be regulated so the extraction and documentation is done under archaeological standards. There is a need to find a common place because new cases unforeseen by underwater cultural heritage policy makers question principles taken from granted.

This chapter has explored the ethical issue of uses of underwater cultural heritage. Traditionally, this heritage has to be preserved for the benefit of humankind. However, this chapter has demonstrated that there are unexpected uses of underwater cultural heritage that need to be considered. This challenge will be explored in other chapters of the book: for instance, States use underwater cultural heritage for political aims or the management of underwater cultural heritage can serve to protect the natural heritage. All the uses have to be evaluated and respected.

Note

1 Reproduced from Perez-Alvaro, E. and Gonzales-Zalba, M. F. (2015). The role of underwater cultural heritage on dark matter searches: ancient lead, a dual perspective. *Ocean & Coastal Management* 103: 56–62. Copyright © 2015, published by Elsevier Masson SAS. All rights reserved.

Bibliography

Aitchison, K. (2009). Archaeology and the global financial crisis. *Antiquity* 83(319): 319–326.

Alessandrello, A., Allegretti, F., Brofferio, C., Camin, D., Cremonesi, O., Fiorini, E., Giuliani, A., Pavan, M., Pessina, G., Pizzini, S., Previtali, E., Sverzellati, P. and Zanotti, L. (1993). Measurements of low radioactive contaminations in lead using bolometric detectors. *Nuclear Instruments and Methods Physics Research B* 83(4): 539–544.

Alessandrello, A., Arpesella, C., Brofferio, C., Bucci, C., Cattadori, C., Cremonesi, O., Fiorini, E., Giuliani, A., Latorre, S., Nucciotti, A., Orvini, E., Pavan, M., Parmeggiano, S., Perego, M., Pessina, G., Pirro, S., Previtali, E., Romualdi, B., Rotilio, A., Tatananni, E. and Zanotti, L. (1998). Measurements of internal radioactive contamination in samples of roman lead to be used in experiments on rare events. *Nuclear Instruments and Methods Physics Research B* 142(12): 163–172.

Ananthaswamy, A. (2010). *The Edge of Physics: A Journey to Earth's Extremes to Unlock the Secrets of the Universe*. Boston: Duckworth Overlook.

Aznar-Gómez, M. J. (2010). Treasure hunters, sunken state vessels and the 2001 UNESCO Convention on the Protection of Underwater Cultural Heritage. *International Journal of Marine and Coastal Law* 25(2): 209–236.

Bernabei, R., Belli, P., Cappella, F., Caracciolo, V., Castellano, S., Cerulli, R., Boiko, R. S., Chernyak, D. M., Danevich, F. A., Dai, C. J., d'Angelo, A., d'Angelo, S., Di Marco, A., He, H. L., Incicchitti, A., Ma, X. H., Mokina, V. M., Montecchia, F., Poda, D. V., Polischuk, O. G., Sheng, X. D., Wang, R. G., Ye, Z. P. and Tretyak, V. I.

(2013). Crystal scintillators for low background measurements. *AIP Conference Proceedings* 1549(1): 189–196.

Butler, D. (2006). *Distant Victory: The Battle of Jutland and the Allied Triumph in the First World War*. Westport, CT: Greenwood: 229.

Callataÿ, F. (2005). The Graeco-Roman economy in the super long-run: lead, copper, and shipwrecks. *Journal Roman Archaeology* 18(1): 361.

Caple, C. (2008). Preservation *in situ*: the future for archaeological conservators? *Studies in Conservation*, 53(supp 1): 214–217.

Carman, J. (2002). *Archaeology and Heritage: An Introduction*. London: Continuum Press.

Channel, D. (2009). Turning Lead into Gold (*treasure quest* session 1. ep. 5. Video).

Churchill, R. and Lowe, A. (1999). *The Law of the Sea*. Manchester: Manchester University Press. Melland Schill Studies in International Law: 152.

Coroneos, C. (2006). The ethics and values of maritime archaeology. In Staniforth, M. and Nash, M. (eds.), *Maritime Archaeology: Australian Approaches*. New York: Springer: 111–122.

Danevich, F. A., Georgadze, A. S., Kobychev, V. V., Nagorny, S. S., Nikolaiko, A. S., Ponkratenko, O. A., Tretyak, V. I., Zdesenko, S. Y., Zdesenko, Y. G., Bizzeti, P. G., Fazzini, T. F. and Maurenzig, P. R. (2003). Activity of natural tungsten isotopes. *Physics Review C* 67(1): 014310.

Directive (2010). 2010/63/EU. European Union legislation for animals used for scientific purposes. Available at: http://eur-lex.europa.eu/legal-content/EN/TXT/?uri=CELEX:32010L0063 (1 July 2018).

Dromgoole, S. (2013). *Underwater Cultural Heritage and International Law*. Cambridge: Cambridge University Press.

Flatman, J. (2007). The origins and ethics of maritime archaeology – Part I. *Public Archaeology* 6(2): 77–97.

Gale, H. (2011). A study of lead ingot cargoes from ancient Mediterranean shipwrecks. Master's thesis, Texas A&M University.

Gerstenblith, P. (2007). Controlling the international market in antiquities: reducing the harm, preserving the past. *Chicago Journal of International Law* 8(1): 169–195.

Gwynne, P. (2013). Physicist and archaeologists tussle over long-lost lead. *Inside Science*. Available at: www.insidescience.org/content/physicists-and-archaeologists-tussle-overlong-lost-lead/1521.

Hamilton, D. L. (2006). Port Royal, Jamaica: archaeological past and development potential. *Underwater Cultural Heritage at Risk: Managing Natural and Human Impacts* 1(1): 49–51.

INFN (2010). *Lead from a Roman Ship to Be Used for Hunting Neutrinos*. Phys. org. Available at: https://phys.org/news/2010-04-roman-ship-neutrinos.html (3 October 2017).

Kaoru, Y. and Hoagland, P. (1994). The value of historic shipwrecks: conflicts and management. *Coastal Management* 22(2): 195–213.

Komatsu, E., Smith, K. M., Dunkley, J., Bennett, C. L., Gold, B., Hinshaw, G., Jarosik, N., Larson, D., Nolta, M. R., Page, L., Spergel, D. N., Halpern, M., Hill, R. S., Kogut, A., Limon, M., Meyer, S. S., Odegard, N., Tucker, G. S., Weiland, J. L., Wollack, E. and Wright, E. L. (2011). Seven-year Wilkinson microwave anisotropy probe (WMAP) observations: cosmological interpretation. *Astrophysics Journal Supplement Series* 192(2): 18.

Lang, R. F. and Seidel, W. (2009). Search for dark matter with CRESST. *New Journal of Physics* 11(10): 105017.

Lee, N. (2000). *Lead-free Soldering and Low Alpha Solders for Wafer Level Interconnects*. Chicago: SMTA International.

Lynch, T. (2007). A historically significant shield for in vivo measurements. *Health Physics* 93(2): S119–S123.

Lynch, T. (2011). In vivo radiobioassay and research facility. *Health Physics* 100: S35.

Maarleveld, T., Guerin, U. and Egger, B. (2013). *Manual for Activities Directed at Underwater Cultural Heritage: Guidelines to the Annex of the UNESCO 2001 Convention*. Paris: UNESCO.

Manders, M. (2003). Safeguarding: The physical protection of underwater sites. *MoSS Newsletter* 4(4): 18–20.

Manders, M. (3 May 2004). Why do we safeguard shipwrecks? *MoSS Newsletter* 3: 4–5.

Manders, M. (2008). *In situ* preservation: 'the preferred option'. *Museum International 240* 60(4): 31–41.

Manders, M. (2013). Capacity building in underwater heritage management. Setting standards with the UNESCO foundation course, Chanthaburi, Thailand. AIMA 13 Conference: Towards Ratification: Australia's Underwater Cultural Heritage, Canberra, 4 October 2013.

Moskowitz, C. (2013). Ancient Roman metal used for physics experiments ignites science feud. [online]. *Scientific American*. Available at: www.scientificamerican.com/article/ancient-roman-lead-physics-archaeology-controversy/.

Moskowitz, C. (2014). Lead treasure. *Scientific American* 310(3): 20.

M.R.E. (2010). El plomo español de un barco romano servirá para detectar neutrinos. [online]. *El Pais. Sociedad*. 15 April 2010. Available at: http://sociedad.elpais.com/sociedad/2010/04/15/actualidad/1271282406_850215.html.

Nosengo, N. (2010). Roman ingots to shield particle detector. [online]. *Nature*. Available at: www.nature.com/news/2010/100415/full/news.2010.186.html (3 March 2018).

Perez-Alvaro, E. (2013a). Experiments on particle physics using underwater cultural heritage: the dilemma. *Rosetta* 13(5): 40–46

Perez-Alvaro, E. (2013b). Unconsidered threats to underwater cultural heritage: laying submarine cables. *Rosetta* 14: 54–70.

Perez-Alvaro, E. and Gonzalez-Zalba, F. (2014). The role of underwater cultural heritage on dark matter searches: ancient lead, a dual perspective. *Ocean and Coastal Management* 103: 5–62.

Pringle, H. (2013a). Troubled waters for ancient shipwrecks. *Science* 340: 802–807.

Pringle, H. (2013b). Random sample: particle physicists seek a Roman shield. *Science* 342: 541.

Revol, J. (2007). Fundamental research: the engine of innovation and example of particle physics. In Kahn, A., Qurashi, M. and Hayee, I. (eds.), *Basic or Applied Research: Dilemma of Developing Countries*. Islamabad: Commission on Science and Technology for Sustainable Development in the South: 41–52.

SAA (1990). Ethical principles of the Society for Historical Archaeology. Available at: www.saa.org/career-practice/ethics-in-professional-archaeology (17 March 2019).

Scarre, C. and Scarre, G. (2006). *The Ethics of Archaeology: Philosophical Perspectives on Archaeological Practice*. Cambridge: Cambridge University Press: 1–14

Smith, M., Bignell, L., Alexiev, D., Mo, L. and Harrison, J. (2008). Evaluation of lead shielding for a gamma-spectroscopy system. *Nuclear Instruments and Methods Physics Research A* 589(2): 275–279.

Stemm, G. (2000). Differentiation of Shipwreck Artifacts as a Resource Management Tool. Association of Dive Contractors/Marine Technology Society UI 2000 Conference, January 2000. Available at: www.shipwreck.net.

Sturges, M. L. (1998). Who should hold property rights to the human genome? An application of the Common Heritage of Humankind. *International Law Review* 13: 219–261.

Tenenbaum, E. (1990). A world park in Antarctica: the common heritage of mankind. *Virginia Environmental Law Journal* 10(1): 109–112.

Throckmorton, P. (1998). The world's worst investment: the economics of treasure hunting with real-life comparisons. In Babits, L. E. and Van Tilburg, H. (eds.), *Maritime Archaeology: A Reader of Substantive and Theoretical Contributions.* London: Plenum Press: 75–83.

Tong, H.-M., Lai, Y.-S. and Wong, C. P. (2013). *Advanced Flip Chip Packaging.* New York: Springer.

Trubek, D. M. (1972). Toward a social theory of law: an essay on the study of law and development. *The Yale Law Journal* 82(1): 1–50.

UNCLOS (1982). United Nations Convention on the Law of the Sea. Available at: www.un.org/depts/los/convention_agreements/texts/unclos/unclos_e.pdf (21 January 2019).

UNESCO (2001). Convention on the Protection of the Underwater Cultural Heritage. Paris, 2 November 2001. Available at: http://unesdoc.unesco.org/images/0012/001260/126065e.pdf (22 January 2019).

Villegas Zamora, T. (2008). The impact of commercial exploitation on the preservation of underwater cultural heritage. *Museum International* 60(4): 18–30.

Yorke, R. (2013). Commercial exploitation of underwater cultural heritage issues, consequences and options for control. AIMA 13 Conference: Towards Ratification: Australia's Underwater Cultural Heritage, Canberra, 4 October 2013.

5 Preservation
Climate change[1]

Predictions forecast changes in climate that may affect cultural heritage in the future. Not only our underwater cultural heritage will become exposed, but also our land tangible cultural heritage will be submerged: entire nations and their cultural heritage may disappear, losing their identity. In fact, climate change has the potential to increase the sea level enough by 2100 to inundate 136 sites considered by UNESCO as cultural and historical treasures. However, climate change damage on cultural heritage is not only a warning for the future as already it has caused damages to some cultural heritage.

Introduction

Climate change is warming the oceans, the ice at the poles is melting, and sea levels are rising. We are also witnessing changes in the chemical composition of oceans, for example in their acidity or salinity. Moreover, currents are changing their patterns and, as a consequence, ecosystems are becoming increasingly more endangered (Climate Central, 2015).

Climate change, therefore, is likely to have to have a direct impact on tangible cultural heritage (Hall, 2016; Dunkley, 2013a). Higher global surface temperatures will dry out some submerged heritage items and, contrariwise, sea level rises will flood many coastal areas, creating new underwater cultural heritage (Climate Central, 2015). On the one hand, each one of the changes—namely, warmer waters, changes in currents, rising oceans and chemical changes—will have a different effect on the various materials constituting currently submerged archaeological sites. On the other hand, if the global temperature continues to rise at its current rate over the next two centuries, 40 of the UNESCO Cultural World Heritage sites will be affected by 2100. Of the 720 sites listed in the cultural and mixed categories in the UNESCO World Heritage list, 136 will be impacted by the rise in sea level (Marzeion and Levermann, 2014). In addition, 3–12 countries will lose more than half of their current land surface (Marzeion and Levermann, 2014). Sheridan and Sheridan (Sheridan and Sheridan, 2013) state that civilisation is heading for informed self-destruction. They define culture as 'the last cab off the climate rank'.

Issue

Water covers 71% of the Earth's surface (Rahmstorf and Richardson, 2009). As climate change warms the earth, oceans respond more slowly than land environments, but marine ecosystems have proven to be far more sensitive (Ganje et al., 2011). It is unclear what changes, if any, will occur to the oceans in the future. What complicates the picture, in this regard, is that scientists are working mostly under suppositions: the temperature of the water, the sea levels, and the changes to currents and chemical composition are difficult to measure. In addition, the geographical variety of the globe means that seawater has different properties in different seas and oceans. Nonetheless, a review and analysis of the climate change literature allows this chapter to identify the four main effects of climate change on the oceans and, consequently, on cultural heritage. These are illustrated in Figure 5.1 and they will be discussed in the following subsections.

Warming of the waters

There have always been fluctuations in water temperature, especially in the surface layer of water that is in direct contact with the atmosphere (the top 50–200 metres) (Rahmstorf and Richardson, 2009). However, the temperature in this layer has increased by more than 3°C in the last 50 years. Such an increase in temperature will most likely gradually spread to deeper ocean layers, where shipwrecks and other heritage sites are located. This oceanic warming could result in changes such as coral bleaching and species

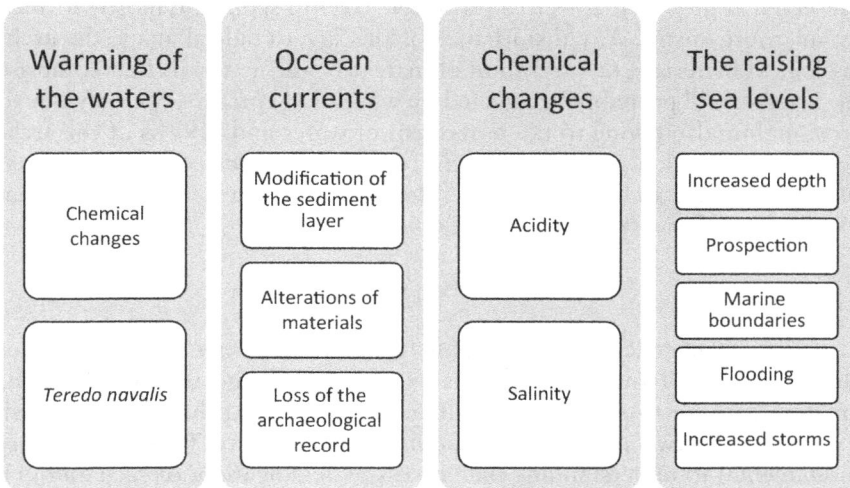

Figure 5.1 Climate changes.

migration. Other issues will also affect underwater tangible heritage such as chemical changes since any chemical change occurs faster at a higher temperature and as a consequence, the deterioration of heritage due to chemicals in seawater will occur at an increasing rate, and the proliferation of *teredo navalis* since increasing water temperature could be crucial in aiding shipworms (termites of the sea or *teredo navalis*) to adapt to lower salinity. The *teredo navalis*, according to Hoppe (Hoppe, 2002), is a harmful marine invader that settles on wooden ships and boats. In fact, a major reason for the shipwrecked *Vasa*'s survival after 300 years on the seabed was the absence of the shipworm in the Baltic, whose freshwater the *teredo* finds inhospitable. In warmer water, the *teredo* is better able to survive low salinity (Willis, 2008).

Ocean currents

Ocean currents are kept in continual motion by the gravitational pull of the moon and the sun, the water level being higher when the moon is overhead (Rahmstorf and Richardson, 2009). Ocean temperature differentials and wind patterns are also recognised as causes of tide equilibrium. In addition, there is a driving force of current changes, referred to as *thermohaline forcing*—the exchange of heat and freshwater at the surface that makes the water warmer or colder or saltier or fresher (Rahmstorf and Richardson, 2009). Some experts predict that climate change could cause a possible interruption of the thermohaline circulation, largely responsible for regulating the earth's temperature (Fernandez, 2013). Such change would affect the submerged heritage in different ways, such as (1) modification of the sediment layer: much underwater cultural heritage in the oceans is partially preserved at present thanks to a protective layer of sediment, mostly formed by microorganisms. Any disturbance of this layer could damage the archaeological materials, (2) alteration of materials: the materials that comprise the artefact will probably be affected by waves and currents, not only due to erosion, but also owing to the movement of water and (3) loss of the archaeological record: a change in current can displace some or all the material of a submerged archaeological site, decontextualising it from its original location or otherwise dispersing the objects.

Chemical changes

A variety of chemical changes might occur in the oceans as a result of climate change. However, since changes in acidity and salinity cause the greatest damage to submerged heritage (Dunkley, 2013b), this study will focus on these two factors only. The first one is acidity. Two concepts are fundamental to understanding the process of acidification: oxygen and pH. Oxygen acts as an accelerator of metal corrosion, both on land and underwater (Florian, 1987a). pH measures the acidity of liquids. Seawater typically had a pH of around 8, but it has dropped to 7.9 in the past century. Due to increasing levels of atmospheric CO_2, a drop to 7.4 in polar and sub-polar water is predicted (Daly, 2011). If the pH of seawater decreases and the oxygen increases, it will become more acidic. As a consequence, underwater material is more likely to corrode (Daly, 2011). In addition, according to Hamilton (Hamilton, 1997), textiles dissolve more readily in acidic water, meaning any archaeological textiles remaining under water would likely be lost. The second factor is salinity: in the open sea, salinity is around 32–33%. Higher salinities occur in enclosed seas subject to high evaporation (the Mediterranean has 38.6%, the Red Sea, 41%) (Florian, 1987b). Scientists still do not know whether salinity will decrease or increase as a result of the melting of the polar ice. What it is known, however, is that salinity accelerates corrosion. Changes in salinity will almost certainly have a direct effect on cultural heritage.

The rising sea levels

Increased global temperatures melts land ice, which adds water to the sea. Similarly, an increase in water temperature results in the expansion of the sea, since warm water occupies a larger volume than colder water. Sea levels react only very slowly, and it takes many centuries, or even millennia, for large continental ice masses to melt (Rahmstorf and Richardson, 2009). However, since ice masses are becoming wetter because of the contact with water, they will almost certainly melt at a much faster rate. Ice masses are like a 'ticking time bomb'. The authors estimate that there will be a rise in the sea level of between 18 and 59 cm by the year 2100; but it could exceed one metre (Rahmstorf and Richardson, 2009). This rising sea level would be the most difficult challenge facing cultural heritage. Not only it could submerge the land-based cultural heritage, but underwater cultural heritage might also be affected. Some of the issues recognised in this regard are: (1) increased depth: more water means greater depth and shipwrecks lying on the seabed will be subject to greater pressure, which may be more than they can withstand, (2) prospection: an increase of only one metre may not affect the search for shipwrecks with radar. However, it will affect the amount of time a diver can remain safely under water (Dunkley, 2013b), (3) marine boundaries: higher sea levels will result in legal maritime boundaries becoming less well-defined. Political issues and legal disputes are expected to arise in the affected areas (to be discussed below), (4) flooding: some land-based archaeological sites will flood, meaning that some land cultural heritage will become *underwater* cultural heritage (Murphy et al., 2008), and (5) increased storms: higher sea levels will cause more powerful storms (Sivan, et al., 2004) that will devastate low-lying areas. These will be in the form of tropical storms and hurricanes/cyclones, at best eroding at worst destroying both land and underwater heritage. Although these are largely predictions for the future, some cultural heritage sites are already experiencing some of these changes, as this chapter will demonstrate.

State of knowledge

Humans have been travelling at sea for at least 60,000 years (Willis, 2008). Naval engineering has continuously improved in a way that ships are built with strong materials, resistant to water and marine organisms and that do not corrode in salt water (which becomes an electrolyte solution). From the first ships (logs together to form a raft around 10,000 BC) to the ships today (war, carriers, luxury, research ships) many different materials have been used to build them (Macdonald, 2008: 8). According to Smith and Couper (2003) from the 1850s there was an emphasis on durable iron rather than perishable wood. And in the 1880s iron was replaced by steel. In general, both iron and steel ships are much better preserved than wood ships, although some of them are already suffering changes, for instance the *Titanic*, as it will be explained.

Of all materials, iron and wood are the ones that cause more problems in its preservation. Usually these materials form a layer of encrustation. The natural moulds formed by corroded metal artefacts are also present in wooden objects containing metal, for instance, nails (Delgado, 1998). If this concretion is cracked or damaged, CO_2 ingress can cause irreparable damages (Green, 1990). Artefacts recovered from a salt water environment are often well preserved but of a very fragile nature (Hamilton, 1997). In addition, it is necessary to distinguish between permanent damage (like a destroyed artefact) or damage that can be fixed by the conservator (like a layer of sediments) when talking on protection and conservation of underwater archaeological remains. However, all the material, if recovered, must be quickly conserved because they will easily deteriorate when they leave their stable environment. In the same way, this will make a difference to the material when affected by climate change, since they are of a very fragile nature and any change that makes them leave their undisturbed environment will deteriorate them.

This section will analyse one by one very material that can be found in an underwater archaeological site and how and which of the climate changes affecting the oceans will affect these materials.

Waterlogged wood

Wood is a major component of ships and was used for hulls, decks, masts and personal items such as combs, bowls, tables or furniture. *Waterlogged* means the complete filling with water of the pore spaces. This fully saturated wood that is removed from under the sea and exposed to the air may be rapidly deteriorate since the excess water evaporates and the surface tension of the evaporating water will cause the weakened cell walls to collapse (Grattan, 1987; Hamilton, 2000). However, wood from marine wrecks tend to be very impermeable. Being of organic origin, wood normally decays under combined biological and chemical attack when buried in the ground, but it can survive prolonged exposure to extremes of dryness or wetness (Hamilton, 1997). In shipwreck sites underwater the wooden components of the hull and small artefacts of wood often survive in good condition. Damage to submerged wood can range from as a result of wave action to alterations of the ultrastructural level (Grattan, 1987). Also, there can be damage by biodegradation, like the attack by marine borers and crustaceans, ligniferous marine fungi or by marine bacteria. Marine worms mine the original wood of the shipwrecks leaving organic-rich sediments behind. However, the damage will depend on the chemistry of the environment of the wreck, of the duration of the burial and mostly of the presence of iron. On the seabed floor the environment that forms the perimeter of a wooden shipwreck tends to be very different from the surrounding seabed. The large mass of decaying wood left by the hull alters the chemistry of the sediment profoundly (Piechota and Giangrande, 2008). The raising of sea levels does not seem to be the major threat to wooden remains. However, because of current changes, the erosion of protective sediments on wood exposes it to oxygenated water and exacerbates existing bacterial action (Daly, 2011). Acidity can also cause serious problems. Another of the main problems will be salinity, since shipworms (which can deteriorate the shipwreck within a few months; Manders, 2012) require high salinity: the increase in global warming may help the shipworm to survive destroying the wooden remains of shipwrecks or artefacts (Manders, 2012).

Organic material other than wood

There is not too much published research on organic material surviving marine burial although it was a material widely used: cordages, rope, textiles, leather, basketry or rubber shoes (Florian, 1987a). In the process of sinking, these materials have been waterlogged, swollen, covered with sediments, heavily encrusted with calcium concretion and impregnated with iron oxide, tar or calcium salts.

Cellulosic material

For instance, fibres or leaves. According to Florian (1987a) this is a naturally watery material but much of the natural water within the material is lost during fabrication and usage. This material may have been preserved because of the restriction of swelling due to the presence of sodium chloride (table salt) in seawater (Florian, 1987a). Only changes in ocean currents would affect the cellulosic material by spreading it or stretching it.

Plant products

Such as resin or rubber. Microorganisms may be important in the very slow degradation of these elements (Florian, 1987a). Only would be changed by microorganisms, maybe generated by the warming of the oceans.

Animal origin

Such as skin, hair or feathers. Each one of these elements has a specific structural organisation. However, in general, if extreme swelling and stretching occurs, the inner more vulnerable layers and cells are exposed, and degradation may start. Bacteria and fungi can attack these materials (Florian, 1987a). Chemical reactions would cause depolymerisation of the molecules and disintegration (Florian, 1987a). Change in ocean currents or rises in sea levels do not seem to be factors that would deteriorate the materials. However, direct growth of microorganisms due to warmer water could destabilise them.

Textiles

All textiles are deteriorated by light, insects, microorganisms and air pollution. Also, the oxygen in the atmosphere affects all organic substances to varying degrees (Hamilton, 1997) by being able to cause disintegration. The speed of the deterioration varies according to the nature of the fibres and existing local conditions. The main factors that promote disintegration can be organic (subject to attack by moulds and living bacteria), physical (like exposure to ultra-violet light or excessive heat) and chemical (exposure to noxious gases) (Hamilton, 1997). The level of the sea would affect it because it could expose it to ultra-violet light. Fibres, cotton, wool and silk can only live in alkaline conditions. If there is an acidification, these textiles disappear. Warming of the oceans would affect the growth of moulds and living bacteria. Chemical changes could cause disintegration.

Teeth and ivory

These materials are easily preserved and the most mineralised (Florian, 1987a). Heat affects ivory which can even be fossilised because of the salt (Hamilton, 1997). Acid may disintegrate them as well as warming the oceans. No other factors seem to complicate their preservation.

Bone

Acid and inorganic salts are what would affect it most (Florian, 1987a). Bone is warped by heat and moisture and decomposed by prolonged exposure to water. It can even be reduced to a sponge-like material or fossilised because of the salt (Hamilton, 1997). Satisfactory restoration is often impossible. Bones are decomposed by hydrolysis and inorganic structures are disintegrated by acids. They also become easily stained. Chemical changes would affect its preservation, as well as changes in the temperature of the water. Because of these reasons, bone would disintegrate more easily. Also changes in ocean currents would mean that the bones would be disturbed and possibly uncovered from the layer of sediments.

Leather

There are many processes involved in its fabrication and its preservation depends on them (Florian, 1987a). It experiences complex changes in a marine environment. Leather seems to be affected by chemical changes and water temperatures. Other changes should not affect it.

Metals

Metal shipwrecks are in danger. A 10 mm thick hull can be perforated or even totally corroded within 100 years (Memet, 2008). Less oxygen means less corrosion (Manders, 2012). From the moment of manufacture, the various metals and their alloys, except for gold, react with their environment and begin a corrosion process (Hamilton, 1997). Corrosion of metal artefacts is different but often has interrelated factors depending on metal composition, water composition, temperature, marine growth, seabed composition, position of objects, depth of burial beneath the seabed and extent of water movement (North and MacLeod, 1987). In sea water, temperature, pH and the presence of aggressive anions, such as chloride in the water, determine the rates and types of corrosion (Hamilton, 1997). Warmer water produces a protective concretion on the metal surface, except in the case of the copper (North and MacLeod, 1987). When a piece of metal is place in seawater, a large number of oxidation and reduction reactions can occur on the metal's surface. Metal also show accelerated deterioration at the mud line due to oxygen gradients. The oxidising stage lasts from 1000 to 100,000 years and may extend to depths from one to 100 metres. It is in this depth and time range of sediment that wreck sites usually occur (Florian, 1987a). Metals are commonly encrusted with thick layers of material such as conglomerations, from a single coin to masses weighing several thousand pounds. Also, in those conglomerations it is usual to find other artefacts, like ceramics, glass, wood, leather or bone (Hamilton, 2000).

Iron

Iron presents a difficult problem because once exposed to air on the surface, the corrosion rate will accelerate (Green, 1990). Metal shipwrecks may deteriorate more quickly than wooden vessels given the same conditions. Iron tends to create massive concretions since iron is not a biologically toxic material and immersed in seawater is rapidly colonised by marine organisms (North and MacLeod, 1987). Iron corrodes five times faster in sea water than in soil and ten times faster in sea water than in air (Hamilton, 1997). As said, high temperature has an effect on biological growth. Corrosion expects to be double for every 10°C increasing in temperature (North and MacLeod, 1987). Movements of water across the wreck site can affect corrosion rates through metal erosion, destruction of protective films or changing the amount of oxygen. Also, metal corrosion rates increase with increasingly salinity. The growth of marine organisms can produce a protective barrier between the artefact and the seawater, although this can also transfer chemical species creating a microenvironment. As the level of salt increases, water becomes more corrosive (Hamilton, 1997).

Copper

Copper is one of the most common material on ships. It is toxic to marine organisms, so it reduces the growth of such organisms. As a consequence, copper is found unconcreted. For this reason, covering wood by copper was a way to protect wooden vessels from attack by the *teredo* worm and from fouling by marine organisms (North and MacLeod, 1987). Therefore, copper objects are usually partially covered by wood fragments. Beneath the wood the oxygen supply is depleted and causes increased corrosion. As stated warmer water makes copper corrode approximately twice as fast for every 10°C of temperature rise (North and MacLeod, 1987). However, it is a noble metal that survives adverse conditions (Hamilton, 1997). Pressure may also affect the corrosion mechanisms and water movement increases the effect of a corrosion attack.

Brass and bronze

These materials can be found, for instance, in most cannon balls. At a normal pH most corrosion of these elements would not affect them (North and MacLeod, 1987). Only the warming of the seawater temperature and changes of pH would deteriorate this material.

Pewter, lead and tin

On those materials, and even after nearly 350 years in turbulent condition, the depth of corrosion can be less than 1mm (North and MacLeod, 1987). However, high temperatures might affect its preservation. Pure tin items are seldom encountered in archaeological sites: it is found more often used in various alloys. Lead is commonly found as it was used for weights, cannon balls, sheeting and striping. It is a stable metal in neutral or alkaline solution. It usually forms a protective layer that prevents oxidation. Lead free pewter suffers extensive corrosive attack in aerobic seawater (Hamilton, 1997). High temperatures in the seawater and change in pH would cause corrosion to these materials.

Silver

Most of the silver artefacts found are coins, and consequently the majority of silver corrosion and concretion information is derived from coins (Hamilton,

2000). It is one of the finest metals, but chloride and sulphite ions found in marine environments increase the reactivity of the metal. The metal does not appear to be as toxic as copper to many marine organisms. However, the cold makes coins susceptible to stress corrosion and cracking. Also, the reduction of oxygen increases corrosion rates (North and MacLeod, 1987). However, it is not attacked by dry air (Hamilton, 1997). Silver is completely stable in aqueous solutions of any pH, so acidification will not affect it. Only changes in salinification could cause changes to the material.

Gold

It is corrosion resistant. Only if it is in combination with other alloys can the gold surface weaken. In general, the combination of two materials (metal and ceramic, for instance) is dangerous as factors not damaging on one material can affect greatly the other material (Hamilton, 1997). As a consequence, any changes in a material that contains gold, can also damage the gold. Gold, as silver, is a really stable metal. It would not suffer from any of the climate change if not combined with other materials.

Aluminium

It is stable at room temperature and is usually immune to general corrosion attack in the pH range of seawater (North and MacLeod, 1987). Few old shipwrecks have aluminium unless the vessel was lost later than 1920s but due to its light weight it was used in the aircraft industry, especially from the World War II. Water temperature and sea level change would mostly affect aluminium.

Others

Ceramics, glass and stone objects don't deteriorate rapidly from submersion in seawater. The most significant problem is physical damage. A further problem is the accumulation of marine deposits (Pearson, 1987).

Ceramics

Low-fired pottery is the most common and is large in number and dimensions. Objects made from clay not fired will readily dissolve and will not be preserved. However, earthenware survives well in marine environments. Ceramics are invariably covered with organic concretion resulting from marine organisms. Breakage is common from water and sand or sediment movement (Pearson, 1987). It is advisable to reduce the salinity of the water slowly (Green, 1990) but it will not have affected the pieces deeply since they do not absorb soluble salts as they are impervious to liquids (Hamilton, 1997). Change on temperature does not seem affect ceramics.

However, rises in sea levels and change in currents would affect them as they are mechanical elements that could cause breakage. Chemical changes will not have a great effect.

Glass

Glass fragments buried in the surface show greater deterioration than suspended or deeply buried glass (Florian, 1987a). Ion leaching will cause the glass to become opaque. The deterioration is increased with increases in pressure, temperature and time of exposure. Also, the pH of the surrounding environment will affect deterioration. However, this is usually damage that can be repaired by the conservator. Glass can survive reasonably well underwater apart from breakage (Pearson, 1987). All changes except salinity would affect glass. However, there is no risk of disintegration but of damage, like leaching.

Stone

The deterioration of stone is associated with its properties: porosity, water absorption, hardness, strength, thermal expansion and composition. Chemical deterioration depends on the mineral composition and it can be susceptible to dissolution. It will be influenced by salinity. It is susceptible to erosion by water and sediment movement. Also, to some chemical changes.

Table 5.1 summarises the effects of climate change on underwater cultural heritage materials. As it can be observed, of the eighteen elements that we can find in a shipwreck, twelve of them would be affected by the warming of the waters, six by the rises in sea levels, seven by the change of ocean currents, seven by changes in salinity and twelve by changes in acidification. Rises in sea levels, would be, therefore the less aggressive change that underwater cultural heritage faces. However, it would cause irreparable damage to ceramics and glass, an important source of information for archaeologists (Renfrew and Bahn, 2008).

The only element that would not suffer with the effects of climate change is pure gold. Paradoxically this is the element that is most sought by treasure hunters, so its preservation is not either way guaranteed. Textiles, copper and glass would be the most fragile elements in the event of future changes. However, for most materials, only by being affected by only one change could make them disappear, as in the case of iron that would suffer massive concretions from chemical changes. For the reader's convenience, Figure 5.2 summarises the amount of materials that would be affected by the different climate changes:

Ethical dilemmas: preservation

Climate change may affect cultural heritage in two substantial ways:

Table 5.1 Effects of climate change on underwater cultural heritage material

	Main problems	Warming of the waters	Rises in sea levels (more pressure)	Ocean currents (erosion)	Chemical changes Salinity (higher)	Chemical changes Acidity (less pH)
1. Waterlogged wood						
Wood	Waterlogged and evaporation	✓		✓		✓
2. Organic material, no wood						
Cellulosic material	Stretching	✓		✓		✓
Plant products	Microorganisms	✓			✓	✓
Animal origin	Swelling and stretching	✓			✓	✓
Textiles	Light, insects, pollution, microorganisms	✓	✓		✓	✓
Teeth and ivory	Heat and salt	✓			✓	✓
Bone	Warped by heat and decomposed by water	✓			✓	✓
Leather	Complex changes	✓			✓	✓
3. Metals						
Iron	Massive concretions / Organisms	✓		✓	✓	✓
Copper	Unconcreted / Heat	✓	✓	✓		✓
Brass and bronze	Need of normal pH	✓				✓
Pewter, lead and tin	Alloys are the main problem	✓				✓
Silver	Stable				✓	
Gold	Stable					
Aluminium	Unstable to heat	✓	✓			
4. Others						
Ceramics	Breakage		✓	✓		
Glass	Breakage	✓	✓	✓		✓
Stone	Chemical changes can cause dissolution		✓	✓		✓

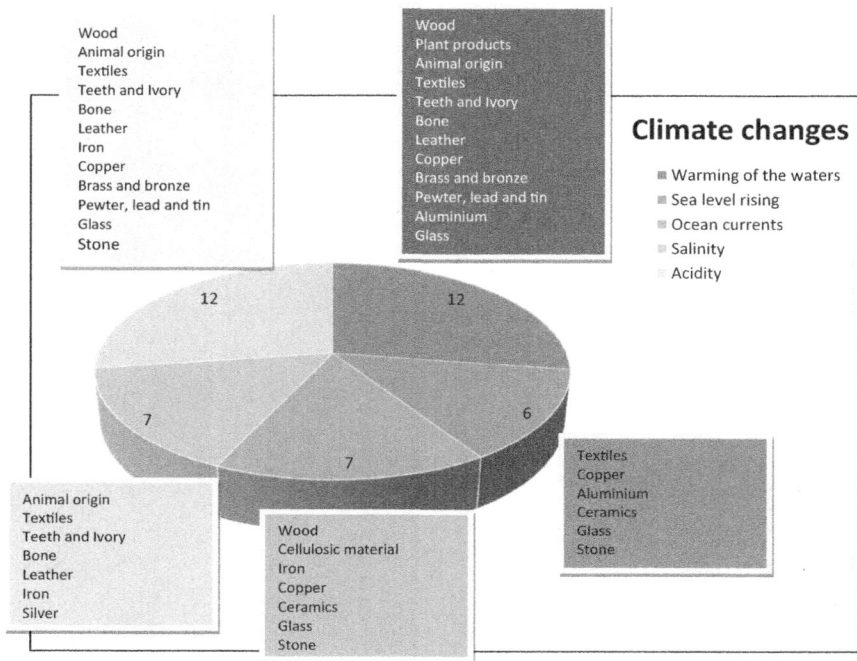

Wood
Animal origin
Textiles
Teeth and Ivory
Bone
Leather
Iron
Copper
Brass and bronze
Pewter, lead and tin
Glass
Stone

Wood
Plant products
Animal origin
Textiles
Teeth and Ivory
Bone
Leather
Copper
Brass and bronze
Pewter, lead and tin
Aluminium
Glass

Climate changes

■ Warming of the waters
■ Sea level rising
■ Ocean currents
░ Salinity
░ Acidity

12

12

7

6

7

Textiles
Copper
Aluminium
Ceramics
Glass
Stone

Animal origin
Textiles
Teeth and Ivory
Bone
Leather
Iron
Silver

Wood
Cellulosic material
Iron
Copper
Ceramics
Glass
Stone

Figure 5.2 Diagram of the effects of climate change on underwater cultural heritage material.

The exposing, damage or movement of current underwater cultural heritage

As said in previous chapters, the most important source of archaeological information about an underwater site is not only the ship or underwater city itself, but also the objects associated with it, such as those found at the location, the ship's inventory, personal belongings and cargo. The various types of object have different reactions to water because they are composed of different materials. Cultural heritage, once submerged, is covered by coral, mud, microorganisms and sand. Once thereby stabilised, there is little further physical disturbance by post-depositional forces (Piechota and Giangrande, 2008). At 400–800 metres' depth, archaeological sites experience a low and near-constant water temperature all year around (Daly, 2011). Sunlight, recognised as a biodeterioration accelerator, does not penetrate below 200m. At the seafloor, the current speeds are often very low, with minimal tidal effects and sediment transfer rates. Cold temperatures and currents in a deep-water environment have a strong preservative effect. As a consequence, shipwrecks are often situated in the ideal conditions for preservation (Willis, 2008). In addition, such positions are free from most human interference. Underwater cultural heritage is, therefore, well protected under the water. It is only when objects are disturbed that the equilibrium due to burial is lost (Piechota and Giangrande, 2008). For this reason, leaving heritage *in situ* is usually the archaeologists' first option for preserving heritage in both land and underwater sites. As next chapter will demonstrate, new ways are being developed to make underwater cultural heritage accessible to the public, such as diving down to a site that has been curated as an underwater park or reserve. However, the disruption caused by making underwater cultural heritage more accessible to the public as it lies *in situ* is minimal in contrast with the threat to this heritage posed by climate change. Chapman (Chapman, 2003) emphasises that its implications are likely to be far-reaching, although he recognises that they are not yet fully understood.

There are already some examples of the pernicious effect of global warming on cultural heritage. For instance, in Spain, a Phoenician shipwreck is becoming exposed due to the change of ocean currents. The shipwreck, which was at a depth of 6 metres 25 years ago, is now at a depth of only 1.8 metres (Rubio, 2014). Its preservation *in situ* may no longer be the best option since it is now readily accessible to human interference and to further damaging changes in the currents. The rising sea level is also already having effects and it has disturbed the underwater graves of soldiers killed in World War II on the Marshall Islands (McGrath, 2014). The tides have exposed a grave containing 26 human bodies, and the coffins and human remains are being washed away. This case raises further ethical concerns: water graves are being disturbed, causing all types of ethical issues related to the preservation of human remains (Perez-Alvaro, 2014). The wreck of the *Titanic* is also suffering damage due to chemical changes, and it is destined to disappear. Mann (Mann, 2012) reports:

> The scientists of the *Titanic* observed that the ferrous-iron structures, such as cast iron, wrought iron and steel were corroded and covered, draped with rust-like precipitates [...]. Unfortunately, due to rusticle consumption, the *Titanic* wreck cannot be preserved forever as an underwater heritage site [...].

As a consequence, sites that have been protected and preserved, thanks to the layers of sediments, are already being exposed or damaged.

Cultural heritage transformed into underwater cultural heritage

When there is destruction, there also is creation. The question is not only how destruction of underwater sties can be prevented but what cultural heritage destruction creates. We may be losing some cultural heritage, but we will also be *gaining* underwater cultural heritage. The 2001 UNESCO

Convention on the Protection of the Underwater Cultural Heritage, Article 1.1 (UNESCO, 2001) defines underwater cultural heritage as:

> [...] all traces of human existence having a cultural, historical or archaeological character which have been partially or totally under water, periodically or continuously, for at least 100 years such as: (i) sites, structures, buildings, artefacts and human remains, together with their archaeological and natural context [...]

A total of fifteen of the world's twenty megacities are situated by the sea. 'If water levels rise even further, by 3, 4 or 5 metres in centuries to come, we will have to give up some of the cities' (Rahmstorf and Richardson, 2009). These underwater cities will become future underwater cultural heritage since they will meet all the conditions for protection under the 2001 UNESCO Convention; namely, there will be traces of human existence having a cultural character totally underwater for 100 years (from 2100).

To obtain a clearer idea, the following images from Climate Central (Climate Central, 2015) project a potential scenario for post-2100 sea-level rise. The first image of the pair show projections based on 2°C of warming from carbon pollution, corresponding to the target limit set by the United Nations. The second image shows projections based on 4°C (see Figures 5.3–5.8).

The images show different possibilities for the cities in the future. This recently published research has to do with the long-term sea-level rises that near-term emissions can lock in by 2100, based on different emission scenarios. Although these are future predictions, we already have some examples of sea-level rises affecting cultural heritage. In fact, according to a leaked diplomatic cable (The Guardian, 2010) the Dalai Lama has called attention to the climate change Tibet is suffering. Although Tibet is entirely landlocked, its temples are already being inundated, which will convert them to underwater cultural heritage in the future—an example that could be repeated with other monuments and sacred places around the world:

> The Dalai Lama argued that the political agenda should be side-lined for five to ten years and the international community should shift its focus to climate change on the Tibetan plateau. Melting glaciers, deforestation and increasingly polluted water from mining projects were problems that 'cannot wait.' The Dalai Lama criticized China's energy policy, alleging that dam construction in Kham and Amdo have displaced thousands of Tibetans and left temples and monasteries underwater.

Also shifting the delimitation of the seas can be a problematic issue: although a specific example has not yet materialised, legal disputes concerning sea boundaries are a diplomatic source of conflict nowadays: just metres of sea can be the object of disputes in international tribunals, such as the

Figure 5.3 London (UK) underwater.

Figure 5.4 Durban (South Africa) underwater.

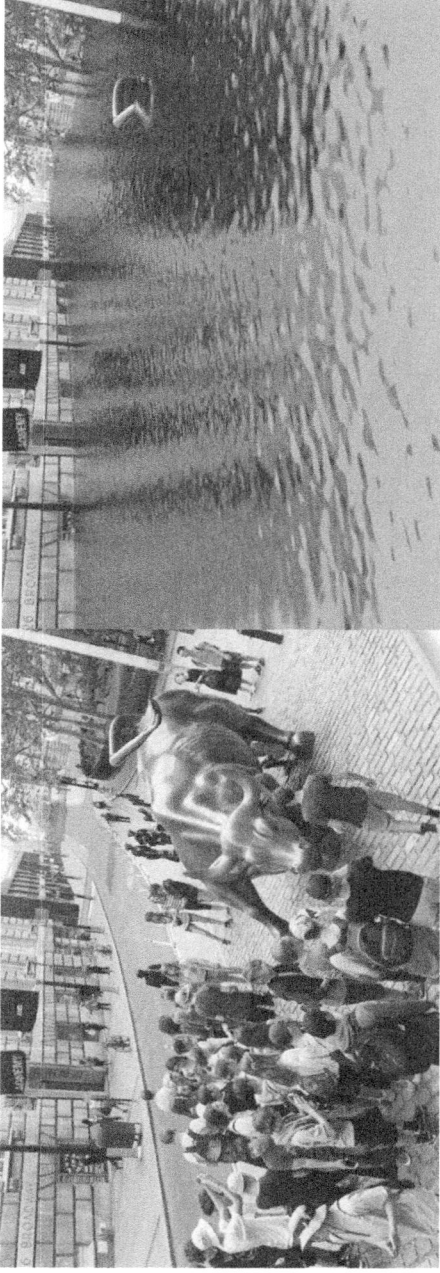

Figure 5.5 New York (USA) underwater.

Figure 5.6 Mumbai (India) underwater.

Figure 5.7 Rio de Janeiro (Brazil) underwater.

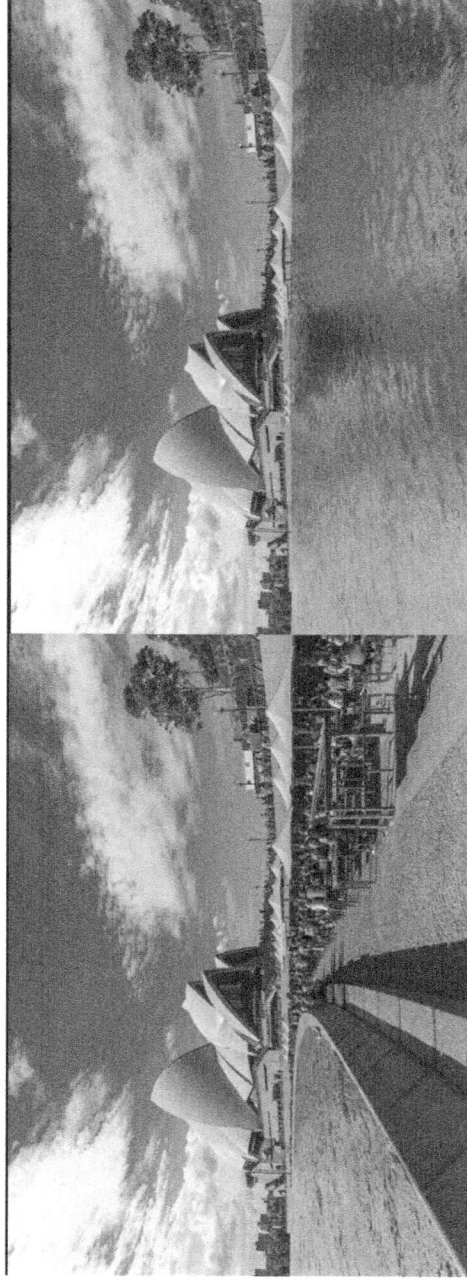

Figure 5.8 Sydney (Australia) underwater.

International Tribunal for the Law of the Sea. The delimitation of the seas is mainly derived from the baseline taken from the coast. Should such baselines change as a consequence of climate change, this would mean not only new disputes, but also that 'islands and archipelagos could modify their territories and may lose the benefit of their maritime zones'. In addition, the melting of the Arctic would open new commercial maritime routes, which will most certainly bring about new economic possibilities and the claiming of new territories (Fernandez, 2013). In addition, and according to Milman (2017) more than 13,000 archaeological and historic sites in America will be wiped out by sea-level rise, forcing the potential relocation of the White House and the Lincoln Memorial in Washington DC. Florida, which is more vulnerable to sea-level rise, has the most sites in danger from the raising of the oceans. Sea-level rise is also expected to displace millions of people form the US coasts. Around a dozen towns in Alaska are already being abandoned or relocated due to diminishing sea ice.

A very concerning issue is that Small Island Developing States (SIDS) are vulnerable to rises in sea levels and may even become uninhabitable (UNESCO, 2008). For instance, the Pacific Islands, a region that comprises 22 countries and territories, nine of them fully independent (Barnett and Campbell, 2010). It is divided into three regions: Melanesia (of large cultural diversity and more than 800 languages spoken), Polynesia (more homogeneous, with 'only' 30 languages) and Micronesia (with strong links to the United States; Barnett and Campbell, 2010). This cultural diversity may change for the effects of climate change. The IPCC 4th assessment report identified small island states as being the most vulnerable countries of the world to the adverse impacts of climate change and the Pacific is in fact one of the world's most vulnerable regions. Not only their cultural heritage will be affected but also their agriculture, water resources, forestry, tourism and other industry-related sectors. However, the impact of climate change in these communities will not only be noticeable on flooding lands, but also in its effects on agricultural production and fisheries, and, as a consequence, in the availability of food. However, there has been little research on understanding how people is going to adapt to climate change. For instance, the Tuvalu State is already losing not only its territory because of the flooding, but also its identity and heritage: its culture as a nation is transforming (Fernandez, 2013). Communities on the Torres Strait are also suffering king tides and flooding that make life non-viable (Kelly, 2014). The islands will probably be completely submerged in the future, meaning 7000 people already have to adapt to climate change. Australia has invited them to live on Australian territory, but this would mean that the land of such states—and, therefore, their tangible culture—will be lost. People may move to another country to start a new life, but their identity as citizens of their cities, as members of a community with their own tangible past, complete with their cultural heritage, will completely change. In this regard, climate change will probably modify social and cultural behaviours, with communities changing the ways in which they live and work, migrating and abandoning their heritage and losing their identity. In fact, the problem is much larger than it may seem at first glance: as already explained, 'identity' is a concept intrinsically linked to the concept of heritage. Identity is the process of inclusion and exclusion that defines communities, and the process is led by heritage (Graham and Howard, 2008: 5). Heritage is, therefore, necessary for an individual or a society to be able to reinforce its socio-cultural identity. If climate change robs a culture of the land where its physical heritage is located, it would mean, not only the loss of territory, such as a sunken island, but also the transformation of a culture.

Proposal: natural/cultural partnership

There are two basic responses to climate change: mitigation and adaptation. Mitigation includes all policies and laws that have been drafted on climate change. Adaptation has its origins in evolutionary biology, seen as the basis for natural selections and it implies long-term processes. This chapter proposes a mix of mitigation and adaptation actions in order to understand and face the effects of climate change on underwater cultural heritage.

As Chapman (2003) points out, references to archaeology in climate change arenas are rare. The most common proposal, consisting of monitoring underwater cultural sites (Chapman, 2003; Dunkley, 2013a), will help to understand the problem but will have little effect. However, as Hall (Hall, 2016) states, heritage may be employed to further develop climate change awareness. Some organisations advise on guidelines to follow to avoid climate change. English Heritage recommends a limitation of further dangerous emissions and of working on projects such as risking assessment, adaptation and mitigation.[2] It also recommends broader actions such as advice for home owners, energy efficiency or renewable energy. However, more specific actions in relation to underwater cultural heritage have to be taken. The present study focuses the required actions in four steps: recognising the loss, starting the debate, creating a legal framework in which situate the debate and recognising underwater cultural heritage as a natural resource. Recognising the loss means that there have already been two periods of climate change in the past which could have affected the heritage. It is essential to understand that although climate change does destroy the heritage, it also creates new heritage—for instance, flooded cities or islands will become underwater cultural heritage in 100 years. Again, this is the ethical issue of heritage as a process: understanding that it is inevitable to lose some cultural heritage but that we will also gain some. On these premises it is again the time to evaluate the importance of the sites and to undertake actions to preserve the selected ones. The next step is starting the debate: climate change debate has occupied few concerns in the archaeological and heritage arena. Whatever the causes, the effects may be devastating (Chapman, 2003). This chapter has tried to trigger the debate, which needs to be discussed and disseminated through academic, social and political agendas. Once the topic has been discussed, it is important creating a legal framework: the 2001 Convention that guides States on the management of their underwater cultural heritage does not include climate change as a danger to the heritage. As with any other international instruments, the authors of the Convention would hope to become an example to the states (Carman, 2013). If this Convention does not take climate change into consideration neither States will. In this regard, the regulations governing terrestrial matters, which always appear before those governing underwater matters, can help to offer solutions. However, this chapter includes underwater cultural heritage as a part of the oceans and as a consequence underwater cultural heritage preservation has more similarities to *underwater natural* heritage than to *terrestrial cultural* heritage. Although the methodology—archaeology—and the ethical concerns that both underwater and land heritage face have a major equivalence, in the aspects of preserving and facing climate change, underwater cultural heritage has to fight the same battles as the natural heritage in the oceans. The changes that will affect them are the same. As a consequence, the same legal and political agendas on climate change affecting the oceans should already include (as coral reefs are included) underwater cultural heritage on their agendas. This leads to the final point of action: it is essential recognising underwater cultural heritage as a natural resource since the seabed and the sand is covering the archaeological objects. Also, the non-sedentary fishing species live around artificial reefs made by shipwrecks. For this reason, some authors (Rössler, 2006) have tried to link cultural and biological diversity for the better preservation of underwater cultural heritage. In fact, the 1972 Convention Concerning the Protection of the World Cultural and Natural Heritage (UNESCO, 1972) is one instrument designed for the preservation of both cultural and natural heritage. Chapman (2003) also reiterates the close relationship between ecological and archaeological site management and suggests a liaison between archaeologists and other parties interested in the natural environment. Lixinski (2008: 379) claims that the 'nature and culture dichotomy' listed in the 1972 Convention is simply artificial. It is necessary, therefore, to adjust environmental policies on the oceans in an effort to accommodate cultural heritage. As Flatman (2009) highlights, the 'green lobby' is proving successful in ensuring that good consideration is given to the environment. Wildlife biologists make concerted efforts to promote the need for ocean conservation: messages about saving whales and dolphins, protecting coral reefs or promoting catch-and-release fishing have not only been well received by the public but creates hordes of people defending such principles (Scott-Ireton and McKinnon, 2015). If underwater cultural heritage is treated as one more element in the ocean, its protection would be guaranteed. This could be of mutual benefit: if underwater cultural heritage is preserved, the natural heritage will also gain.

Conclusions

All heritage is already considered vulnerable to natural disasters (UNESCO, 2008). As this chapter has tried to demonstrate, rising sea levels, warmer waters, ocean acidification and changes in currents will almost certainly affect cultural heritage. Warmer waters mean more chemical changes and the proliferation of *teredo navalis*. Ocean currents may cause disturbances to the layer of sediment protecting underwater cultural heritage sites, alteration of the materials and the potential loss of the archaeological record. Although the direct effects of chemical changes (particularly acidification and salinification) are still not well understood, the current rates of metal corrosion and damage to materials may well increase due to their climate change–induced fluctuation (Dunkley, 2013b). Lastly, the rises in sea levels would reduce the amount of time an air-breathing diver can safely spend under water and hence their productivity. Rises would also mean expansion, which could raise the problem of ocean delimitation. It will also increase the depths of oceans and increase the frequency and magnitude of storms, which may further erode or damage heritage. It may also lead to flooding of cultural heritage that is now on land.

Each site deserves unique treatment, and it is difficult to design a general set of criteria to cover all cases. Some authors predict that future generations will face the climate change damages and loss of underwater cultural heritage or make great efforts to protect them (Marzeion and Levermann, 2014). In view of these examples, new management policies need to be planned: it is ultimately a moral challenge, and cultural heritage managers have to be prepared for policy changes (Sheridan and Sheridan, 2013). As Sheridan and Sheridan (Sheridan and Sheridan, 2013) observe, people may well need to see their cultural heritage threatened, temples washed away, or cathedrals destroyed by flooding, in order to be convinced of the effects of climate change and finally evaluate the situation honestly and propose workable solutions. This chapter has directed its efforts towards triggering this debate, which needs to be discussed and disseminated through academic, social and political channels. It is erroneous to assume that the most visible remains are the most threatened. Accordingly, there is a need for a practical and political response to the effects of climate change on underwater cultural heritage but raising awareness of such impacts ought to be the priority. Since there is a lack of creativity in managing cultural heritage, some inter-agency cooperation might be necessary (Van de Noort, 2013), and there may be some difficulty convincing climate policy makers to include the impact of climate change on cultural heritage in their planning: legislation can be used to minimise human threats to underwater cultural heritage. There is only 1.9 million km^2 of ocean area where nature conservation regulations apply. There is some Marine Protected Areas (MPA) but some authors (Rahmstorf and Richardson, 2009) believe that at least 20 to 30% of the world's oceans should be protected. The Intergovernmental Panel on Climate Change (IPCC, 2007), Group I concluded that the oceans are warming and the salinification of water is changing. Although they are not visible ocean circulation changes, the ocean biogeochemistry is changing since there is evidence of decreased oxygen concentrations. And the sea level is definitely rising (IPCC, 2007). Despite of all this information, international instruments fails to protect cultural heritage from climate change forces (Sheridan and Sheridan, 2013). There are gaps in the capacity of the legislation for future protection. Only the 1972 Convention has some response to climate change (Sheridan and Sheridan, 2013). The 2001 Convention does not mention climate change as an adverse factor for underwater cultural heritage. However, Dromgoole (2013) feels that the term in the definition 'partially or totally underwater, periodically or continuously, for at least 100 years' is of importance for the predicted sea-level changes due to climate change. However, and despite this minor concession, the Convention does not explicitly mention 'climate change' and as a consequence, it does not propose solutions. The *United Nations Framework Convention on Climate Change* (1994) has no direct reference to underwater cultural heritage either, nor does the *Kyoto Protocol* (1997) which aims to reduce the levels of greenhouse gases. However, these instruments that try to cover the topic provide good intentions rather than solutions. They make a good starting point for the development of the field, although they tend to be vague and imprecise and no remedies are proposed. As a consequence, there is a need for ranking the potential impact of climate change on individual heritage and determining the vulnerability, sensitivity and resilience to future changes (Howard, 2003).

Climate change actions have a central moral component and the ethical dilemma is the core of all challenges (Sheridan and Sheridan, 2013). What is the right thing to do now? (Sheridan and Sheridan, 2013). Different ethical dilemmas arise from this chapter. First one is imperativeness: the impact of climate change on underwater cultural heritage is real and although it might be a point of no return, it can be a manageable one. The nub of the problem is not the necessity of evaluating and deciding predominant values to determine what we should preserve but why we should preserve it and how. The problem is the necessity of prompt decisions since climate change is already happening (Corfield, 1996). The second dilemma is that the effects that climate change will have in the oceans have been the leading clue to understand the effects that, as a consequence, climate change will have on underwater cultural heritage. If efforts by international and national organisations are aimed at helping to avoid climate change, are we also avoiding damage to underwater cultural heritage? The oceans are being used as a cure for climate change through ocean nourishment (feeding algae with iron oxide) (Flatman, 2009: 6). Therefore, the oceans as well as cultural heritage are facing the same issues. Uniting efforts to fight against climate change will offer broader solutions: the legal instruments governing underwater cultural heritage should include policies to mitigate the effects of climate change. This could include allowing ocean-based energy systems even if their installation damages in the short term underwater cultural heritage. The pillars of prevention might be mitigation, adaptation and climate engineering (Ganje et al., 2011). This adaptation could include also an open mind on the preservation of underwater cultural heritage because there is a close interrelationship between the environment, culture and human behaviour (Sheridan and Sheridan, 2013). Whereas the term 'marine environment' has traditionally been applied to refer to the natural environment and the living resources therein, it is now recognised that cultural heritage resources are part of that environment as well and the inextricable link between both means that the protection and treatment of one must contemplate the consequences for the other. Maybe it is time to adopt the concept of sustainability from environmentalism as the prime motivator for underwater cultural heritage protection (Kingsley, 2011). Treating underwater cultural heritage as a completely different element to natural heritage such as fish, reefs or flora prevents the seas being understood as a unique object to protect. The third dilemma is that it is essential to analyse if preserving underwater cultural heritage can help to mitigate climate change effects. Metal corrosion, pollution or munitions on board of the wrecks can damage local areas which may be small parts of the global picture but still important. Cooperation between different organisations—biologists, oceanographers and engineers—creates a synergy on actively reporting processes and proposing adaptation measures that could establish solutions for, as previously said, rowing in the same direction (UNESCO, 2008).

This chapter has reviewed the concept of preservation applied to underwater cultural heritage and the possible consequences of climate change on this heritage. Preservation and how to preserve will be examined in other chapters of this book underwater cultural heritage can be managed according to different needs: watery graves, tourism and preservation of migrant shipwrecks are topics that will re-examine this concept.

Notes

1 Reproduced from Perez-Alvaro, E. (2016). Climate change and underwater cultural heritage: impacts and challenges. *Journal of Cultural Heritage* 21: 842–848. Copyright © 2016, published by Elsevier Masson SAS. All rights reserved.
2 English Heritage. Advice: Climate Change. Available at: www.english-heritage. org.uk/professional/advice/advice-by-topic/climate-change/.

Bibliography

Barnett, J. and Campbell, J. (2010). *Climate Change and Small Island States: Power, Knowledge, and the South Pacific*. London: Earthscan.

Carman, J. (2013). Legislation in archaeology: overview and introduction. In Smith, C. (ed.), *Encyclopaedia of Global Archaeology*. New York: Springer: 4469–4485.

Chapman, H. (2003). Global warming: the implications for sustainable archaeological resource management. *Conservation and Management of Archaeological Sites* 5(4): 241–245.

Climate Central. (2015). *Mapping Choices: Carbon, Climate and Rising Oceans: Our Global Legacy*. Climate Central. 29 November 2015. Available at: http://sealevel. climatecentral.org/research/reports/mapping-choices-carbon-climate-and-rising-seas-our-global-legacy.

Corfield, M. (1996). Preventive conservation for archaeological sites. *Studies in Conservation* 41(1): 32–37.

Daly, C. (2011). Climate change and the conservation of archaeological sites: a review of impacts theory. Conservation and Management of Archaeological Sites 13(4): 293–310.

Delgado, J. (ed.) (1998). *British Museum Encyclopaedia of Underwater and Maritime Archaeology*. London: British Museum Press.

Dromgoole, S. (2013). *Underwater Cultural Heritage and International Law*. Cambridge Studies in International and Comparative Law 101. Cambridge: Cambridge University Press.

Dunkley, M. (2013a). The potential effects of oceanic climate change on the management and curation of underwater archaeological remains. *The Archaeologist* 89: 60–62.

Dunkley, M. (2013b). *Ocean Climate Change and Underwater Archaeology*. English Heritage. 12 September 2013. Available at: https://heritagecalling.com/2013/09/12/oceanic-climate-change-and-underwater-archaeology/.

Fernandez, P. (2013). Cambio climatico y derecho del mar. In Franch, J. J. (ed.), *Derecho del mar y sostenibilidiad ambiental en el Mediterraneo*. Valencia: Tirant Lo Blanch: 271–317.

Flatman, J. (2009). Conserving marine cultural heritage: threats, risks and future priorities. Conservation and Management of Archaeological Sites 11(1): 5–8.

Florian, M.-L. (1987a). The underwater environment. In Pearson, C. (ed.), *Conservation of Marine Archaeological Objects*. Cornwall: Butterworth: 1–20.

Florian, M.-L. (1987b). Deterioration of organic materials other than wood. In Pearson, C. (ed.), *Conservation of Marine Archaeological Objects*. Cornwall: Butterworth: 21–54.

Ganje, F., Hezbkhah, E. and Maashkar, B. (2011). Evaluation of the effects of climate change in destruction procedure on Iran's historic buildings. *World Academy of Science, Engineering and Technology* 5(11): 1718–1720.

Graham, B. and Howard, P. (2008). Introduction. In Graham, B. and Howard, P. (eds.), *The Ashgate Research Companion to Heritage and Identity*. Cornwall: Ashgate: 1–17.

Grattan, D. W. (1987). Waterlogged wood. In Pearson, C. (ed.), *Conservation of Marine Archaeological Objects*. Cornwall: Butterworth: 55–67.

Green, J. (1990). *Maritime Archaeology: A Technical Handbook*. San Diego: Academic Press.

The Guardian. (2010). US Embassy cables: Dalai Lama says prioritise climate change over politics in Tibet. [online]. *The Guardian*. 16 December 2010. Available at: www.theguardian.com/world/us-embassy-cables-documents/220120.

Hall, C. (2016). Heritage, heritage tourism and climate change. *Journal of Heritage Tourism* 11(1): 1–9.

Hamilton, D. (1997). *Basic Methods of Conserving Underwater Archaeological Material Culture*. Texas A&M in partnership with the US Department of Defense Legacy Resource Management Program, Department of Anthropology. Washington, DC: Nautical Archaeology Program.

Hamilton, D. L. (2000). Conservation of cultural materials from underwater sites. In Williamson, R. A. and Nickens, P. R. (eds.), *Science and Technology in Historic Preservation*. New York: Kluwer Academic/Plenum Publishers: 193–229.

Hoppe, K. (2002). Teredo navalis: the cryptogenic shipworm. In Leppakoski, E., Gollasch, S. and Olenin, S. (eds.), *Invasive Aquatic Species of Europe. Distribution, Impacts and Management* Netherlands: Springer: 116–119.

Howard, P. (2003). *Heritage: Management, Interpretation, Identity*. London: Library of Congress Cataloguing-in Publication Data.

IPCC (2007). Intergovernmental Panel on Climate Change Fourth Assessment Report on Climate Change. Available at: www.ipcc-wg1.unibe.ch/ (3 April 2019).

Kelly, E. (2014). Rising seas pose a cultural threat to Australia's 'forgotten people'. [online]. *The Conversation*. 26 November 2014. Available at: http://theconversation.com/rising-seas-pose-a-cultural-threat-to-australias-forgotten-people-34359.

Kingsley, S. (2011). Challenges of maritime archaeology: in too deep. In King, T. F. (ed.), *A Companion to Cultural Resource Management*. Chichester: Wiley-Blackwell: 223–244.

Kyoto Protocol (1997). United Nations. Available at: http://unfccc.int/kyoto_protocol/items/2830.php (11 March 2018).

Lixinski, L. (2008). Book review by F. Francioni and F. Lenzerini: The 1972 World Heritage Convention: a commentary. *European Journal of Legal Studies* 2(1): 371–386.

Macdonald, F. (2008). *Shipwrecks: 100 Facts*. Essex: Miles Kelly.

Manders, M. (2012). Unit 9: in situ preservation. In Manders, M. and Underwood, C. (eds.), *Training Manual for the UNESCO Foundation Course on the Protection and Management of Underwater Cultural Heritage in Asia and the Pacific*. Bangkok: UNESCO.

Mann, H. (2012). The appearance of new bacteria and metal corrosion: new bacterium species discovered on RMS Titanic rusticles. In *UNESCO Scientific Colloquium on Factors Impacting Underwater Cultural Heritage, UNESCO Regional Meeting on the Protection of the Underwater Cultural Heritage: Conference*. Brussels: Book Royal Library of Belgium: 62.

Marzeion, B. and Levermann, A. (2014). Loss of cultural world heritage and currently inhabited places to sea-level rise. *Environmental Research Letters* 9: 1–7.

McGrath, M. (2014). Climate change helps seas disturb Japanese war dead. [online]. *BBC News: Science and Environment*. 7 June 2014. Available at: www.bbc.co.uk/news/science-environment-27742957.

Memet, J. B. (2008). Conservation of underwater cultural heritage: characteristics and new technologies. *Museum International* 60(4): 42–49.

Milman, O. (2017). Buried in marshes: sea-level rise could destroy historic sites on US east coast. [online]. *The Guardian*. 29 November 2017. Available at: https://www.theguardian.com/uk (accessed 6 July 2018).

Murphy, P., Pater, C. and Dunkley, M. (2008). Out to sea: climate change and the maritime historic environment. *Conservation Bulletin* 57: 17–19.

North, N. A. and MacLeod, I. D. (1987). Corrosion of metals. In Pearson, C. (ed.), *Conservation of Marine Archaeological Objects*. Cornwall: Butterworth: 68–98.

Pearson, C. (1987). Deterioration of ceramics, glass and stone. In Pearson, C. (ed.), *Conservation of Marine Archaeological Objects*. Cornwall: Butterworth: 99–104.

Perez-Alvaro, E. (2014). The management of human remains on shipwrecks: ethical attitudes and legal approaches. In *Proceedings of the Second Asia-Pacific Regional Conference on Underwater Cultural Heritage*. Honolulu: Electric Pencil: 39–48.

Piechota, D. and Giangrande, C. (2008). Conservation of archaeological finds from deep-water wreck sites. In Ballard, R. (ed.), *Archaeological Oceanography*. Princeton, NJ: Princeton University Press: 65–92.

Rahmstorf, S. and Richardson, K. (2009). *Our Threatened Oceans: The Sustainability Project*. London: Haus Publishing.

Renfrew, C. and Bahn, P. (2008). *Archaeology: Theories, Methods and Practice*. London: Thames & Hudson.

Rössler, M. (2006). World heritage: linking cultural and biological diversity. In Hoffman, B. T. (ed.), *Art and Cultural Heritage: Law, Policy and Practice*. Cambridge: Cambridge University Press: 201–205.

Rubio, M. (2014). Peligro: el mar devuelve el barco fenicio. [online]. *La verdad*. 6 May 2014. Available at: www.laverdad.es/murcia/v/20140505/mazarron/peligro-devuelve-barco-fenicio-20140505.html.

Scott-Ireton, D. A. and McKinnon, J. F. (2015). As the sand settles: education and archaeological tourism on underwater cultural heritage. *Public Archaeology* 14(3): 157–171.

Sheridan, R. and Sheridan, J. (2013). *International Heritage Instruments and Climate Change*. Champaign, IL: Common Ground Publishing.

Sivan, D., Lambeck, K., Toueg, R., Raban, A., Porat, Y. and Shirman, B. (2004). Ancient coastal wells of Caesarea Maritima, Israel: an indicator for relative sea level changes during the last 2000 years. *Earth and Planetary Science Letters* 222(1): 315–330.

Smith, H. D. and Couper, A. D. (2003). The management of the underwater cultural heritage. *Journal of Cultural Heritage* 4(1): 25–33.

UNESCO (1972). Convention concerning the protection of the world cultural and natural heritage. Paris, 16 November 1972. Available at: http://whc.unesco.org/en/conventiontext/ (2 June 2018).

UNESCO (2001). Convention on the Protection of the Underwater Cultural Heritage. Paris, 2 November 2001. Available at: http://unesdoc.unesco.org/images/0012/001260/126065e.pdf (2 June 2018).

UNESCO (2008). *Policy Document on the Impacts of Climate Change on World Heritage Properties*. UNESCO World Heritage Centre Publications on Climate Change. Available at: http://whc.unesco.org/document/10046 (2 June 2018).

United Nations Framework Convention on Climate Change (1994). United Nations 'Rio Conventions'. Available at: http://unfccc.int/essential_background/convention/items/6036.php (3 April 2019).

Van de Noort, R. (2013). Wetland archaeology in the 21st century: adapting to climate change. In O'Sullivan, F. M. (ed.), *The Oxford Handbook of Wetland Archaeology*. Oxford: Oxford University Press: 719–732.

Willis, S. (2008). *Shipwrecks: A History of Disasters at Sea*. Oxford: BCS Publishing.

6 Sustainability
Preservation *in situ*

One of the commonly agreed principles of preservation of underwater cultural heritage named by the 2001 UNESCO Convention on the Protection of the Underwater Cultural Heritage is the preservation *in situ* as the first option (Preamble, Article 2.5. and Rule 1 of the Annex) (UNESCO, 2001).

> Committed to improving the effectiveness of measures at international, regional and national levels for the preservation *in situ* or, if necessary for scientific or protective purposes, the careful recovery of underwater cultural heritage [...]
>
> Article 2.5. The preservation *in situ* of underwater cultural heritage shall be considered as the first option before allowing or engaging in any activities directed at this heritage.
>
> Rule 1. The protection of underwater cultural heritage through *in situ* preservation shall be considered as the first option.

The reason for this being mainly because archaeological objects are better preserved under layers of mud and in saline water. The ship, once she has sunk and lies at the sea-bed, reaches a state of equilibrium with the upper parts destroyed and the buried remains covered (Green, 1990). After reaching this state of equilibrium, the wreck will be only disturbed either by human intervention or by geological changes—physical, chemical and biological threats (Wachsmann, 2011). This is the reason why underwater archaeologists consider preservation *in situ* as the first option, although is not always the preferable or only option, as this chapter will examine.

Introduction

Preservation *in situ* has been commonly adopted for archaeological sites both in land and under water (Corfield, 1996). However, one of the most common mistakes is considering that underwater cultural heritage has to be preserved at all times in the place where it lies (Aznar-Gómez, 2017). In addition, the term does not have a precise definition and can raise problems with the interpretation: is relocation of the site (ex situ preservation) also preservation *in situ*? In terrestrial archaeology, this principle has a clear answer: any decontextualisation of the archaeological objects from the site is always a loss of information (Renfrew and Bahn, 2008). In underwater archaeology, the answer is not so straight forward: for enjoyment of the site some parts may be displayed, but if it is decided that the site has to be protected for keeping the information safe, it may be needed to be completely covered (Manders, 2012b). In addition, preservation *in situ* is preferred to reserve the opportunity to apply future techniques and innovations (Khakzad and Van Balen, 2012) since underwater techniques of preservation may be more advanced in the future. However, there will always be a future with more developed techniques. Should we always wait?

The issue has been well discussed in relation to terrestrial sites. In fact, international legislation, like the Valetta Treaty (1992), calls for the 'conservation and maintenance of archaeological heritage, preferably *in situ*'. The *Training Manual for the UNESCO Foundation Course on the Protection and Management of Underwater Cultural Heritage in Asia and the Pacific* (Manders and Underwood, 2012) considers some reasons of why preservation *in situ* should be the first option: because a representative proportion of our maritime past has to be preserved for future enjoyment and research; because most countries nowadays have a well-developed law and regulation system concerning the protection of maritime archaeological heritage; because the amount of shipwrecks discovered grows fast and there is not enough capacity to do the research; because the excavation of an underwater wreck is very expensive; because even if a wreck is likely to be excavated, there is usually a prolonged period of time between the discovery of objects and the actual excavation; and because of the lack of knowledge on how to treat certain processes of deterioration. However, as Caple (2008) proves, archaeological remains under water are degrading and the corrosion rates of buried metal artefacts, for instance, are increasing. The balance between protection and accessibility—funds, human resources and economic development pressures—has to be combined with urgent, unexpected needs brought, for instance by climate changes.

Issue

Preservation *in situ* is the first option under the 2001 UNESCO Convention (UNESCO, 2001). However, 'it forms just one part of management and not (as often interpreted) the only right way forward' (Manders, 2003: 31). As a consequence, different possibilities for the conservation of underwater cultural heritage can be identified (Khakzad and Van Balen, 2012):

Displacement

Displacement of the underwater heritage objects or even site to shallow waters or moving it onto land for relocation or incorporation in museums: the disadvantage is the difficulty to safeguard the values of the heritage since it is deprived of its archaeological and environmental context, which makes it lose significance.

In situ

In situ methods that complies with the Convention and preserve it for the future generations but that may not be the best option in the future due to threats such as climate change. Preservation *in situ* may include different techniques, like sandbags, polypropylene debris netting, sand deposition or artificial sea grass (Manders, 2012a). Preservation can also be benefited from technology, like the development of underwater vehicles to clean the hull of large ships (Ballard and Durbin, 2008), although the artefacts would not remain intact. The contra of this option is the difficulty of the exhibiting to the public. However, with the improvement of technology, *in situ* public access to submerged cultural sites can be achieved through telepresence technology, for instance, high-speed data communications on a real time basis (Ballard and Durbin, 2008) preserving the remains in undersea museums. However, if *in situ* preservation is chosen, shipwrecks would have to be monitored and regularly examined to avoid deterioration, as some authors stress (Manders, 2012a; Khakzad and Van Balen, 2012). With this method, preservation *in situ* can be a reality but still some threats to the cultural heritage such as climate change will have an effect. Different options are available inside this possibility for a best preservation depending on the site characteristics (Khakzad and Van Balen, 2012): *in situ* protection (exploring the site, covering it and restricting access), *in situ* conservation (intervening the site and stabilising it but still making it accessible to visitors), reburial the site (covering the site but continuously monitoring it which can recreate the original condition of the site), and *in situ* preservation and presentation (transforming the site in underwater parks, aquariums or submerged museums; Aguilar, 2013), an option that will be more common when technology and techniques develop and the ideas for its access will evolve.

However, to be able to preserve *in situ* one must first know what it entails (Manders, 2012a). Some authors state that the essence of *in situ* preservation is equally debatable for land or under water (Khakzad and Van Balen, 2012). However, the changes that climate change will bring to the oceans will be different to the ones that will take place on land. Some factors would determine if underwater artefacts should be left under the sea or be recovered, such as the size of the artefact since it is not the same economic and archaeological trying to lift a huge ship than a small boat. The scale of the excavation and preservation measures is going to be different and as a consequence the funding and the research interests will be poles apart. Also, the depth will be a deciding factor: artefacts can be totally submerged, almost at the surface or totally on land. This preservation on land could be more accessible to the public and still have the necessary preservation measures like humidity, worm and microbe protection. Finally, the state of preservation will also determine what to do: lifting a corroded artefact or an object in perfect conservation condition will have different outcomes.

State of knowledge

As previously explained, the most important source of information for the archaeologists of an underwater site is not only the ship or underwater cites but also her associated objects: context, inventory, personal belongings and cargo (Manders, 2012a), each one of them having a different reaction to water and changes. Shipwrecks can become trapped on rocks or be washed ashore, although the most common scenario is that they sink beneath the waves (Willis, 2008). After, they may be broken by currents, crushed by water pressure or covered by corals, mud, microorganisms and sand. Some wrecks have reached the sea bottom in a more or less intact condition, since the natural buoyancy of a wooden hull does not immediately sink, but slowly floats until reaching the bottom (Wachsmann, 2011). Anchors, for instance, might end up beneath the ship since whey would hang below the ship during the descent. However, as said, after being stabilised, there is little physical disturbance by post-depositional forces (Piechota and Giangrande, 2008). However, how well a shipwreck is preserved depends on various factors such as weather, temperature, salinity, pH, or depth where is located. It is not the same scenario to conserve material from freshwater that from marine sites (Hamilton, 2000). Encrustation is one of the main problems in all materials: the degree and extent of the encrustation depends on the local sea environment. It does not form in fresh water and it is extensive in tropical sea water. As a consequence, in cold water, the encrustation is minimal (Hamilton, 1997). Also there are other relevant environmental attributes (Muckelroy, 1978): how close is the wreck to the coast, the average slope of the sea-bed, the sedimentary deposits, the size of the tidal streams and the nature of the sea-bed, which may be really diverse such as sandy shores, rock shores or shores with submerged cliffs.

The ideal condition for preservation is with no daylight, in deep water and where the temperature is cold and marine animals cannot live (Willis, 2008). In addition, they are free from human interference and treasure hunters. In normal conditions, the preservation of the hull will be limited to those portions buried in the anoxic sediment soon after the sinking (Wachsmann, 2011). If there is any part of the organic cargoes or shipwrecks that are not covered by sediments, they will disintegrate. There have also been cases of survival of the shipwreck in shallow and warm water if it is buried on mud (materials like human or plant remains and even clothes). As the previous chapter has demonstrated, in adverse environmental conditions, stone, gold, silver, mercury or platinum have appeared to be almost unaffected (Willis, 2008). This is not only because of its chemistry but also because heavy objects will obviously tend to drop faster through layers of deposit remains.

Ethical dilemmas: sustainability

In situ *preservation arguments*

Preservation *in situ* is the first option under the 2001 UNESCO Convention for both pragmatic and philosophical reasons (Manders, 2012a). Aplin (2002) argues that preservation *in situ* on land is best for two main reasons: to save the items and for the item to be accessible and visited by the public. However, the *in situ* option was not a new principle in the 2001 UNESCO Convention but an archaeological option unanimously already adopted by the archaeology scientific community in the Sofia Charter (1996) a non-legal text. However, the term was adopted for land archaeology, where both accessibility and preservation was guaranteed. In this regard, and in order to evaluate the principle, Wreckwatch (2011), sent a questionnaire to experts in the area for their opinion about the preservation *in situ* strategy adopted by the 2001 UNESCO Convention. According to the questionnaire, 57% felt, that as an overall fundamental management policy, the application of *in situ* preservation to underwater cultural heritage is a positive strategy. A further 43% felt that it was not. In answer to this questionnaire, Maarleveld (2011) replied that he would not complete the questionnaire since it was based on a faulty assumption:

> the idea of the *in situ* preservation of underwater cultural heritage is the most dominant managerial concept in marine archaeology today. Centre stage of the *2001 UNESCO Convention on the Protection of the Underwater Cultural Heritage* (Article 2.5, 2.10, Annex Rule 1), it generates strong opinions about what this tool is intended to do and its repercussions on fieldwork.

This is because for Maarleveld (2011), the rule of preservation *in situ* does not reduce a central principle to a management tool. For Forrest (2010: 341–342),

> the principle of *in situ* preservation does not therefore mean that underwater cultural heritage is never recovered, only that it is recovered for a sound reason, and only after pre-disturbance archaeological investigation has been undertaken

Considering the ethical dilemmas of preservation of underwater cultural heritage, the next section summarises the main pragmatic and philosophical reasons in favour of preservation *in situ*. It will next analyse the counter-arguments for *in situ* preservation.

One pragmatic reason for preservation *in situ* of the material is the number of discovered sites: as both, technology and development on the fields happen, the number of archaeological sites underwater discovered is growing fast, although they cannot be all studied (Manders, 2004) and of course, not all can be lifted. But also cost effectiveness needs to be taken into account: first, there is not enough funding to preserve every under-water archaeological remain on land. Second, interventions under the sea are expensive because special equipment is necessary (Manders, 2003). Last, costs of assessing, analysing, conserving and recording the material *ex situ* is considerable, and, if recovered, the remains conserved in a museum must be curated in perpetuity (Corfield, 1996). Another reason for preservation *in situ* is the time gap between discovery and excavation: the main aim in under-water archaeology is to create an accessible archive underwater, and not to recover every site. Excavations will be carried out only if necessary and, in this case, after time studying the site *in situ*. In addition the deterioration processes are not still completely understood as is the case of the rusticles of the *Titanic* (Mann, 2011) or the sulphur problems threatening both the hulls of the *Vasa* and the *Mary Rose* (Manders, 2008), and preserving the sites *in situ* could save them in the future, when these processes are better under-stood. Furthermore, projects, such as MoSS (*Monitoring of Shipwreck Sites*) and BACPOLES (*Preserving cultural heritage by preventing bacterial decay of wood in foundation poles and archaeological sites*) have proven that *in situ* preservation can slow down degradation (Manders, 2012a). As it has already explained, shipwrecks have become artificial reefs attract loads of species of plants and animals. Researches indicate that shipwrecks in deep water are likely to serve as hard surfaces, supporting hundreds of life forms and as a consequence their preservation *in situ* is necessary. Another reason for preserving sites *in situ* is that some studies can be investigated only under the sea: what is the environment of the ship, the exact location, pos-sible reasons for sinking or how some materials are preserved under the sea after several years. Also, by taking away the source, it will be impossible to answer other questions (Manders, 2004). Underwater sites should be treated as underwater archives (Manders, 2003). But also robotics and telepresence technology to preserve and make a submerged cultural site accessible for the public (Ballard and Durbin, 2008) will be more developed in the future: it will also provide high-speed data communications on a real time basis on the state of the shipwreck, and its current state of deterioration, proceeding with the preservation right away if the shipwreck or the item is in immediate peril after a change of current, for instance. Finally, another reason for pres-ervation *in situ* is the precautionary principle: as a general rule, it seems to be best preserved under water.

However, there is not only pragmatic reasons to support the preservation *in situ*. It is also necessary to consider some philosophical thoughts such as the need for evaluation and significance in its context: the shipwreck in an archaeological context, where all the remains share homogeneity of the event and conditions (Gibbins and Adams, 2001). This context is where it can be best evaluated. In addition, preserving it is the best for the future: intro-duction of the 2001 UNESCO Convention states that States Parties should guarantee that underwater cultural heritage will be preserved for the future and *in situ* (UNESCO, 2001). It seems the way to be best preserved for future generations. Finally, decontextualising the object means the loss of part of its authenticity: it is different seeing an anchor in a museum and seeing it under water. Delgado (2009: 56) states that 'the best and largest museum of all lies in the bottom of the sea'.

In situ *preservation counter-arguments*

There are also some counter-arguments for preservation *in situ*. The first one would be that some artefacts are better preserved outside the sea: some materials better withstand water exposure than others. *In situ* preservation as a first option has been doubted by some authors who indicate that the corrosion rates of buried metal artefacts are growing (Caple, 2008). In addition, some studies can be only carried out in special laboratories, whether for preservation or for research. As a consequence, the piece of underwater cultural heritage has to be recovered and taken to one of those laboratories. Another argument is that some ships are a danger to the environment or to current navigation: some shipwrecks can still have fuel or ammunition which carries potential health, safety, and environmental risks (Sayle et al., 2009). Furthermore, some metals pollute the water (Mann, 2011). Plenderleith and Werner (1971) considered as the most contaminant materials aluminium, silver, cadmium and copper. These materials are usually used in ship construction. One more counter-argument is that underwater cultural heritage is for the benefit of humanity (Article 3.2; UNESCO, 2001). As a consequence, it has to be enjoyed by all. Under water, it is less accessible. In addition, preservation *in situ* can slow degradation, but does not stop deterioration (Manders, 2012a). As Gearey and Chapman (2006) state not only direct process affect wet deposits, such as development, but also indirectly, such as water abstraction, for instance. As a consequence, underwater cultural heritage will inevitably disappear in the future if preserved *in situ*. Also, different resources are being used for new energies, such as osmotic power (energy obtained from the difference in the salt concentration between seawater and river water), oceanic winds or wave power (Fernández, 2013). These resources arising from the sea can be used as natural energies helping to stop climate change, but this use of the oceans can conflict with underwater cultural heritage *in situ* protection. In this line, the freedom of the high seas allows companies to lay submarine cables in any part of the high seas even if there are archaeological deposits underneath. In 2010 some shipwrecks were discovered in the Baltic Sea when preparing the seabed for installation of the Nord Stream natural gas pipeline. Some of these shipwrecks were more than 1000 years old.[1] The shipwrecks were not in the path of the pipeline, but they were in the anchor corridor, which is the area where the ships lying down the pipeline would anchor. The planned works had to be changed. And these paths are multiplying: thousands of kilometres of submarine cables lie on or under the seabed carrying telephone calls and internet data (only 1% of telecommunications are established via satellite). In 2013, 283 cables are active with 29 new routes planned (Perez-Alvaro, 2013: 14). Another counter-argument is that technology is continuously improving which will benefit the progress of underwater archaeology and it may be that the pieces will not be damaged when recovered and studied. And a final reason for not preserving a site *in situ* is climate change: as said, if climate change keeps progressing, underwater archaeological remains will be affected.

Proposal: sustainable blue cultural heritage

The 2001 UNESCO Convention highlights the importance of public awareness and public enjoyment of the underwater cultural heritage. In its introduction, Articles and Rules of the Annex, the Convention seems to acknowledge the touristic side of the underwater cultural heritage but only if is not incompatible with the protection and management of underwater cultural heritage.

> […] Convinced of the public's right to enjoy the educational and recreational benefits of responsible non-intrusive access to *in situ* underwater cultural heritage, and of the value of public education to contribute to awareness, appreciation and protection of that heritage […]
>
> Article 2.10. Responsible non-intrusive access to observe or document *in situ* underwater cultural heritage shall be encouraged to create public awareness, appreciation, and protection of the heritage except where such access is incompatible with its protection and management.
>
> Article 18.4. A State Party which has seized underwater cultural heritage shall ensure that its disposition be for the public benefit, taking into account the need for conservation and research; the need for reassembly of a dispersed collection; the need for public access, exhibition and education; […]
>
> Article 20 — Public awareness. Each State Party shall take all practicable measures to raise public awareness regarding the value and significance of underwater cultural heritage and the importance of protecting it under this Convention.
>
> Rule 7. Public access to *in situ* underwater cultural heritage shall be promoted, except where such access is incompatible with protection and management.

As a consequence, the Convention is already implicitly pointing out the necessity of a sustainable use of this heritage: it tries to balance the desire to conserve and protect versus the desire to exploit. This compatibility of tourism with cultural heritage has been largely explored in the literature: while it has been accepted that the heritage needs to be available to all, its availability sometimes could threat its integrity. Mass tourism can bring pollution, economic exploitation and mass transit: the rise of tourism has position it in the world's number one industry. In fact, the World Tourism

Organization estimates the growth of tourist trips from approximately 842 million in 2006 to 1.5 billion in 2020 (Barthel-Bouchier, 2016).

This book proposes the idea of a 'Blue Cultural Heritage', a concept that comes from the recent model of 'Blue Economy', an idea based on the sustainable use of the sea to meet human needs, embracing environmental as well as economic interests (Michel, 2016). This theory considers that the sea has been misused and that it has not been used as creatively as the land. It also considers the continents as large islands, instead of the traditional 'landcentric' vision of the land bordered by sea rather than the sea with land interspersed, highlighting that the amount of land available for human use is diminishing because of the predicted climate change. The idea is a sustainable management of the oceans should include fisheries, aquaculture, coastal and island tourism, renewable energy, sea-bed mining, shipping and maritime security, biotechnology, waste management, research and biodiversity. As a consequence, 'Blue Economy' needs to be an evolving and multidimensional concept. Our proposal is applying this concept for an ethical and sustainable use of the heritage. Sustainability means living in a way that do not endanger the life chances of people alive tomorrow by exhausting the earth's resources and destroying its environment (Barthel-Bouchier, 2016). In this case, it means enjoying the underwater cultural heritage today in a way that do not endanger it for tomorrow (Carman, 2016). The term 'blue cultural heritage' offers challenges and opportunities for the enjoyment of this heritage, protecting it but opening the door to enterprise contribution and people willing to take a financial risk: underwater cultural heritage can be places to visit and learn, giving economic benefits to local communities. While archaeological museums exhibiting objects from land only need to show and explain the object, museums showing archaeological objects from underwater sites have, in addition another goal: not only showing the objects but also educating on the archaeological process of recovering them. These museums are an appealing cultural attraction that can help to urbanism development and its use as attractions can help to educate visitors about the history and preservation of underwater sites (Scott-Ireton and McKinnon, 2015). In the past, the enjoyment and accessibility of underwater cultural heritage seemed to be kept just for the ones who were able to professionally dive since they are a powerful touristic driving force: there are six million active divers around the world and more than 20 million snorkellers which are also interested in protecting the natural and cultural heritage of the seas. Their help, their interest and their money can be very important for managing the underwater cultural heritage. In fact, the federated associations of divers are the users that are more in contact with this heritage. By involving them in the protection of the underwater cultural heritage, it is guaranteed that divers will be educated in the same precepts of awareness and protection of this heritage. The reward will be reciprocal. The creation of underwater parks and reserves of underwater cultural heritage will initiate interest on visiting the site diving (or snorkelling in shallow sites) (Aguilar, 2013) which will bring a large amount of tourism. This option is not only educative for the tourists -the visitors usually receive information beforehand on what they are about to visit- but it also regulates the amount of tourist visiting the place, what makes its protection sustainable with its exploitation. These underwater parks can also be underwater itineraries with replicas, ensuring that the visitor receives a positive experience but that the 'real' heritage is not damaged. These options are experiences that visitors cannot acquire with any other form of heritage: underwater trails can change mindsets and engage emotions, where the visitor can experiment the tragedy of the maritime disaster in its habitat with historic shipwrecks but also surrounded of the natural environment. Also, the location of this heritage in ever-changing environments can bring new meanings to the site, transforming the visitor into interpreter, curator and educator, learning from its own experience and interaction with the site (Scott-Ireton and McKinnon, 2015). In addition, to be so close to a tragic human even can evoke powerful feeling, connecting the visitor to those who lived and perished as a result of its sinking.

In addition, in the last decades, new options are being developed for making underwater cultural heritage accessible to all public since underwater cultural heritage stakeholders have understood that involving society is a good way to preserve the underwater cultural heritage. As a consequence, this heritage can be experimented in more accessible ways, such as walking through museums that take you underwater (the unexcavated ship inside the *Maritime Silk Road Museum* in Guangdong, China) or taking the museum out of the building, like the planned above water museum in Alexandria with an underwater area (Manders, 2003). Shipwrecks encapsulated in museums such as *The Mary Rose* in the UK and the *Vasa Museum* in Sweden are examples of record-breaking number of visitors. The *USS Arizona* in Hawaii is another example of sustainable tourism on an underwater cultural site: both a touristic attraction and an underwater cemetery, the memorial consists of a platform over the sunken ship. Visitors can see the vessel through the glass platform below their feet. The site preservation options have traditionally been focused on maintaining the integrity of the site as an historic monument and a war grave. The shipwreck remains perfectly preserved *in situ* and monitored. The year of the opening, 1962, more than 178,000 people visited the site. It attracts today more than 1.5 million visitors per year (Slackman, 2012). This combination of emotions and historical perspective on the shipwreck has been a key to the museum's success on attracting tourism.

Digital technologies also promise new improvements in raising awareness and access to underwater cultural heritage. State-of-the-art, low-budget digital technology records, analyses and disseminates data from these submerged sites. This option respects *in situ* preservation, creating virtual reality museums and building 2D and 3D digital models (Varinlioglu, 2016). These advances promote the awareness of underwater cultural heritage in an age where visualisation is so important.

Underwater cultural heritage is a kind of heritage which, since it is surrounded by an aura of mystery, can easily attract tourism. However, its accessibility has to be weighted with its preservation. Tourism can be an opportunity to protect the heritage but can also be a threat: many historic shipwrecks are been moved from beaches to foment other kind of touristic industries, such as water sports or promenades, water pollution from leisure ports can damage underwater cultural heritage and leisure diving can threaten preservation because unaware divers can recollect underwater objects as souvenirs or dive boats can anchor on wreck hulls. However, this proposal has suggested some preservation examples where its management complies with a sustainable development: they provide education, protection and accessibility: it is the sum of various parts. With new technologies these steps forward in the field with bring us new solutions: these developments have barely skimmed the surface of what is possible. It is necessary to keep an open mind to attract new ideas where not only the preservation of the heritage but also its enjoyment by all can become a reality: the sustainable use of underwater cultural heritage is possible.

Conclusions

The precept of preservation *in situ* that has been long established in cultural heritage management does not take into account possible future changes that may challenge that preservation *in situ* is the preferable option. There are several arguments and counter-arguments for this preservation *in situ* but the reality is that each case must be studied individually and with a future projection in mind considering the possibility of future threats, such as climate changes. Monitoring the site is essential but we need to be ready to act with several tools and new ideas. A cross-disciplinary and inter-agency collaboration is necessary since preservation *in situ* will be an option if joint efforts from the different actors protecting and enjoying the seas. The preservation of underwater cultural remains has to be formally challenged. It cannot only be the responsibility of underwater cultural heritage stakeholders: divers, museums, ONG, agencies and communities also have to be part of the action. If the importance of this heritage is understood by all, its enjoyment can attract more diversity of background of tourists, making the experience more positive for everyone and its protection shared by all.

Managing an underwater cultural site requires a plan that combines preservation with dissemination. Its sustainability is essential for its understanding, appreciation and conservation and although preservation *in situ* is the first option of archaeologists for preserving heritage, both, land and underwater. However, expanded regimes of exploration through the seas, mining of precious and non-precious metals, fishing, marine engineering, the use of the oceans as a cure for climate change through 'ocean nourishment' and the production of marine-zone renewable energy are new threats to the submerged heritage (Flatman, 2009). As Gribble et al. (2009)

questions, underwater cultural heritage could be a risk or a resource. If it is a risk, its preservation does not need to be guaranteed since can pose a hazard to the environment (pollution), commerce (impeding navigation) or human life (unsafe diving or sailing). If it is a resource, it means that it can be 'used' for research, education and tourism. And although it may be thought that underwater archaeological remains are held to be finite and non-renewable, it also can be argued that the new ships are sunken every day, new shipwrecks are being discovered and new ways to explore the past are investigated, making the past renewable and non-finite.

The process of heritage is shifting from an objectified, glass-covered and static heritage to a more alive, interactive and dynamic heritage. As Kingsley (2011) observes, nobody wants or can afford another *Mary Rose* (which brings the ship out of context, anyway) and as a consequence new paths need to be explored. New agreements and new perspectives have to be taken. As Renfrew and Bahn (2008) states, the past is a big business which can be used to serve many masters, such as economic ends, national ends, or for gaining knowledge. It is necessary to look at alternatives for the management of underwater cultural heritage, since preservation of cultural heritage needs to be combined with tourism and sustainable options to make this heritage enjoyable and available to all. As this chapter has reviewed, sustainability in the management of underwater cultural heritage is a balanced concept between enjoyment and preservation. Sustainability is a term that will be continuously used in other chapters of this book: preservation of the violin of the *Titanic* under private ownership or for its enjoyment by all humanity, the rights of colonised countries or balancing the economic value of underwater cultural heritage are all issues that need to be weighted to find the right balance.

Note

1 *The Free Library*. (2010). S.v. Nord Stream pipeline probe uncovers shipwrecks in Baltic Sea. 27 April 2015. Available at: www.thefreelibrary.com/Nord+Stream +pipeline+probe+uncovers+shipwrecks+in+Baltic+Sea.-a0225588584 (17 March 2017).

Bibliography

Aguilar, C. (2013). La colaboración de las federaciones deportivas de buceo en la actualización de las Cartas Arqueológicas Subacuáticas y la protección del patrimonio cultural subacuático (PCS). *Ministerio de Educación, Cultura y Deporte: ARNSE: Congreso de Arqueología Náutica y Subacuática Española*. 1024–1031. Madrid. Available at: https://dialnet.unirioja.es/servlet/libro?codigo=567158 (accessed 5 September 2017).

Aplin, G. (2002). *Heritage Identification, Conservation and Management*. Oxford: Oxford University Press.

Aznar-Gómez, M. (2017). Aspectos jurídicos de la protección *in situ* del patrimonio cultural subacuático (su incidencia en el caso del Mazarrón II). In Alcalde, M. M. A., Cano, J. M. G., Pérez J. B. and Sanmartín, A. S. (eds.), *Mazarrón II: Contexto arqueológico, viabilidad científica y perspectiva patrimonial del barco B-2 de la bahía de Mazarrón (Murcia)*. Madrid: UAM Ediciones: 133–173.

Ballard, R. D. and Durbin, M. J. (2008). Long-term preservation and telepresence visitation of cultural sites beneath the sea. In Ballard, R. D. (ed.), *Archaeological Oceanography*. Princeton, NJ: Princeton University Press: 249–261.

Barthel-Bouchier, D. (2016). *Cultural Heritage and the Challenge of Sustainability*. London: Routledge.

Caple, C. (2008). Preservation *in situ*: the future for archaeological conservators? *Studies in Conservation* 53(Supplement 1): 214–217.

Carman, J. (2016). Educating for sustainability in archaeology. *Archaeologies* 12(2): 133–152.

Corfield, M. (1996). Preventive conservation for archaeological sites. *Studies in Conservation* 41(1): 32–37.

Delgado, J. (2009). *Adventures of a Sea Hunter: In Search of Famous Shipwrecks*. Vancouver: Douglas & McIntyre.

Fernández, P. A. (2013). Cambio climático y derecho del mar. In Juste Ruiz, J. and Bou Franch, V. (eds.), *Derecho del mar y sostenibilidad ambiental en el Mediterráneo*. Valencia: Tirant Lo Blanch.

Flatman, J. (2009). Conserving marine cultural heritage: threats, risks and future priorities. *Conservation and Management of Archaeological Sites* 11(1): 5–8.

Forrest, C. (2010). *International Law and the Protection of Cultural Heritage*. London: Routledge.

Gearey, B. R. and Chapman, H. P. (2006). Planning policy, in situ preservation and wetland archaeology in the United Kingdom: some present concerns. *Conservation and Management of Archaeological Sites* 7(3): 179–182.

Gibbins, D and Adams, J. (2001). Shipwrecks and maritime archaeology. *World Archaeology* 32(3): 279–291.

Green, J. (1990). *Maritime Archaeology: A Technical Handbook*. San Diego: Academic Press.

Gribble, J., Parham, D. and Scott-Ireton, D. (2009). Historic wrecks: risks or resources? *Conservation and Management of Archaeological Sites* 11(1): 16–28.

Hamilton, D. L. (1997). *Basic Methods of Conserving Underwater Archaeological Material Culture*. Nautical Archaeology Program. Washington, DC: Department of Anthropology, Texas A&M University Spring 1997 Prepared in partnership with the U.S. Department of Defense Legacy Resource Management Program.

Hamilton, D. L. (2000). Conservation of cultural materials from underwater sites. In Williamson, R. A. and Nickens, P. R. (eds.), *Science and Technology in Historic Preservation*. New York: Kluwer Academic/Plenum Publishers: 193–229.

Khakzad, S. and Van Balen, K. (2012). Complications and effectiveness of in situ preservation methods for underwater cultural heritage sites. *Conservation and Management of Archaeological Sites* 14(1–4): 469–478.

Kingsley, S. (2011). Challenges of maritime archaeology: in too deep. In King, T. F. (ed.), *A Companion to Cultural Resource Management*. Chichester: Wiley-Blackwell: 223–244.

Maarleveld, T. J. (2011). Open letter to Dr. Sean Kingsley Wreck Watch International regarding his questionnaire on in situ preservation. *Journal of Maritime Archaeology* 6(2): 107–111.

Manders, M. (2003). Safeguarding: the physical protection of underwater sites. *MoSS Newsletter* 4: 18–20.

Manders, M. (2004). Why do we safeguard shipwrecks? *MoSS Newsletter* 3: 4–5.

Manders, M. (2008). In situ preservation: 'the preferred option'. *Museum International* 60(4): 31–41 (no. 240).

Manders, M. (2012a). Unit 9: in situ preservation. In Manders, M. and Underwood, C. (eds.), *Training Manual for the UNESCO Foundation Course on the Protection and Management of Underwater Cultural Heritage in Asia and the Pacific*. Bangkok: UNESCO.

Manders, M. (2012b). Unit 3: management of underwater cultural heritage. In Manders, M. and Underwood, C. (eds.), *Training Manual for the UNESCO Foundation Course on the Protection and Management of Underwater Cultural Heritage in Asia and the Pacific*. Bangkok: UNESCO.

Manders, M. and Underwood, C. (eds.) (2012). *Training Manual for the UNESCO Foundation Course on the Protection and Management of Underwater Cultural Heritage in Asia and the Pacific*. Bangkok: UNESCO.

Mann, H. (2011). New bacterium species discovered on *RMS Titanic* rusticles. [online]. *UNESCO Scientific Colloquium on Factors Impacting the Underwater Cultural Heritage 10th Anniversary of the Convention on the Protection of the Underwater Cultural Heritage*. Available at: www.unesco.org/new/fileadmin/MULTIMEDIA/HQ/CLT/pdf/Henrietta_Mann_Paper.pdf.

Michel, J. A. (2016). Rethinking the oceans: towards the blue economy. *Maritime Affairs: Journal of the National Maritime Foundation of India* 12(2): 115–117.

Muckelroy, K. (1978). *Maritime Archaeology*. Cambridge: Cambridge University Press.

Perez-Alvaro, E. (2013). Unconsidered threats to underwater cultural heritage: laying submarine cables. *Rosetta* 14: 54–70.

Piechota, D. and Giangrande, C. (2008). Conservation of archaeological finds from deep-water wreck sites. In Ballard, R. D. (ed.), *Archaeological Oceanography*. Princeton, NJ: Princeton University Press.

Plenderleith, H. J., and Werner, A. E. (1971). *The Conservation of Antiquities and Works of Art: Treatment, Repair and Restoration*. Oxford: Oxford University Press.

Renfrew, C. and Bahn, P. (2008). *Archaeology: Theories, Methods and Practice*. London: Thames & Hudson.

Sayle, S., Windeyer, T., Charles, M., Conrod, S. and Stephenson, M. (2009). Site assessment and risk management framework for underwater munitions. *Marine Technology Society Journal* 43(4): 41–51.

Scott-Ireton, D. A. and McKinnon, J. F. (2015). As the sand settles: education and archaeological tourism on underwater cultural heritage. *Public Archaeology* 14(3): 157–171.

Slackman, M. (2012). *Remembering Pearl Harbor: The Story of the USS Arizona Memorial*. Hawaii: Pacific Historic Parks.

Sofia Charter (1996). Charter on the protection and management of underwater cultural heritage. *ICOMOS*. Available at: www.international.icomos.org/charters/underwater_e.pdf (2 May 2018).

UNESCO (2001). Convention on the Protection of the Underwater Cultural Heritage. Paris, 2 November 2001. Available at: http://unesdoc.unesco.org/images/0012/001260/126065e.pdf (2 May 2018).

Valetta Treaty (1992). European Convention on the Protection of the Archaeological Heritage. Available at: http://conventions.coe.int/Treaty/en/Treaties/Html/143.htm (2 May 2018).

Varinlioglu, G. (2016). *Digital in Underwater Cultural Heritage*. Cambridge: Cambridge Scholars.

Wachsmann, S. (2011). Deep-submergence archaeology. In Catsambis, A., Ford, B. and Hamilton, D. L. (eds.), *The Oxford Handbook of Maritime Archaeology*. Oxford: Oxford University Press: 202–221.

Willis, S. (2008). *Shipwrecks: A History of Disasters at Sea*. Oxford: BCS Publishing.

Wreckwatch (2011). The sunken past: shipwrecks lost in translation. [online]. *Wreckwatch*. Available at: http://wreckwatch.wordpress.com/2011/09/28/the-sunken-past-shipwrecks-lost-in-translation (1 April 2017).

7 Intangibility
Watery graves

Although human remains on land archaeology has been a debated topic, in the realm of underwater heritage the references are almost non-existent. However, the importance of the topic has already been highlighted since some nations have already established legal frameworks to protect those human remains. In addition, the term is included in the definition of 'underwater cultural heritage' under the 2001 UNESCO Convention on the Protection of the Underwater Cultural Heritage (UNESCO, 2001). However, the ethical dilemmas around the topic have not been discussed and protocols for management of shipwrecks with or without human remains have not been established. The chapter, as a consequence, hopes to fill the legal and ethical gaps on the topic as well as offer solutions introducing three concepts applied for the first time to human remains in base at this variety of cultural attitudes: absent, invisible and intangible heritage.

Introduction

The treatment of human remains is one of the most complex areas of archaeology—on land and underwater (Mays, 2008). Its management depends both on legal and ethical considerations. Although this controversy has been largely discussed for land archaeology, marine contexts are different and deserve special consideration. Shipwrecks are usually caused by catastrophes that in most cases also cause deaths, mostly fatalities claiming several lives (Perez-Alvaro and Carman, 2011). Vessels were used to transport passengers and cargo and were operated by a crew so every ship, big or small, carried human lives on board. The event that usually converts a vessel into a shipwreck is an accident; an accident that provides us with a document of scientific value and with a direct connection with the past.

For Flatman (2007: 81) shipwrecks have an inherent 'stench of the morgue', even if they have not caused a loss of life. In fact, not in all shipwrecks there are human remains preserved: if human remains are still preserved on the shipwreck, they can be left untouched, they can be recovered or they can be managed, creating an underwater cemetery or memorial. This last option, the treatment of shipwrecks as graveyards and memorials, is an option that has started to be applied in practical cases since the recognition of a wreck as a resting place for human remains acknowledges the need for a treatment of respect. In addition, this treatment of shipwrecks as watery graves has proved to be effective for protection in some countries, although it is still controversial (Perez-Alvaro, 2014). However, if there are no human remains preserved but there were human bodies on the shipwreck, we would be dealing with absent/invisible/intangible heritage and its management would be different, as the proposal of this chapter will show.

Issue

Management and protection of human remains as part of underwater cultural heritage is a complex ethical issue—as it is in land archaeology—untangled with technical considerations for being underwater. The problem in underwater cultural heritage is that being a relatively new discipline, the issues are starting to appear now, as opposed to land archaeology that has already faced these issues some time ago. However, underwater heritage managers cannot find all the answers in land heritage since both archaeologies—land and underwater—face different situations. The first difference is the cause of death: usually in shipwrecks all died at once and for the same reason. It is not common to find shipwrecks with only one or two bodies on board. Usually shipwrecks are a consequence of accidents and create catastrophes. Mays (2008) differences between additional burials (accumulated over a period of time with varying causes of death) and catastrophe samples (individuals died at the same time, sharing a common cause). Human remains on shipwrecks are included in the last type. On land, battlefields, disasters or fires are the only examples of this type. There is a second main difference between both disciplines: establishing identities of the human bodies on shipwrecks can be easier than in land archaeology, since in most cases passengers and crew were registered in the log books of the ship. A third main difference is that microbial destruction of bone in maritime contexts differs from those buried on land and, as a consequence, preservation and treatment have to be different. In a maritime environment, for instance, human remains tend to be incomplete and co-mingled (Mays, 2008) with some other remains floating freely away from the ship. In land archaeology, with exceptions such as prehistoric tombs or the Towton mass grave (Sutherland and Schmidt, 2003), human remains tend to be preserved together. Another difference is that a ship is a mobile means of transport usually carrying people of different cultures on board, which could have sunk in the waters of the flag state, other nation's waters or high seas' water and these factors load the issue with several complexities. In land archaeology, death people are easier to belong to the same community or culture—except in battlefields—and its posterior management will be easier than in underwater archaeology. The final difference is that it is more difficult for families to pay their respects to their relatives when in the ocean, since some parts are practically inaccessible. For families, a wreck may represent the last resting place of those that perished but can be a place that they will not be able to visit (Perez-Alvaro, 2013). Some land sites may also be difficult or impossible to access, although is not the usual situation.

Any policy making or management decision on underwater cultural heritage often faces complicated and delicate decisions. However, the management of human remains also implies an emotional component that has to be looked at through various values contained in ethical principles. The protection of human remains contained in underwater cultural heritage reveals differences in the management between countries established by aspects of culture, such as tradition, mentality or habit (Perez-Alvaro, 2014). Consequently, states develop their policies according to their collective values—human remains and the rest of underwater cultural heritage—and those values are the ones that decide what deserves to be preserved. Only by recognition, human remains transform from trash to grave sites. The different options of management when finding a shipwreck with or without human remains (excavating it any way, leaving it as a watery grave, recovering the human remains, etc.) will depend on the archaeologists. Its management after the remains are recovered will depend on museum managers and policy makers (O'Keefe, 2002).

State of knowledge

The very first question should be related to the possibility of finding human remains under water on a submerged archaeological site. It is confirmed that human remains can still be found at sites that are several hundred years old (Dromgoole, 2013), although skeletal remains are the only human remains usually found—soft tissues discoveries are exceptional (Mays, 2008). However, the preservation of human remains depends on various factors and environmental conditions. Its deterioration can be due to different processes, such as impacts with rocks when the shipwreck, encrustation by organisms or sediments that abrade the surfaces of the bones (Mays, 2008). At the end of the day, shipwrecks have many causes: storms, damaged hulls, poor navigation or collision with other ships or with objects for instance (Fenwick and Gale, 1998).

Cunningham and Tolson (2010) state that the normal changes and decomposition of a body are delayed in cold, deep water so that bodies may be surprisingly well-preserved after a long period of immersion. Although biological activity results in advanced decomposition within 12 years, even in cases of the most durable skeletal parts (Cunningham and Tolson, 2010), some human bones on shipwrecks are preserved if and when the body became trapped below deck—for instance, beneath a cannon or the cargo. This situation prevents degradation of the remains until a sealing layer is deposited to conserve it within an anaerobic environment. Therefore, the degree of preservation will depend on whether the burial site is oxygen free and how quickly the remains become sediment-inundated. However, for Pickford (1994) it is the exception and not the rule for bodies to be trapped inside a hull, since this usually happen when the sinking is very quick. According to him the vast majority of people lost at sea float free from the ship itself.

MacLeod (2008) sets out some examples of preserved shipwrecks containing human remains. For instance the *Mary Rose* (1545), which was built in Portsmouth between 1509 and 1511 and it sank during an engagement with the French fleet. The surviving section of the ship was raised in 1982 and is now on display in *Portsmouth Historic Dockyard* along with an extensive collection of well-preserved artefacts. One hundred seventy-nine human remains were recovered as skeletal material and 91 as intact bodies. Experts examined the skulls of 18 crew members to determine their origin and concluded that many of them came from southern Europe. The ship *Vasa* (1628) capsized and sank in Stockholm harbour on her maiden voyage and was raised from the seabed in 1961. Skeletal remains were recovered from at least 25 individuals, with teeth and jaws from 17 of them (Mays, 2008). The *HMS Pandora* (1797) wrecked in the Torres Strait in Australia, transported captured mutineers. A mix of human and animal bones in advanced states of decay were recovered in 1987. The *HL Hunley* (1864) was a submarine sank in Charleston Harbour with eight members of the crew on board. The reason for an expedition to the wreck in 2000 was not only to determine the physical reasons for the sinking but also the recovery of the bodies. The *RMS Titanic* (1912) entombed some 1,250 people. Some of the bodies were recovered in the following days to the sinking but most of them still lie around the wreck site. The emotional link to the wreck has made some authors (Elia, 2000; Delgado, 2009) claim it as a mass grave. It is also worth remembering the Japanese suicide motorboats known as the Shinyo. These Japanese suicide attack vessels used during World War II were equipped with explosives that detonated by switch or impact. The vessels, operated by kamikazes, were used as weapons. Some of these boats have been discovered (Macdonald, 2017). Being kamikaze vessels there is not doubt that there will be human remains on board. Also the shipwrecks in Truk lagoon contain human remains: the destruction of this Japanese Naval Base at Truk included more than 60 ships. Although the site is considered a sacred cultural site, divers from all over the world dive the shipwrecks. Although some Japanese human remains have been recovered, some still remain to preserve the idea of war grave (Jeffery, 2004). The controversy is if these sacred places should be allowed to be touristic attractions, since they attract what has been called as 'dark tourism' and which will be explained later. Finally, it is worth highlighting the *USS Arizona* (1941) that contains the remains of over thousand sailors. Their bodies have not been recovered, and as a consequence, the site is an historic monument and a war grave, as well as a memorial. The *USS Arizona* deserves special mention because it solves respectfully preservation and management of human remains: the USS *Arizona Memorial*, built over the wreck, serves as a lasting tribute to the 1,177 men who lost their lives on that 'Day of Infamy' under the motto 'How shall we remember them, those who died?' But it is not only an emotional answer to an attack on national identity; in 1992 more than 1.5 million visitors toured the site of the shipwreck (Slackman, 2012). In addition, the museum is a place of trust and respect for the families of the perished crew and the survivors themselves. Families assume the shipwreck as a cemetery for their deceased relatives (Figure 7.1).

Regarding the legal status of human remains, the fact that human remains are included on the 2001 UNESCO Convention definition means that human remains under water for at least 100 years *are* underwater cultural heritage and fall under the umbrella of the Convention and as a consequence every article and every rule of the Convention is applicable to human remains (Dromgoole, 2013; Perez-Alvaro, 2014). However, there is not reference to human remains in the United Nations Convention on the Law of the Sea (UNCLOS, 1982). In this regard, Bryant (2001) argues that because the laws of finds and salvage do not prohibit the salvaging of wrecks containing human remains, nothing in UNCLOS would prohibit salvaging vessels containing human remains.

Figure 7.1 USS *Arizona* memorial, USA.
Source: Authors' photo.

2001 UNESCO Convention on the Protection of the Underwater
Cultural Heritage.
Article 1 — Definitions
For the purposes of this Convention:

1.   (a) 'Underwater cultural heritage' means all traces of human existence having a cultural, historical or archaeological character which
have been partially or totally under water, periodically or continuously, for at least 100 years such as:
(i) sites, structures, buildings, artefacts and *human remains*, together
with their archaeological and natural context; [...]

Three main concerns arise from explicitly mentioning human remains in the
2001 UNESCO Convention. First, the explicit mention of 'human remains'
in multiples articles of the Convention which are mentioned in two more
articles besides the definition. The fact that human remains have specific
articles in the Convention differentiates human remains from the rest of
underwater cultural heritage. Buildings or vessels, for instance, do not have
specific articles. Some authors (Aznar-Gómez, 2013) argue that it does
not discriminate but it emphasises the need for respect for human remains
(Article 2.9 of the 2001 UNESCO Convention reads: 'States Parties shall
ensure that proper respect is given to all human remains located in maritime waters'. In this regard, Rule 5 of the Annex specifies that activities
directed at underwater cultural heritage shall avoid the unnecessary disturbance of human remains or venerated sites). For O'Keefe (2002) human
remains are specifically mentioned for their significance to the eyes of the
general public. However, do not specify how to manage human remains if
the shipwreck has to be excavated and/or raised. Neither they do specify
if the remains should be reburied, should remain at the bottom of the sea or
if they should be repatriated to their country of origin (Perez-Alvaro, 2014).
The second concern is that every single article of the Convention is applied
to 'human remains': it seems clear that since human remains *are* underwater
cultural heritage, every article of the Convention is applicable to human
remains, such as preservation for the benefit of humanity, preservation *in
situ*, prohibition of commercial exploitation or international cooperation
for the preservation of the remains (Perez-Alvaro, 2014). However, these
general rules conflict with ethical concerns. If human remains have to be
preserved for the benefit of humanity, it means that they are available for all
and not only for the families. If they have to remain under water as the first
option, it conflicts with its use for scientific investigation or for the importance of their recovery for some cultures. If they cannot be commercially
exploited, it conflicts with their use in touristic places such as museums,
and if they have to be managed under a policy of international cooperation,
it ignores those shipwrecks with human remains without a nation, such as
nationless shipwrecks or refugees' shipwrecks. Last issue of the inclusion of

human remains in the Convention is that since human remains are under-water cultural heritage and the Convention suggests keeping the collection together, human remains should be stored with the rest of the collection. In this regard, some authors defend that human remains are in fact part of the whole collection, and as a consequence, they should not be separated (Manders, 2012). This would mean that if other objects of an archaeological site are recovered, the human remains should also be recovered, without consultation to living descendants. If the archaeological site is to be left untouched, then the human remains would be untouched and kept at the bottom of the sea.

The Convention does not provide more guidelines about the management of human remains because it was a politically sensitive issue when negoti-ating the Convention (Dromgoole, 2013). Maritime states required a special status for military graves, and other states required the same statues for civil graves. However, Dromgoole (2013) concludes that although it does not say it specifically, the 2001 UNESCO Convention implies that a site with human remains should be preserved with respect as a maritime memorial *in situ* with limited or prohibited access. The issue is what 'respect' means.

Other legal agreements, although not specific to human remains on shipwrecks, can be applied and combined for the protection of human remains. For instance, the Vermillion Accord on Human Remains (1989) requires the respectful treatment and consideration of indigenous commu-nities. It asks for respect for the human remains, for the wishes of the dead, for the wishes of the local community and of relatives and for scientific research. It acknowledges the possibility of negotiation with ancestors and descendants for the uses of the remains for science and education. Since it does not limit the scope of the Accord, and since it is intended to apply to all archaeologists, it automatically extends to human remains under water. The Tamaki Makau-rau Accord on the Display of Human Remains and Sacred Objects (2005), also devoted to archaeologists, establishes eth-ical measures on the display of human remains, such as permission by the affected community: if this permission is refused the decision should be respected; if it is granted the display should be culturally appropriate. Also the, UNESCO Convention on Intangible Heritage (UNESCO, 2003) can help to protect human remains: if, as explained later, shipwrecks that once contained human remains which are still tangible are also seen as under-water cemeteries, since the remains are not tangible anymore they may be considered intangible heritage and as a consequence this Convention needs to be considered as a possible legal instrument and to have an annex on human remains in shipwrecks or to consider as sacred places those sites where there were they used to contain human remains. The treatment of human remains as intangible heritage will be studied in detail below under the epigraph 'dilemmas'. Finally, some regulations on the exploitation of natural resources have already mentioned the possibility of finding human remains and archaeological sites. Specifically, it is important to mention two regulations that are, however, limited to 'the Area' (high seas, beyond any state jurisdiction): the Regulations on prospecting and exploration for poly-metallic sulphides in the Area (2010) and Regulations on prospecting and exploration for cobalt-rich ferromanganese crusts in the Area (2012) read:

> Regulation 37. Human remains and objects and sites of an archaeological or historical nature. The contractor shall immediately notify the Secretary-General in writing of any finding in the exploration area of any *human remains of an archaeological or historical nature*, or any object or site of a similar nature and its location, including the preservation and protection measures taken. [...]. Following the finding of any such human remains, object or site in the exploration area, and in order to avoid disturbing such human remains, object or site, no further prospecting or exploration shall take place, within a reasonable radius, until such time as the Council decides otherwise after taking account of the views of the Director-General of the United Nations Educational, Scientific and Cultural Organization or any other competent international organization.

In addition to these international regulations, some countries have created their own national legal instrument to protect their archaeological human remains. It is not the purpose of this chapter to analyse this legislation, but it is worth highlighting that some national laws on heritage and the protection of human remains have been created as acknowledgement of indigenous cultures (Australia) and some others have been developed as a consequence to the rampant looting of archaeological sites (Spain) (Hutt and Riddle, 2007: 224). In Japan, human remains not claimed by living descendants are no longer subject to protection. This rises several issues since human remains are important, not only for the descendants but in some cases also as a symbol of a nation, or a community or a hero (Iwabuchi, 2014). In addition, and as the author reminds us, according to traditional Asian beliefs, human remains will never become underwater cultural heritage since if human remains are seen by someone in an underwater site, it is imperative to rescue and bury them on land. According to Pickford (1994) the Japanese, for instance, pay large sums of money for World War II losses to be recovered since their bodies have to be buried properly. This contrasts with the preservation *in situ motto* claimed by the 2001 UNESCO Convention.

Ethical dilemmas: intangibility

Underwater cultural heritage has a value, not only as an archaeological, economic or scientific source, but also as a 'container' of human remains. The dilemmas in this chapter will be organised on the basis of a three-concept relationship: *values* awarded to the submerged human remains, *guardians* of the deceased (cultural or genetic) and *subjects* (human remains) of these shipwrecks.

Values

Cultural value

From the nineteenth century, the world's reality has been seen through the eyes of our own cultural believes and values inside a spiral of ethnocentrism (Pojman and Fieser, 2012: 12). However, what it is good in one culture may be bad in another: what is sacred for one culture may be superficial for another. And since ethics on the subject of death is an area loaded with emotions (Mays, 2008), remains of the dead can offend religious or secular sensibilities (Mays, 2008). However, definition of 'respectful treatment' is different in different cultures. In the *UNESCO Manual for Activities Directed at Underwater Cultural Heritage* (Guerin and Egger, 2011) it is highlighted that respect and significance means different things to different nations, and within a nation, to different people. Respect for the dead is acknowledged by most religions but also by people with no religion. Some cultures may need ceremonies to honour death or private access to human remains (Teague, 2007). Other cultures may choose rivers or seas as their graves for their dead (Guerin and Egger, 2011). And what it is even more complicated, soldiers in wars and crews of naval ships included people from many faiths and ethnicities and may be together in the same site. Wight (2009) observes that the issue of remembering—or not—tragic events depends on a number of ethical codes such as the consideration of death, where there are usually superstitious perceptions, and a general attitude to the 'respect of the dead' and their remains, the religious considerations with transcendental character and its impetus in life after death, the consideration of memories as an instrument to continue life after death, the consideration of the past as an example—positive or negative—for the present and for the future associated with the collective memory of the human being. One particular aspect of this consideration is that it uses memories as a tool for the benefit of social cohesion, to create or strengthen a national, regional or local identity. The concepts of monument and hero acquire, in those contexts, an emotive capacity which can strengthen the goals and actions for the protection of the heritage (Nora, 1996–1998). But also, the religious perception of the death or the different philosophies on the consideration of the body may be different for different people.

Temporal value

Respect for the deceased not only depends on traditions or cultures but also on time. What in the same culture was respectful yesterday may not be respectful today. We have to bear in mind the changing contexts of the present. In addition, there is a dichotomy between the protection of human remains and the protection of the rest of underwater cultural heritage. Under the 2001 UNESCO Convention, as explained, shipwrecks have to be under water for more than 100 years to be protected. And human remains *are* underwater cultural heritage. On the other hand, some authors (Dunkley, 2011) suggest that before our ancestors from submerged warships are of archaeological interest and can serve science and be investigated at least four generations (100 years) should have passed. Underwater cultural heritage is better protected if older (more than 100 years after the tragedy) but human remains are better protected if more recent (less than 100 years after the tragedy). In other words, the human remains deserving respect and protection and which should be untouchable are the most recent and the shipwrecks deserving protection are those that have been submerged for more time after the tragedy. On these basis, human remains contained in shipwrecks in the World War II should be kept undisturbed, although the ship itself can be recovered, plundered or salvaged, since she is not protected for instance under the 2001 UNESCO Convention. Following the same line of thought, a 200-year-old shipwreck should be kept intact although the human remains contained in it could be used as examples of catastrophe once four generations have passed.

Scientific value

The recovery of human remains (sometimes there are a large number of civil and/or military victims) is a source of controversy on the way that both the bodies and the shipwrecks containing them should be managed. Some opinions are opposed to the treatment of human remains while other ones are related to the need of historians and public opinion to understand the facts and through these to gain knowledge of history. The question of leaving the human remains alone, to be researched by scientists in the present or be preserved for the archaeologist of the future is not a new debate (Saunders, 2002). However, it seems commonly acknowledged that although contributions to science can carry some beneficial results, it cannot justify ignoring the dignity of the dead and their relatives (Teague, 2007). Other disciplines such as medicine have gone through the same process of thought. One of the justifications of archaeologists and museum managers for the recovery and/or exhibition of human remains is the appeal to science and education (Curtis, 2003), which raises other ethical issues, for instance the role of museums as keepers of human remains. However, archaeologists or museum guardians are not the only stakeholders of these remains (Coroneos, 2006: 122). The establishment of respect for the dead or the development and education for the future faces complicated moral questions (Garratt-Frost, 1992). In order to establish a fair comparative analysis, this section aims to list the main/core arguments in favour of and against the use of human remains for education and/or science purposes:

Arguments in favour of the use of human remains for education and science are, for instance, that, as Bryant (2001) remarks that it is widely acknowledged that gaining knowledge about the past requires examining ruins from earlier cultures, including human skeletal remains. Human remains are the source that offers us the most information about the past (Mays, 2008). In fact, human remains in shipwrecks can give us a variety of information such as demographic information, origin of the crew, specific roles of the crew (rowers, archers, etc.), diseases and injuries—such as scurvy or bone injuries—and the diet of the crew. This information from the past is helpful in developing science in the present day, for instance, by understanding diseases better (Bryant, 2001). Also, and according to Tarlow (2006), the knowledge that we obtain from dead bodies for medical research and research on human tissue cannot be obtained otherwise. Cheek and Keel (1984) have summarised the types of information obtained from human remains (Cheek and Keel, 1984): archaeological (physical characteristics, biological and genetic elements, demographic, pathological evolutionary processes and treatment of the dead), medical (diseases and disorders) and forensic. The ambiguity of the concept of 'respect' for the deceased is another argument in favour of the use of human remains: it can be what archaeologists consider as 'respect', what cultural descendants of the dead claim or what the scientific community considers respectful. In an archaeological excavation (land or marine) if human remains are expected to be found, a human osteologist is appointed, recording and tracing every step, from the location (their grave) to the point of recovery—if they are recovered (Mays, 2008). A final argument in favour of the use of human remains is that some visitors expect to see human remains on display in a museum (Curtis, 2003) since museum experiences are part of a necessary educational process.

The first arguments against the use of human remains for science and education is that curators and archaeologists do not own human remains (Curtis, 2003): ownership of human remains is controversial (Saunders, 2002). Dromgoole (2013) reminds that whether a dead body is property is subject to debate. This is why Teague (2007) establishes a process of consultation to those interested in human remains: interview, deciding who speaks, meeting, analysis of new discoveries, recording bearing in mind when a form of study is specifically offensive to cultural traditions, restriction on the use of photographs and other records, reasonable private access to human remains for their ceremonies and allowing those ceremonies. Another argument against the use is the idea of authenticity: if an authentic skeleton in a window of a museum is really informative or if it is just a source of appeal for the public. What would be the difference in showing in the window a plastic skeleton? This, as in the case of the violin of the *Titanic*, is an issue of authenticity. And although a fake skeleton in a museum would not be 'authentic' with regard to material, it would be regarding to experience. However, as Leinhardt and Crowley (2002) remark, previously objects in museums were selected for their high cultural value, were showed for being unique examples or impressive or for encouraging reactions. However, present-day mentality in museums is changing: it is more interactive, including touching the objects that can only be made from copies of the real object. This intention and authenticity has to be clear for the public: in 2004 a museum in China closed for displaying fake objects (Dasgupta, 2014). In addition, how objects are displayed affects their sanctity. The same material can be sacred for different people depending on how it is presented (Curtis, 2003). A museum, especially an occidental museum, will display the object according to its criteria, which does not have to agree with the way that an indigenous community, for instance, would display (or not display) it. Another argument for not using human remains is that deciding on which authority can order to recover the dead is a complicated issue (Tarlow, 2006). During years it has been the religious authority who took the decision, but it does not seem to be any more. One more argument is that although in medicine the use of human bodies for research is a common and accepted practice, there is a difference with archaeological use which is that in medicine the bodies are obtained only through body donation and if the donor agreement is not signed, only in special and interesting cases for science, such as rare illness, the doctor will look for permission to the deceased's relatives (Goold, 2014). This barely happens in archaeology. Finally, finding a limit on the use of human remains is a complicated issue, since its use may increase in medical and scientific research (Magnusson, 1992).

Funerary value

> Finding a country willing to accept the remains of the world's most wanted terrorist would have been difficult. So he was buried at sea.[1]

There are various and different reasons for leaving bodies undisturbed such as the spirit finding rest, the necessity to pray or show dignity, that tampering with remains is sacrilegious or reasons of tradition or culture (Scarre, 2006). For instance, some beliefs disregard mortal remains but some think that the soul is tied to the remains as long as there is a body (Cheek and Keel, 1984). In some cultures, any kind of disturbance of human remains is disrespectful (Scarre, 2006). The example of mummification or building the pyramids (Scarre, 2006) proves that for some cultures how the deceased are disposed and buried is important. In the case of shipwrecks, leaving them undisturbed as watery graves would mean leaving the human remains untouched. However, as Dromgoole (2013) points out, in a recovery of cargo from a shipwreck, even if it does not disturb the remains of the human beings, there is still a case of disturbing the sanctity of the site as a gravesite. In favour of treating shipwrecks as watery graves is that declaring shipwrecks as funerary monuments or underwater cemeteries in most cases attract tourism if the shipwreck is accessible, such as the *USS Arizona*. It also conveys the unique meaning of sacred places, and in addition complies with some 2001 UNESCO Convention principles, such as preservation *in situ* (Perez-Alvaro, 2013). However, this option will depend both on the collective interest in remembering the tragedy, and the weight of opinion to consider the shipwrecks as a sanctuary for the dead. A shipwreck represents a loss: personal or cargo. However, the symbolic value of the shipwreck is only awarded if there is an effort to prolong its memory (Gibbs, 2005). Converting these burials to heritage is, as a consequence, a process and commemoration is part of this process. Says Delgado (2009):

> Despite years of shipwreck exploration as a maritime archaeologist and a decade as director of a maritime museum, *Titanic* was never high on my list of lost ships to visit. I'd never considered it an archaeological site, but rather an underwater museum and memorial.

According to Howard (2003) commemoration is the alternative to conservation: we can demolish a building or leave a memorial. In terms of tourism, leaving a memorial can attract people, where they can go to remember the victims, honour them or just see it as a curiosity or a historical memory, like war memorials (Howard, 2003). States can manage and protect their underwater cultural heritage to shape public memory through the various forms of memorials and sites (Nora, 1996–1998): memorials are highly selective in terms of what they portray as worthy of being remembered. Part of our identity is based on our cultural identity. This is the feeling of a group of people or of an individual which is influenced by their culture.

However, there are also arguments against treating shipwrecks as watery graves. In fact, some authors are opposed to the treatment of shipwrecks as cemeteries (Bryant, 2001) for several reasons. First, it is argued that neither history nor the law treats shipwrecks, historic or otherwise, as protected underwater cemeteries, stating that the historic, social, scientific and monetary value of historic shipwrecks dictates that they should not be treated as underwater cemeteries protected from salvage or recovery. This fact is well documented. However, if as we will claim, human remains *are* underwater cultural heritage, they would be protected and managed by the 2001 UNESCO Convention, meaning that they have to be preserved *in situ*. In addition, it is also suggested (Bryant, 2001) that since underwater shipwrecks are not natural and do not belong on the bottom of the sea—they belong at their home ports and intended destinations—neither do human remains belong on the bottom of the seas. As a consequence, recovery is acceptable where circumstances permit, the reason being that while cemeteries are the intended resting places for the dead, shipwrecks are not and because shipwrecks have other diverse values, they should not be labelled as cemeteries and kept off-limits to salvors and others. Historic shipwrecks containing human remains deserve respect, although not so far as to treat them as underwater cemeteries that cannot be salvaged, Bryant (2001) concludes. However, in this regard, it is open to debate that, while cemeteries are the intended resting place for the dead, shipwrecks are not. Throughout history, cemeteries have changed their context according to the circumstances: from churches, which are not meant to be cemeteries, to main squares in the village when there were mass deaths. It has been the fatalities of the sunken wrecks that have converted them into submerged cemeteries. A final argument is that management of shipwrecks as watery graves can lead to dark tourism, attracting tourists to a place with special meaning to the friends and relatives of the people who lost their lives in the disaster. Dark tourism is defined as a different type of touristic attraction: it is the act of travel and visitation to sites of death, disaster and the seemingly macabre (Stone, 2009). If shipwrecks as watery graves attract this tourism, tragedies would be exploited, not only to convey political messages but also for commercial gain (Sharpley, 2009). A ship is a vehicle but can also be a place of catastrophe and with a range of spiritual values with which we want to award it (Gibbs, 2005). In addition, Dr Iain Scobbie, an expert in maritime law at Glasgow University, said (Anonymous, 2003)

> there are those who believe that the site is a grave, but that is normally the case only when you are talking about military ships when it is a war grave. I understand that people might be upset because their ancestors died when the ship went down, but where do you stop? Do you refrain from excavating Bronze Age ships because those who died were someone's ancestors?

Guardians

Surviving relatives

For some authors, biologically and culturally related groups must have a substantial role (Teague, 2007). However, it is different to honour the ancestors and another to honour their descendants (Scarre, 2006). It is understood that the descendants are the ones having the obligation of care of the human remains (Hutt and Riddle, 2007). However, for that, there should be an 'unwritten social contract' that for instance, does not exist with Tutankhamen (Scarre, 2006). In fact, Dunkley (2011) argues that the only argument to respect human remains is if there are living descendants who knew the victims. Dromgoole (2013) also suggests that if there are interested parties, their feelings have to be taken into consideration, and as a consequence, being taken into consideration for consultation. However, relatives of the dead have often been excluded from decision making (Teague, 2007). In addition, the issue of ownership of a shipwreck also affects the human remains contained in it. A shipwreck in other nations' waters loses nationality if it is not a State vessel. Repatriation of bodies is the common practice for accidents that happen nowadays, both on land and in water. Repatriation of cultural heritage is a topic that has been largely discussed in the literature

(Bator, 1981). The only issue is if human remains arising from incidents more than 100 years underwater should or could be repatriated.

Indigenous communities

There are communities that until recently have been excluded from their countries decisions in particular on the treatment and preservation of human remains (Teague, 2007). A prime example of this approach is the case of the Kennewick Man, a 9,300-year-old skeleton found in 1996 (Chatters, 2000: 291). Five Native American tribes claimed it as an ancestor, under the Native American Graves Protection and Repatriation Act (1990), a law that allows Native Americans to remove ancestors' bones from museum collections (Bruning, 2006). However, in February 2004, the United States Court of Appeals for the Ninth Circuit ruled that a cultural link between any of the Native American tribes and the Kennewick Man was not genetically justified, allowing scientific study of the remains to continue (Bruning, 2006). The case, however, is still unresolved (Bruning, 2006). Opposite to this approach, however, is Zimmerman's opinion (1994). For the author the collection and study of Indian remains have grown with the development of American archaeology. From the moment that the actions of the collectors were improper and offensive to Indians, archaeologists took action to become more scientifically sophisticated and more ethically aware of the indigenous communities. In this line of thought, Teague (2007) reminds that the recent repatriation law is an approach to prohibit the scientific research in favour of traditional concerns, especially when talking of indigenous communities. In this regard, Forrest (2010) remarks that in some countries such as the US, Canada, Australia and New Zealand issues on the return of human remains to indigenous communities are of particular political importance. The author reminds that a considerable number of aboriginal remains have been already returned from these states.

Subjects

War graves vs civil graves

Human remains not only have a scientific value or a cultural value, but sometimes also a political value (Gibbs, 2005). The issue is more evident in the case of war graves. According to Williams (2005), the debate surrounding war graves has been clouded more by emotion than reason. The advances on technology for underwater explorations on the decade of 1980 was the catalyst not only for underwater archaeology, but also for the concern of disturbance to 'war graves' which has always created more interest than other types of grave, maybe for being assigned to a particular group or organisation. It can also be due to the feeling of 'those who died for us, for their country' (Slackman, 2012). Declaring shipwrecks as war graves is a mixture of salvage principles and legislation relating to military remains (Williams, 2005). Under international law, the captain of any ship, regardless of size or nationality has the authority to conduct an official burial service at sea. According to Aznar-Gómez (2010) sunken State vessels in non-commercial mission are grave sites and are protected by general rules protecting human remains, including *jus in bello* rules—or international humanitarian law in the law of war. National laws are changing on this direction. In the UK, for instance, the *Imperial War Graves Commission* established in 1917 that the Commission is not responsible for unrecovered human remains and that referring to ships with those human remains as 'war graves' is a mistake, since they do not constitute a 'burial' as such, leaving the war remains unprotected. However, in 1986, the *Protection of Military Remains Act* (1986) was drafted. It differentiates between protected places—designated by name but not locations—where diving is permitted, and controlled sites, where damaging, moving or unearthing any remains is an offence. Under this Act, any excavations that contain the remains of any military aircraft or vessel of any nationality or age is forbidden. The United States in another nation that protects war graves:

> … salvors should not presume that sunken U.S. warships have been abandoned by the United States. Permission must be granted from the United States to salvage sunken U.S. warships, and as a matter of policy, the U.S. Government does not grant such permission with respect to ships that contain the remains of deceased servicemen[…][2]

This legal protection contrasts with the protection awarded to other kinds of watery graves. No specific legislation in any country has been established to protect the fishers from wrecks of fishing boats or the victims of accidents on oil platforms.

Underwater cultural heritage nationless

As it will be explained in the next chapter shipwrecks from nations with complicated status or shipwrecks carrying slaves or refugees offer many ethical issues on its preservation as watery graves. The fact that the remains cannot be claimed by any group because of the confusion on its nationalities are still an unresolved matter.

Proposal: intangible, invisible and absent heritage

The fact that human remains should not be disturbed without good reason seems to be covered by common law and generally accepted. However, we cannot protect all sites and we may not be able to protect all the human remains under water (Manders *et al.*, 2012). The examples on land show this: cemeteries are transformed by cities. For instance, in Sheffield there is not a single cemetery site unaffected by modern construction and exhumation projects are common (Sayer, 2010). Shipwrecks may suffer the same fate. However, if a shipwreck is evaluated and it is decided to be worth preserving because it contains human remains, a new approach has to be taken.

The scope of heritage has been admitted internationally to include tangible and intangible heritage and their surrounding environment. As said, two situations can arise from human remains on shipwrecks: that the human remains are preserved and that the human remains are not preserved but there were people who perished on board of the shipwreck. If the human remains are still conserved they can be recovered for reburial, repatriation, museum exhibitions or for retrieving information or leaving them untouched as watery graves. However, if the human remains were known to be there but they are not conserved, the options for preservation complicated the issue. This study proposes three options for the possibility of new policies for the treatment of these shipwrecks:

Intangible heritage

Graham and Howard (2008: 4) argue that intangible heritage is as powerful as tangible material, although protecting it is particularly difficult. One option explored in this chapter is if those shipwrecks that once contained human remains should maintain their status of 'sacred places' as intangible heritage. According to the UNESCO Convention for the Safeguarding of the Intangible Cultural Heritage (UNESCO, 2003), intangible heritage is defined as:

1. The 'intangible cultural heritage' means the practices, representations, expressions, knowledge, skills—as well as the instruments, objects, artefacts and cultural spaces associated therewith—that communities, groups and, in some cases, individuals recognise as part of their cultural heritage. This intangible cultural heritage [...], provides them with a sense of identity and continuity, thus promoting respect for cultural diversity and human creativity.
2. The 'intangible cultural heritage', as defined in paragraph one above, is manifested inter alia in the following domains: [...] (c) social practices, rituals and festive events.

Intangible heritage does not include physical material that has been destroyed and a wreck does not constitute a ritual practice. As Lixinski (2013) argues, due to the organic evolving nature of intangible cultural heritage, legal protection may be difficult. However, Rule 5 of the Annex of the 2001 UNESCO Convention introduce the word 'venerated sites' when discussing the management of human remains. For O'Keefe (2002) 'venerated sites' means those ones that have spiritual attachment for certain people, being the graves of people. As a consequence, shipwrecks considered 'venerated sites' would be included on the definition of intangible heritage for being 'cultural spaces associated with a community'. Its preservation as intangible heritage, therefore, can be not only monuments to the great journey or heroic combat, but also a tool to shape the collective memory. Underwater cultural heritage can act as a trigger for a set of emotions and historical memory (Perez-Alvaro, 2013) and that is considered intangible cultural heritage. In addition, watery graves fall right in the middle of the delicate issue between the definition of intangible cultural heritage—living cultural practices passed from generation to generation—and human rights.

Invisible heritage

A new approach to an undiscovered form of heritage has been recently raised. This is the example already explained: the reuse of vessels as harbour structures (Ford, 2013). A vessel loses its original function (transportation) and is transformed into barracks, prisons, hospitals, store ships or hotels. The ship left in these harbours remain in existence: cans, syringes, pots and all kinds of objects that can carry archaeological interest. These semi-permanent structures left full archaeological fields in the same spot. This is what we have called 'invisible heritage': the heritage that has been there and has left its footprints behind. In this regard, when Odyssey Marine Exploration found the wreck of *Nuestra Senora de las Mercedes*, claimed that the shipwreck was not a shipwreck, but a field of debris, so as a consequence it was abandoned property (Zorich, 2009). This argument could have contravened the concept of 'invisible heritage': shipwrecks fields that are known to be there but have disappeared and that have left invisible human remains. As a consequence, the human remains that were once there contained in shipwrecks that have disappeared would be considered as cemeteries of 'invisible heritage'. It is the idea of the heritage as a footprint. The shipwrecks fields have as a consequence adopted the function of cemetery whose human remains where once there and need to be respected.

Absent heritage

It is the memorialisation of places and objects whose significance relates to their destruction or absence (Harrison, 2013). It was particularly applied by the author to the destruction of the Great and Little Buddhas of the Bamiyan Valley (Afghanistan). The pieces of heritage are the niches that once contained the Buddhas and that have remained as a memory of the destruction. This theory, applied to human remains on shipwrecks would transform the shipwrecks into 'absent niches' where the human remains are not preserved but the shipwreck is preserved for its memorialisation. It is what we can consider as an 'absent presence'.

These three ideas would show respect for human remains while con-serving underwater cultural heritage. However, although the archaeological community would acknowledge these concepts, for the concepts to work for the protection of human remains both on land and underwater they should be incorporated into a legal instrument.

Conclusions

The articulation of the dilemmas surrounding the management of human remains on underwater cultural heritage has been based on three pillars: values, guardians of the deceased, and subjects—human remains. Each one of these pillars generates different ethical dilemmas. However, while the values awarded to these shipwrecks and its management depend on historical, sociological, cultural and traditional particularities of every country (Perez-Alvaro, 2014) and the priorities and goals of the authorities, the guardians of the deceased should be the ones in charge of taking the decisions. However, these decisions get tangled with the subjects—the human remains—that generates contro-versial issues such as the kind of passengers that the shipwreck carried or the ownership of the shipwreck which will produce particularities and objectives of every kind. The triangle, as a consequence, will live on.

However, these dilemmas are common to two different circumstances that can be found in relation to the conservation of human remains; first, shipwrecks still containing human remains since this chapter has shown that shipwrecks from almost five hundred years ago still contain tangible human remains. Not only heritage managers and archaeologists but also communi-ties, ancestors and descendants should collaborate on what to do with them whether research, museology, reburial or leaving where they are. However, benefits from the study of human remains would come to an end if some of these human remains are not recovered and/or studied. The real com-plexity arises from the choice of the remains that will be disturbed. Second, shipwrecks not containing human remains although they once did. These shipwrecks will only be preserved by recognition of them as watery graves, even if the remains are not conserved. These shipwrecks offer a complex dis-course for being respected.

As MacLeod (1993) stated, the management of the ethical, religious and social implications, and also the recovery and preservation of the human remains in aircraft and shipwrecks, will contribute to help the public be more aware of the real value of this heritage (MacLeod, 1993). Dialogue and the consideration of other actors interested on the management of human remains are the keys to the question of respect. Not only can the shipwreck preserve the human remains but the treatment that we give to the human remains can help preserving the shipwreck. Respecting the wishes of the owners of human remains means that some activities have to be for-bidden (Aplin, 2002). And although Bryant (2001) claims that since historic shipwrecks are unlikely to contain human remains so they can be salvaged and the grave disturbed, this chapter has proved that several shipwrecks still contain human remains and as the shipwrecks sunken get closer in time, it will be more likely to contain them.

Since most of the earth is covered with water, burial at sea can be seen as an accepted norm for seamen all over the world. And those buried human remains can offer knowledge to archaeologists not reachable by other means. Different legal agreements in relation to archaeological practices have been established as common ground for the treatment of human in the sense of 'respect'. However, what is respectful for some communities or professionals may not be for others. As Saunders (2002) mentions, excavating human remains is a memory-making activity that has to be regulated in order to reach a balance between families of the deceased and benefits for the communities. This case study has proposed a new categorisation of these scenarios under three main labels: intangible heritage, absent heritage and invisible heritage. Under the first treatment, human remains would be considered as 'venerated sites' which are part of a community cultural space and as a consequence would be considered intangible cultural heritage. These shipwrecks would be protected, as a consequence under the 2003 Convention for the Safeguarding of the Intangible Cultural Heritage. The other two treatments of shipwrecks—absent and invisible heritage—would not be protected under the Convention for being new proposed categories of heritage. However, they could be considered as new annexes to any of the UNESCO conventions. The treatment of human remains on underwater cultural heritage as 'invisible heritage' would imply the consideration of shipwrecks fields as cemeteries of those human remains that were once on there but have now disappeared. The shipwreck would then leave their footprint, 'the human remains', that need to be respected. A last option has been considered by this study, which is the treatment of the human remains as 'absent heritage' that would imply that the shipwrecks are seen as a 'frame' of what is not there anymore. These human remains would be considered 'absent presence'. The consequence would be the memorialisation of those shipwrecks as 'containers' of sacred remains.

Intangibility has been used to protect heritage such as practices, representations, expressions, knowledge or skills. However, this chapter has applied it to protect underwater cultural heritage, specifically, human remains. It is the same concept that will be used when protecting nationless or migrant shipwrecks since it is underwater cultural heritage with a significance that exceeds the tangible.

Notes

1 U.S. Official about Osama Bin Laden. Available at: www.theguardian.com/world/2011/may/02/bin-laden-body-buried-sea.
2 Letter from Department of State to Maritime Administration, December 30, 1980, *reprinted in* United States Department of State, *Digest of United States Practice in International Law* 999, 1004 (1980).

Bibliography

Anonymous (2003). Titanic salvage sinks in sea of litigation. [online]. *The Scotsman: Scotland on Sunday.* 28 February 2003. Available at: www.scotsman. com/news/world/titanic-salvage-sinks-in-sea-of-litigation-1-548215.

Aplin, G. (2002). *Heritage Identification, Conservation and Management.* Oxford: Oxford University Press.

Aznar-Gómez, M. J. (2010). Treasure hunters, sunken state vessels and the 2001 UNESCO Convention on the Protection of Underwater Cultural Heritage. *International Journal of Marine and Coastal Law* 25(2): 209–236.

Aznar-Gómez, M. J. (2013). Treasure hunters. In AIMA 13 Conference: Towards Ratification: Australia's Underwater Cultural Heritage, Canberra, 4 October 2013.

Bator, P. M. (1981). *The International Trade in Art.* London: University of Chicago Press.

Bruning, S. B. (2006). Complex legal legacies: the Native American graves protection and repatriation act, scientific study, and Kennewick Man. *American Antiquity* 71(3): 501–521.

Bryant, C. (2001). The archaeological duty of care: the legal, professional and cultural struggle over salvaging historic shipwrecks. *Albany Law Review* 65(1): 97–145.

Chatters, J. C. (2000). The recovery and first analysis of an early Holocene human skeleton from Kennewick, Washington. *American Antiquities* 65(2): 291–316.

Cheek, A. L. and Keel, B. C. (1984). Value conflicts in osteo-archaeology. In Green, E. L. (ed.), *Ethics and Values in Archaeology.* London: Free Press: 194–207.

Coroneos, C. (2006). The ethics and values of maritime archaeology. In Staniforth, M. and Nash, M. (eds.), *Maritime Archaeology: Australian Approaches.* New York: Springer: 111–122.

Cunningham Dobson, N. and Tolson, H. (2010). A note on human remains from the shipwreck of *HMS Victory*, 1744. In Stemm, G. and Kingsley, S. (eds.), *Oceans Odyssey: Deep-Sea Shipwrecks in the English Channel, the Straits of Gibraltar and the Atlantic Ocean.* Oxford and Oakville: Oxbow Books: 281–288.

Curtis, N. G. W. (2003). Human remains: the sacred, museums and archaeology. *Public Archaeology* 3(1): 21–32.

Dasgupta, S. (2014). Chinese museum closed for displaying fake art objects. [online]. *Times of India.* 25 May 2014. Available at: http://timesofindia.indiatimes.com/world/china/Chinese-museum-closed-for-displaying-fake-art-objects/articleshow/35580469.cms.

Delgado, J. (2009). *Adventures of a Sea Hunter: In Search of Famous Shipwrecks.* Vancouver: Douglas & McIntyre.

Dromgoole, S. (2013). *Underwater Cultural Heritage and International Law.* Cambridge: Cambridge University Press.

Dunkley, M. (2011). Catastrophic burials: the study of human remains from sunken warships. *Conservation Bulletin* 6(1): 20–22.

Elia, R. (2000). US protection of underwater cultural heritage beyond the territorial sea: problems and prospects. *International Journal of Nautical Archaeology* 29(1): 43–56.

Fenwick, V. and Gale, A. (1998). *Historic Shipwrecks: Discovered, Protected and Investigated.* Gloucestershire: Tempus Publishing Limited.

Flatman, J. (2007). The origins and ethics of maritime archaeology – Part I. *Public Archaeology* 6(2): 77–97.

Ford, B. (2013). The reuse of vessels as harbor structures: a cross-cultural comparison. *Journal of Maritime Archaeology* 8(2): 197–219.

Forrest, C. (2010). *International Law and the Protection of Cultural Heritage.* London: Routledge.

Garratt-Frost, S. (1992). *The Law and Burial Archaeology.* Birmingham: Institute of Field Archaeologists, University of Birmingham.

Gibbs, M. (2005). Watery graves: when ships become places. In Lydon, J. and Ireland, T. (eds.), *Object Lessons.* Melbourne: Australian Scholarly Press: 50–70.

Goold, I. (2014). Why does it matter how we regulate the use of human body parts? *Journal of Medical Ethics* 40(1): 3–9.

Graham, B. J. and Howard, P. (eds.) (2008). *The Ashgate Research Companion to Heritage and Identity.* Cornwall: Ashgate: 1–17.

Guerin, U. and Egger, B. (eds.) (2011). *UNESCO Manual for Activities directed at Underwater Cultural Heritage.* Paris: UNESCO, Secretariat of the 2001 UNESCO Convention.

Harrison, R. (2013). *Heritage: Critical Approaches.* New York: Routledge.

Howard, P. (2003). *Heritage: Management, Interpretation, Identity.* London: Library of Congress Cataloguing-in Publication Data.

Hutt, S. and Riddle, J. (2007). The law of human remains and burials. In Cassman, V., Odegaard, N. and Powell, J. (eds.), *Human Remains: A Guide for Museums and Academic Institutions.* Oxford: AltaMira Press: 223–244.

Iwabuchi, A. (2014). The shipwreck of the Japanese cruiser *Takachico*. [Unpublished paper]. UNESCO Scientific Conference on the Occasion of the Centenary of World War I, Bruges, Belgium.

Jeffery, B. (2004). World War II underwater cultural heritage sites in truk Lagoon: considering a case for world heritage listing. *International Journal of Nautical Archaeology* 33(1): 106–121.

Leinhardt, G., and Crowley, K. (2002). Objects of learning, objects of talk: changing minds in museums. In Paris, S. G. (ed.), *Perspectives on Object-Centred Learning in Museums.* Mahwah, NJ: Lawrence Erlbaum Associates: 301–324.

Lixinski, L. (2013). *Intangible Cultural Heritage in International Law.* Oxford: Oxford University Press.

Macdonald, C. (2017). The kamikaze motorboats: rare craft used as suicide attack vessels by Japanese troops during World War II found off the coast of Japan. [online]. *Daily Mail.* 18 September 2017. Available at: www.dailymail.co.uk/sciencetech/article-4897094/Underwater-remains-Japan-WWII-kamikaze-boats.html.

MacLeod, I. D. (1993). Metal corrosion on shipwrecks: Australian case studies. *Trends in Corrosion Research* 1: 221–245.

MacLeod, I. D. (2008). Shipwreck graves and their conservation management. *AICCM Bulletin* 31(1): 5–14.

Magnusson, R. S. (1992). The recognition of proprietary rights in human tissue in common law jurisdictions. *Melbourne University Law Review* 18(601): 628–629.

Manders, M. (2012). Unit 9: *in situ* preservation. In Manders, M. and Underwood, C. (eds.), *Training Manual for the UNESCO Foundation Course on the Protection and Management of Underwater Cultural Heritage in Asia and the Pacific.* Bangkok: UNESCO.

Manders, M, van Tilburg, K. H. and Staniforth, M. (2012). Unit 6: significance assessment. In Manders, M. and Underwood, C. (eds.), *Training Manual for the UNESCO Foundation Course on the Protection and Management of Underwater Cultural Heritage in Asia and the Pacific.* Bangkok: UNESCO.

Mays, S. (2008). Human remains in marine archaeology. *Environmental Archaeology* 13(2): 123–133.

Native American Graves Protection and Repatriation Act (1990). United States Federal Law. Available at: www.nps.gov/parknagpra/ (2 October 2017).

Nora, P. (1996–1998). *Realms of Memory I–III.* New York City, NY: Columbia University Press.

O'Keefe, P. (2002). *Shipwrecked Heritage: A Commentary on the UNESCO Convention on Underwater Cultural Heritage.* Leicester: Institute of Art and Law.

Perez-Alvaro, E. (2013). Shipwrecks as watery graves: cultural attitudes, legal approach and ethical implications. In Juste Ruiz, J. and Bou Franch, V. (eds.), *Derecho del mar y sostenibilidad ambiental en el Mediterráneo.* Valencia: Tirant Lo Blanch: 133–144.

Perez-Alvaro, E. (2014). The management of human remains on shipwrecks: ethical attitudes and legal approaches. In van Tilburg, H., Tripati, S., Walker, V., Fahy, B. and Kimura, J. (eds.), *Proceedings of the Second Asia-Pacific Regional Conference on Underwater Cultural Heritage.* Honolulu: Electric Pencil: 39–48.

Perez-Alvaro, E. and Carman, J. (2011). International approaches to Underwater Cultural Heritage: shipwrecks as graves. *Ministerio de Educación, Cultura y Deporte: Actas de las Jornadas de ARQUA:* 201–205 (3 June 2018).

Pickford, N. (1994). *The Atlas of Shipwreck and Treasure.* London: Dorling Kindersley.

Pojman, L. and Fieser, L. (2012). *Ethics: Discovering Right and Wrong.* Boston: Wadsworth.

Protection of Military Remains Act (1986). Legislation UK Government. Protection and Management of Historic Military Wrecks outside UK Territorial Waters. Available at: www.legislation.gov.uk/ukpga/1986/35/contents (2 October 2018).

Regulations on prospecting and exploration for polymetallic sulphides in the Area (2010) and Regulations on prospecting and exploration for cobalt-rich ferromanganese crusts in the Area (2012). *International Seabed Authority.* Available at: www.isa.org.jm/mining-code/Regulations.

Saunders, N. (2002). Excavating memories: archaeology and the Great World War. *Antiquity* 76(291): 101–108.

Sayer, D. (2010). *Ethics and Burial Archaeology.* London: Duckworth Debates in Archaeology.

Scarre, G. (2006). Can archaeology harm the dead? In Scarre, C. and Scarre, G. (eds.), *The Ethics of Archaeology: Philosophical Perspectives on Archaeological Practice.* Cambridge: Cambridge University Press: 181–198.

Sharpley, R. (2009). Shedding light on dark tourism: an introduction. In Sharpley, R. and Stone, P. R. (eds.), *The Darker Side of Travel.* Ontario: Channel View Publications: 3–22.

Slackman, M. (2012). *Remembering Pearl Harbor: The Story of the USS Arizona Memorial.* Hawaii: Pacific Historic Parks.

Stone, P. R. (2009). Dark tourism: morality and new moral spaces. In Sharpley, R. and Stone, P. R. (eds.), *The Darker Side of Travel.* Ontario: Channel View Publications: 56–73.

Sutherland, T. L., and Schmidt, A. (2003). The Towton Battlefield Archaeological Survey Project: an integrated approach to battlefield archaeology. *Landscapes* 4(2): 15–25.

Tamaki Makau-rau Accord on the Display of Human Remains and Sacred Objects (2005). WAC Council. Available at: www.worldarchaeologicalcongress.org/site/about_ethi.php (2 October 2018).

Tarlow, S. (2006). Archaeological ethics and the people of the past. In Scarre, C. and Scarre, G. (eds.), *The Ethics of Archaeology: Philosophical Perspectives on Archaeological Practice.* Cambridge: Cambridge University Press: 199–217.

Teague, L. S. (2007). Respect for the dead, respect for the living. In Cassman, V., Odegaard, N. and Powell, J. (eds.), *Human Remains: A Guide for Museums and Academic Institutions.* Oxford: Oxford AltaMira Press: 245–260.

UNCLOS (1982). United Nations Convention on the Law of the Sea. Available at: www.un.org/depts/los/convention_agreements/texts/unclos/unclos_e.pdf (1 May 2017).

UNESCO (2001). Convention on the Protection of the Underwater Cultural Heritage. Paris, 2 November 2001. Available at: http://unesdoc.unesco.org/images/0012/001260/126065e.pdf (22 May 2017).

UNESCO (2003). Convention for the Safeguarding of the Intangible Cultural Heritage. Paris, 17 October 2003. Available at: http://portal.unesco.org/en/ev.php-URL_ID=17716&URL_DO=DO_TOPIC&URL_SECTION=201.html (1 May 2017).

Vermillion Accord on Human Remains (1989). WA Inter-Congress, South Dakota, USA. Available at: www.worldarchaeologicalcongress.org/site/about_ethi.php (2 October 2018).

Wight, C. (2009). Contested national tragedies: an ethical dimension. In Sharpley, R. and Stone, P. R. (2009). *The Darker Side of Travel: The Theory and Practice of Dark Tourism.* Ontario: Channel View Publications: 129–144.

Williams, M. (2005). 'War graves' and salvage: murky waters? *International Maritime Law* 7(5): 151–158.

Zimmerman, L. J. (1994). Review of battlefields and burial grounds: the Indian struggle to protect ancestral graves in the United States by Roger C. Echo-Hawk and Walter R. Echo-Hawk. *Great Plains Research: A Journal of Natural and Social Sciences*: paper 243.

Zorich, Z. (2009). Television: finding treasure and losing history. [online]. *Archaeology* 62(2). Available at: http://archive.archaeology.org/0903/trenches/odyssey.html.

8 Identity
Nationless shipwrecks[1]

Although concepts of identity, restitution, colonialism or human rights have been well discussed in land cultural heritage debates, the underwater cultural heritage creates a whole new dimension to the topic. During times of colonisation, indigenous peoples were deprived not only of their land and territories, but also of their cultural objects. Therefore, booty on board ships travelling from conquered domains to conquerors' land included not only coins and gold, but also sacred and culturally significant objects. For indigenous people, these objects were part of their community; for the conquerors, they were merely treasures. Consequently, European countries with colonial interests amassed collections of special cultural significance (Greenfield, 1996). While most of the ships loaded with treasures and cultural objects from conquered territories took the journey back to the European mainland, some sank to the bottom of the ocean *en route*.

As Stamatoudi (2011) states, cultural property is a recent and fast-evolving area of law which depends heavily on ethics; these do not involve pure objectivity, and this makes it a difficult field. This chapter will not engage in judgmental considerations over conquests and territory domination. Instead, it will make evaluations on the basis of fact, such as conquest and war, and the ethical and legal considerations regarding cultural heritage objects in the wrecks of ships that left port in a territory that does not exist today.

Introduction

Nowadays, underwater cultural heritage attracts attention not only for its cultural but also for its economic value, and ownership of shipwrecks is a topic of high controversy as demonstrated by the legislation for the protection of underwater cultural heritage that has been drafted in many countries (Aznar-Gómez, 2010). A good example is the Old Spanish Kingdom in South America, which raised difficulties in the courtroom in the case of the *Nuestra Señora de las Mercedes*, a vessel sunk in 1804 off the coast of Gibraltar and recovered by a private company, Odyssey Marine Exploration (Werner, 2013). The *Mercedes* left Lima (then part of the Spanish empire but now in the independent country of Peru) with a crew of 337, including military men, families and civilians of that territory; she was loaded with gold and objects from these territories. A British warship destroyed the ship and killed all but fifty of those aboard. Odyssey Marine asked for permission to salvage the shipwreck but Spain claimed that it was a sunken warship and the 'graveyard of marines'. However, the dispute was not only between these two parties, as Peru and twenty-five other claimants declared an interest in the shipwreck: it originated in Peru and several individuals alleged that they were descendants of some of those that had perished and that they owned their human remains. However, their claims were promptly dismissed, since it was considered that, at that time, Peru was not a nation but part of the Spanish Kingdom. In 2013, Spain won the case and kept ownership of the shipwreck and of the cargo. A similar case has occurred in December 2015, when a galleon called *San José*, with an estimated $1 billion in coins and valuable items on board, was discovered off the coast of Colombia (Drye, 2015). The ship belonged to a Spanish fleet that was carrying gold and precious metals from a former Spanish colony to what is now Spain. The Colombian government hailed the discovery as the 'biggest find of under-water heritage in the history of humanity' (Drye, 2015). However, Spain claims the shipwreck on the grounds that it was a ship that sailed under the Spanish flag (BBC, 2015). The question is if the cargo on board of the galleon is part of Colombia's cultural heritage or if it is part of Spain's cultural heritage: if that cargo defines the cultural identity of one of these countries.

The ethical and legal considerations that both cases raise are considerable. Questions of ownership, restitution or compensation are only some of the issues that these two examples bring. On the one hand, both ships were sponsored by the Spanish king to carry out ventures on what was, at that time, Spanish territory. On the other hand, the gold and other precious metals emanated from the territories of what are now sovereign nations—and which represented their wealth—were found by the labour of those territories' workers—or slaves—and brought to Spain on ships crewed by inhabitants of those territories. In some cases, some of these shipwrecks have been rescued by the current nationals of those territories, for instance in the case of Colombia.

Issue

Location vs Flag State (and sovereign immunity)

Rights over shipwrecks depend not only on the location, but also on their ownership before it sunk—i.e. under which flag state it sailed. As a general rule, coastal states exercise complete sovereignty over the underwater cultural heritage in its archipelagic waters and territorial sea. In the other zones of the sea the rules are controversial since salvage and admiralty laws have been long applied and the 1982 United Nations Convention on the Law of the Sea (UNCLOS, 1982) do not contravene them. Article 303 states:

Archaeological and historical objects found at sea

1. States have the duty to protect objects of an archaeological and historical nature found at sea and shall cooperate for this purpose. [...]
3. Nothing in this article affects the rights of identifiable owners, the law of salvage or other rules of admiralty, or laws and practices with respect to cultural exchanges. [...]

Salvage and admiralty laws have long been seen as detrimental for the protection of underwater cultural heritage and, in fact, the 2001 UNESCO Convention for the Protection of the Underwater Cultural Heritage (UNESCO, 2001), in Article 4 stresses that 'any activity relating to underwater cultural heritage to which this Convention applies shall not be subject to the law of salvage or law of finds'.

In the contiguous zone, the state practice accepts the coastal state's right to legislate on underwater cultural heritage. Beyond the contiguous zone, the regime for the underwater cultural heritage is vague (Aznar-Gómez, 2010). In addition, a flag state has jurisdiction not only over its own state vessels but also over private merchant vessels sailing under its flag (Triay, 2014). Sovereign immunity is another issue. With regards to a shipwreck, if it is owned by a State, it may be protected by sovereign immunity in that it can be immune from the jurisdiction and measure of constraints of other states. Moreover, under customary international law governmental ships operated for non-commercial purposes are immune from coastal state enforcement (Article 32; UNCLOS, 1982) and many former colonial powers have declared that they retain ownership of their warships. In the case of *Nuestra Señora de las Mercedes*, Spain relied on its sovereign immunity based on nature and cargo of the ship.

Private property vs state property

In the *Mercedes* case, twenty-five descendants of persons who owned cargo that was on board the ship claimed ownership (Triay, 2014). In this claim, it was argued that even if the shipwreck was a state Spanish vessel, the cargo was not, since it was the private property of some of the passengers on board. However, the court argued that the ship and its cargo are 'inextricably linked' and as a consequence not only the shipwreck but also the cargo belonged to Spain. Derout (1993) explains the difference between property law, for the protection of the rights of the possessor, and cultural heritage law, for the protection of the heritage for the enjoyment of present and later generations. In most cases, these differ. In the case of underwater cultural heritage, there is a tendency to use property law, in the sense that states claim ownership rights over, for instance, shipwrecks and cargo. However, Article 2 of the 2001 UNESCO Convention states that 'States Parties shall preserve underwater cultural heritage for the benefit of humanity', which contrast with the controversies of ownership between the different countries or between countries and private companies.

Shipwreck vs cargo

Even if the nationality of a shipwreck is known and clear, the nationality of the cargo may be an issue. In most cases, the flag state and the state of origin of the cargo either did not correspond or the latter was a colony. Some of these colonies are now independent states and the state of origin of the cargo is difficult to determine. As it has been stated, in the *Mercedes* case, the court decided that the ship and its cargo were inextricably intertwined, not only for effects of private property but also for effects of separation between cargo and shipwreck (Triay, 2014). Peru raised the argument that international law condemns colonialism, particularly the pillage of the resources of the occupied territory (Vigni, 2012). It also contended that the *Mercedes* cargo was part of its cultural and historic heritage (Triay, 2014). However, the US court dismissed these claims because they were shaping an inter-state dispute which needed to be settled by international means[2] and that Peru should file a restitution claim in Spain. This dispute has not been taken ahead. Three countries claimed ownership over the shipwreck of the *San José*: Peru, Colombia and Spain—besides the private treasure company Sea Search Armada, who said they had located the shipwreck in the 1980s. Colombia claimed that the shipwreck was in its territorial waters, Spain that it was a state vessel and Peru that the silver on board of the ship was coming from its mines—although the Potosi mines are actually in Bolivian territory. Sea Search Armada, on the other hand, claimed the shipwreck on the bases of having found the shipwreck (Shearing, 2016).

In this regard is worth to look at the difference between 'wreck' and 'archaeological site' the latter preserving traces of history that allow interpreting the role a material played for hundreds, even thousands of years. As already emphasised, the most important source of information for the archaeologists of an underwater site is not only the wreck but also her associated objects: context, inventory, personal belongings and cargo (Perez-Alvaro, 2014). On the contrary, the claims in admiralty courts all are based on the salvage tradition, and, as a consequence, the wreck is the object of interest, not the archaeological site. However, the heritage needs to be the centre of the debate in the management of 'nationals shipwrecks', which is what the 2001 UNESCO Convention is based on.

State of knowledge

The Spanish conquerors arrived in the territories of Latin America in 1492, when Christopher Columbus encountered the American continent (Flores, 2003). The conquered territories were not states *per se* before the arrival of the conquerors but very organised communities of indigenous people.

Peruvian, Chilean, Colombian 'nations' did not yet exist. Indeed, when the Spanish conquerors arrived, the region was greatly fragmented into different cultures. When the conquerors settled, the race of the European and the race of the aboriginal ethnic groups merged into a new race called mestizo or *criollo*. The territories were then controlled by the Spanish Kingdom but also part of it: the conquered lands were viceroyalties, considered to be provinces rather than colonies, and the Spanish and the Spanish Americans living there were represented in the Parliament, though the mestizos and indigenous people were denied such representation. When the Spanish Crown was weakened by the conflicts with France, these mestizos started a movement towards self-determination around 1809. Over the next decade most of the Spanish-American territories become independent. By 1830 thirteen independent governments had been established in Latin America (Flores, 2003). Colonialism had lasted for three centuries. In this regard, there are two concepts framed in UNCLOS that complicates underwater cultural heritage in state succession with two terms: state of origin and identifiable owner.

State of origin

Article 149 of UNCLOS, which is titled 'Archaeological and historical objects', reads as follows:

> All objects of an archaeological and historical nature found in the Area shall be preserved or disposed of for the benefit of mankind as a whole, particular regard being paid to the preferential rights of the state or country of origin, or the state of cultural origin, or the state of historical and archaeological origin.

The main problem with this article is that the notions of 'state or country of origin', 'state of cultural origin', and 'state of historical and archaeological origin' have not been defined. It is for this reason that Boesten (2002) stresses that this article is confusing at best. Dromgoole (2013) suggests that these terms overlap and that they do not have exclusive meanings. For the author, the presence of all three formulas means that 'there is a broad basis for states to claim preferential rights [...] including situations where one state has succeeded to another, or where several countries share, or shared, the same culture' (Dromgoole, 2013: 123). The author also clarifies that 'state of origin' implies the fact that underwater cultural heritage originated in a certain place—for instance, where it was built—does not mean that that states is, or ever was, the owner. Watters (1983) declares that this clause is of concern since it gives options for more than one state to claim preferential rights to the objects, and sets out various questions: does the state of origin have preferential rights to the vessel whereas the various states of cultural, archaeological, or historical origin have preferential rights to goods transported by such vessel? Or does that state of origin also have preferential rights to the goods if they originally were legitimately acquired through purchase? What if they were seized as booty? What is done with vessels or cargoes from states that no longer exist? The three formulas allow more than one state to be in a position to claim a preferential right (Dromgoole, 2013).

The 2001 Convention—just as UNCLOS—also grants special preferential rights to 'states of cultural, historical or archaeological origin'. Article 12 of the Convention provides:

> [...] 6. In coordinating consultations, taking measures, conducting preliminary research, and/or issuing authorizations pursuant to this Article, the Coordinating State shall act for the benefit of humanity as a whole, on behalf of all States Parties. Particular regard shall be paid to the preferential rights of States of cultural, historical or archaeological origin in respect of the underwater cultural heritage concerned.

However, it is not only the formulas given by the two Conventions—archaeological, historical or cultural origin—that is the only source of concern but the concept employed in both UNCLOS Convention and the 2001 UNESCO Convention: 'states'. Latin American territories were never 'states' until the independence. Consequently, the terms 'state of cultural origin' or 'state of historical origin' are not easily applicable to the civilisations prior the arrival of the Spaniards. The concept of statehood is quite a contemporary one and can be applied to Peru, Chile or Mexico. Although before the arrival of the Spanish, the Latin American territory was not divided into states—in the modern sense, neither were they just scattered people spread across a territory. They were civilisations: according to Flores (2003) the aborigines were notable for their sense of community, with medicinal knowledge and culture and fine hand-made artefacts—some of these artefacts were shipped to the Old Continent and are now exhibited in museums as cultural relics. These civilisations did not disappear with the arrival of the Spanish. In fact, according to Flores (2003), indigenous society in South America still fights hard to promote indigenous culture and recognition of multiculturalism inside their modern independent states. The term indigenous was first employed by Columbus, who, thinking he had found the West Indies, named the aborigines 'indians' or 'indigenous'. These indigenous peoples were the first peoples in their own land, a land taken by force by those who settled (Higgins, 2003). Currently, the United Nations Sub-commission on the Prevention of Discrimination and Protection of Minorities defines indigenous people as

> [I]ndigenous communities, peoples and nations having a historical continuity with pre-invasion and pre-colonial societies that developed on their territories, considered themselves distinct from other sectors of the societies [...] and are determined to preserve, develop and transmit to future generations their ancestral territories and their ethnic identity.[3]

These indigenous communities are still present in the Latin American territory: it is a continuity from before the Spanish arrived, they remained during the Spanish domination and survived after the independence of the new states. It is, therefore, difficult to see the Spanish domination, from the point of view of cultural heritage, as a breach between the existent cultures and modern nations of i.e. Peru, Chile or Colombia. The indigenous community—and their cultural heritage—is an abiding civilisation that has survived state succession, although losing the material expressions of their culture.

During Spanish domination, the gold and the silver started to be considered precious materials and the mines on the Latin American land started to be exploited to obtain those materials. Also, cultural objects from those indigenous communities were shipped to the mainland. Those objects were transported from one side of the Atlantic to the other side by sea, where museums started to flourish. Some of the ships transporting such precious cargoes sunk accidentally, whereas others sunk because of armed attacks. Some of them sunk in waters close to the shore in the Americas, and some in the Area. From the point of view of modern international law, cultural objects were shipped legally since the land from where they had been taken was under Spanish domination and the objects were moved from one Spanish province on one side of the Atlantic to another Spanish province on the other side, the main Spanish land. From the point of view of cultural identity, the objects were snatched from the indigenous communities who created them or for whom they had been created. Although these objects from the old cultures do not represent the democracy of the current Peru, Chile or Colombia as nations, they are symbols of cultures—such as the Inca or Aztec civilisations, which are profoundly linked to the occupants of the territories. In the last few decades—not only as a result of the interest that the underwater world always generate but also because of the development of underwater exploration—several of these shipwrecks have been found and ownership claims have been made by the private companies that found them and by states. They are continuously in the court rooms. However, the rights of indigenous communities have never been considered. For this reason, the concept that should be employed to refer to the objects coming from the cultures before colonisers arrived is 'territorial provenance' of cultural heritage (Jakubowski, 2015). This territorial provenance refers to the link between the territory, its human communities and the collective cultural identity. It is the relation between the object, the land, and the people who lived therein. Although the shipwreck may be from a territory, the cargo on board may be from another, a territory which is not a state, but a civilisation. It may be that neither Spain nor the new independent states are the owners of the cargo but the indigenous communities.

Identifiable owners

Article 303 of UNCLOS is titled 'Archaeological and historical objects found at sea' and reads:

1. States have the duty to protect objects of an archaeological and historical nature found at sea and shall cooperate for this purpose. [...]
3. Nothing in this article affects the rights of identifiable owners, the law of salvage or other rules of admiralty, or laws and practices with respect to cultural exchanges [...].

According to Boesten (2002), under this article, if a state can demonstrate ownership of the objects—i.e. if it can demonstrate that it is the identifiable owner—its rights are protected. However, in state succession, it may be difficult to find the identifiable owner.

State succession changes the rights of the owners over the territory depending on which kind of state succession has happened. Latin American states claimed their independence unilaterally. Spain did not recognise the independence of any of its independences in South America and in fact the treaties by which Spain recognised the independence of its colonies transferred Spanish debts to the new states (Menon, 1991). As a result, they suffered a succession procession, with a new legal status. In fact, the 1978 Vienna Convention on Succession of States in respect of Treaties[4] defines succession as 'the replacement of one state by another in the responsibility for the international relations of territory' (Article 2).

The transfer of territory from one national community to another produces ethical and legal difficulties (O'Connell, 1956). In Latin America the Roman principle *uti possidetis juris* was applied, under which each new nation inherited the boundaries of what had belonged to its respective colonial entity, called *Cedulas Reales* or royal letters. As a consequence, each new nation had to keep the territorial divisions that had been established during the Hispanic period, a rule that produced numerous conflicts in Latin America (Flores, 2003). In fact, as already said, in the *San José* shipwreck case, Peru claimed that the silver on board of the ship came from its mines—the Potosi mines—which are actually in Bolivian territory. This dispute is a product of the applied principle *uti possidetis juris*.

Cultural heritage ownership in state succession is regulated by a set of non-binding principles applied on a case-by-case basis and reflected in peace treaties (Jakubowski, 2015). In the peace treaties concluded with South American states there is no mention to the obligation of returning objects shipped to the main territory of the Spanish Kingdom.[5] There is no mention either of the obligation of Latin America countries to return cultural objects to their predecessor country: the cultural objects created during the Spanish domination—churches, virgins, sculptures, paintings…—remained in Latin American land, and its return to its 'country of origin', Spain, has never been questioned. The reason is that under customary international law, the property of the predecessor state passes *ipso jure* to the successor (Jakubowski, 2014) (state succession does not affect private property of individuals or non-state entities). This means that, in the case of Latin American independent states, their legal and cultural rights to cultural material were acquired during their colonial occupation, and the property of the Spanish passed *ipso jure* to them (O'Connell, 1956).

The 1970 UNESCO Convention on the Means of Prohibiting and Preventing the Illicit Import, Export and Transfer of Ownership of Cultural Property (UNESCO, 1970) throws some light in this regard. Article 4 of the Convention recognises not only the cultural heritage of each state as the one created by nationals of that state, but also, and more importantly for the purposes of this work, the one created or found within the territory of that state. Stamatoudi (2011) also argues that cultural property found in the territory of a state forms part of that state's cultural patrimony. A telling example relates to Greek Attic amphorae excavated in Turkey: these artefacts belong to Turkey's cultural heritage notwithstanding the fact that they had been created when that territory was controlled by the ancient Greek state, and that the Turkish state was created only in the twentieth century. It follows from the foregoing the importance of the idea of 'territorial provenance'. Stamatoudi (2011) remarks the need of a special link between the property and the state. As a consequence, cultural objects of Maya and Inca civilisations, even if belonged to the Spanish Kingdom during the colonial occupation, are linked to the new states. In other words, the current Spanish state does not have any link with Maya and Inca civilisations, whereas states such as Peru, Colombia or Mexico are profoundly connected to the remains of such people. Also the objects created by the Spanish colonisers in the territories of such states may be important to their history. This linkage also applies to the shipwrecks laying in territorial waters. Therefore, the new states should be considered as the identifiable owners of the cargo on board of the shipwrecks that sailed from Latin American territories.

However there may be an inherent conflict between international salvage law and the suggested territorial provenance doctrine that this chapter suggests, since salvage law gives certain rights in the property to the finder of the artefact or shipwreck. However, salvage is an old concept of maritime laws which rewards the salvor when recovering objects from the bottom of the seas, and the 2001 UNESCO Convention does not agree with this practice. However, there is a further contentious point. According to Stamatoudi (2011) and other authors, and as proclaimed by the 1954 Hague Convention for the Protection of Cultural Property in the Event of Armed Conflict (UNESCO, 1954) cultural property is not linked to a state or nation nor to a particular territory, but it belongs to all mankind. Article 149 of UNCLOS also mentions that the cultural objects 'shall be preserved or disposed of for the benefit of mankind'. Dromgoole (2013) asserts that states need to take the interest of mankind as a whole when deciding how the material is preserved or disposed of. In the light of this argument, it could be submitted that the cultural objects that have been removed during colonialism and that have become part of the museums of former colonial powers, as in the case of the Latin American objects that are in Spanish museums, should not be returned because they exhibited there for the benefit of mankind.

The question is then if the law for returning objects on board of nationless shipwrecks depends only on *when* the objects were obtained, and not so much on *how*—i.e., colonisation.

Verifiable link

Since the terms 'state of origin' and 'identifiable owners' does not fill all the legal vacuums, the 2001 UNESCO Convention introduced the concept 'verifiable link' as an umbrella for the attribution of heritage value by a nation. This umbrella includes the state succession but is a far wider concept. Articles 6, 7, 9, 11 and 18 of the Convention mentions the term as applied to the objects in the territorial sea, exclusive zone and continental shelf, and the Area. Article 6 highlights the importance of bilateral, regional or multilateral agreements inviting States with a verifiable link.

> Article 6. 2. The Parties to such bilateral, regional or other multilateral agreements may invite States with a verifiable link, especially a cultural, historical or archaeological link, to the underwater cultural heritage concerned to join such agreements.

As O'Keefe (2002: 70) states, the older the wreck the less the change of establishing a link, especially when States as currently constituted did not exist. The addition of the words 'especially a cultural, historical or archaeological link', according to the author, can be explained as the sum total of all the possible connecting factors. However, the complexity is larger in the case that this chapter is referring to: where the link is to a site which is now part of a modern State.

Dromgoole (2013) develops the term and emphasises the difference between states of 'origin' and 'linked' states, the latter one coming from the Council of Europe's 1985 draft European Convention which refers to states having a 'particular interest'. Introducing the term 'verifiable link' the 2001 UNESCO Convention reflected the historical and political realities of more than one state having a verifiable link to a particular site. In the *Mercedes* or the *San Jose* cases illustrate, and as it has been argued in the previous sections, the notion of 'origin' may be controversial, but both Spain and Peru can establish a verifiable link to both the shipwreck and the cargo (Dromgoole, 2013). This would assure a multi-level protection of underwater cultural heritage (Scovazzi, 2002) which emphasises precisely the importance of the protection as opposed to the importance of the ownership. In addition, the introduction of the sentence 'States with a verifiable link, especially [...]' opens the door to a state to argue that it has a qualifying and verifiable 'link' that is something other than cultural, historical or archaeological. In our cases, this link could be a 'territorial' link to the archaeological site or object.

These developments addressed in the 2001 UNESCO Convention have not influenced in admiralty courts so in both cases—the *Mercedes* and the *San José*—any verifiable link have been bypassed. Maybe, because as Maarleveld (2009) states, the concept of 'verifiable link' is introduced in order to cater for the involvement of others—particularly states with strong feelings of identification. The admiralty courts' duty is, on the contrary, granting exclusive rights.

Ethical dilemmas: identity

During the process of decolonisation, restoration of dispersed cultural property was essential to reconstruct historical memories and national identities: a change of state sovereignty over a territory affects both tangible and intangible cultural heritage. Jakubowski (2015), in his study on the relationship between identity and heritage, and on the issue of responsibility in state succession, explains that heritage is a vehicle of collective memory and identity, and that it plays a fundamental role in the assertion of rights. However, in the Latin American case, independent states cannot separate the influences of indigenous ancient civilisation from those deriving from the Spanish domination which, over centuries, had shaped their language, culture and historical memories. The national identity of Latin American states cannot be derived only from the indigenous civilisations that existed before the arrival of the Spanish. This leads us to the debate over antiquities acquired by western museums during colonisation and whether these should be returned to their original territory, a controversy that has been discussed widely; although this topic will not be analysed in any depth, some considerations will be drawn.

Repatriation of objects taken from indigenous groups during times of colonialism is a controversial issue that is addressed by a complex web of legal and ethical sources. Some authors address claims over physical 'repatriation' of cultural treasure as a means of reconstructing national identity and collective memory (Jakubowski, 2015). Renfrew and Bahn (2008: 56) illustrate the topic with some well-known examples: the Elgin Marbles in the British Museum; the Nefertiti bust in the Neues Museum in Berlin; and the Venus de Milo in the Louvre. Chechi (2008) supports the idea that the full political emancipation of former colonies very much depends on the repatriation of the materials which are of fundamental spiritual and cultural value to them. Return of cultural objects is affected mainly by agreement between the parties, according to the 1970 UNESCO Convention on the Means of Prohibiting and Preventing the Illicit Import, Export and Transfer of Ownership of Cultural Property (UNESCO, 1970). In 2008, Spain returned by agreement 500 pre-Colombian cultural objects to Ecuador (Stapley-Brown, 2016). Even so, the collection of the Museo de America in Madrid comprises more than 25,000 objects, mostly pre-Columbian. A claim over other artefacts in the collection has not been made so far by any of the other South American states. This may be so because those objects were not 'illegally exported' as they belonged to the Spanish Kingdom, but also there are other obstacles to restitution such as evidence or origin or financial and political weaknesses for Latin American countries. Hence, handing over culturally important objects is usually seen in terms of a gift. However, it is important to not overlook these cases where the law contemporaneous to the removal of cultural materials did not regard such taking as illegal (Chechi, 2014). Focusing only on the legality of the original acquisition does not pay tribute to the cultural significance of the object. However, these claims for the return of cultural heritage raise an interesting debate on the cargo being 'cultural and historic heritage' that nations would like to recover as part of their history. However, some of these are not cultural objects but items with a value in the market; therefore, they are claimed not only for their cultural importance, but also for their economic worth. Are gold coins considered historic objects? They may be archaeological objects, but are they *cultural* objects? Is a claim to coins, for instance, the same as with objects of veneration? What are the limits to claiming certain objects?

In the manifest of the *San José*, its cargo was registered as not only over 5.5 million pesos but also as lamps, diadems and chandeliers (Alarcon, 2015). It is also known that highly valuable objects, such as gold and silver coins and jewellery, were also on board. Also documented are precious stones, cannons, spices and fabrics. It may be argued that the lamps, diadems and chandeliers, as well as fabrics are part of the cultural identity of the civilisation that made them. The quandary is if the pesos as well as the gold and silver coins are part of the cultural identity of a community, this is, if they are cultural heritage. There are two definitions of underwater cultural heritage / cultural property relevant in this regard. Article 1 of the 2001 UNESCO Convention states:

> 1. (a) 'Underwater cultural heritage' means all traces of human existence having a cultural, historical or archaeological character which have been partially or totally under water, periodically or continuously, for at least 100 years such as: (ii) vessels, aircraft, other vehicles or any part thereof, their cargo or other contents, together with their archaeological and natural context; [...]

As a consequence, for the 2001 UNESCO Convention, if the objects of cultural, historical or archaeological character have been under water for more than 100 years, they are cultural objects. This includes coins. On the other hand, Article 1 of the 1970 UNESCO Convention defines cultural property as:

> [...] property which, on religious or secular grounds, is specifically designated by each State as being of importance for archaeology, prehistory, history, literature, art or science and which belongs to the following categories: [...] (e) antiquities more than one hundred years old, such as inscriptions, coins and engraved seals; [...]

The Convention includes coins as cultural property of a country. Therefore, and on this basis, everything on board the *Mercedes* and the *San José* is cultural property and should be returned to its country of origin. However, the 1970 UNESCO Convention is not retroactive and cannot be applied.

UNESCO offers states a way to negotiate restitutions of objects removed during colonialism with the Intergovernmental Committee for Promoting the Return of Cultural Property to its Countries of Origin or its Restitution in case of Illicit Appropriation (ICPRCP).[6] This intergovernmental body has advisory role, providing a framework for discussion and negotiation. It facilitates bilateral negotiations promoting exchanges of cultural property. However, its recommendations concerning inter-State disputes are not legally binding. It is just simply a matter of ethics deciding what is its country of origin and which state is its identifiable owner. Countries should act in an *opinio juris sive necessitatis* bases and believe that they are legally bound to return items and recognise claims over shipwrecks and artefacts found on these shipwrecks. State practice should include specific tangible actions by states of returning artefacts or shipwrecks. and not only return of certain items of cultural property as that only demonstrates state practice recognising specific types of cultural property to be returned.

Proposal: agreements

Nationless shipwrecks and the return of cultural objects that are found on board of those shipwrecks is a complicated issue. The colonising countries may see these objects as legally acquired—because of history or because they legally bought them. In addition, returning some objects to some countries may lead to new claims for returning all objects from other countries. It is a complicated balance for both sides. In the case of illegal acquired cultural objects such as theft or illegal purchases the issue seems more straightforward. However, in the case of cargo proceeding from territories that were colonised and belonged to a different nation, the ethical controversies challenge the law.

Shipwrecks loaded with valuable and cultural items are often a scene of several actors for just one good. Ambiguous wording of laws and concepts such as 'identifiable owner' and 'state of origin, archaeological or historic origin' attract claims of diverse consideration. However, the introduction of the concept 'verifiable link' by the 2001 UNESCO Convention opens the possibility for those communities that were colonised, the ones that do not exist today, or to those states whose territory belongs to a different, new state. In addition, it overcomes the controversy of the term 'states' as applied to new communities that do not exist today. In this line and developing the concept, this chapter defends the term 'territorial provenance' as a link applicable to sunken cultural objects which are involved in state succession.

Returning these objects should be studied in a case-by-case basis. Some objects may be amicable returned, some by force of law and some may be returned as a perpetual loan. However, other options could be of benefit for all parties such as temporary exhibitions or temporary loans. In addition, with new technologies there may be other possibilities: digitalising the collections make the information accessible to a wider public. In addition, virtual accesses to the pieces or virtual exhibitions that can be created by common projects between the countries could transport users to museums that could be far apart. Virtual tours, on-screen maps, navigating through the museum, videos, clips, 360 scans or 3D images are all tools that could make the collection available not only to the countries with a link to the objects but to every user. This would mean that countries having an interest on an object kept in other countries could install in their museums touch-screens, televisions or computers showing those objects so the visitor can 'virtually' visit the pieces. Returning cultural objects does not need to stick to the debate of which country is the owner of the object. If cultural heritage has to be shared and enjoyed by all, that should be the main aim of states and museums. If the discourse is about attracting visitors, the alternatives to owning and showing the object are many. However, it is necessary to open new alternatives that could benefit all parties without sticking to old routines.

Conclusions

This chapter has explored the issue of state succession applied to ownership of underwater cultural heritage. The case of the Latin American territories as former colonies of the Spanish Kingdom is the example used to investigate all the complexities that shipwreck claims present regarding once colonised nations. First, the chapter summed up some issues in pairs, such as location/ownership, private/state vessels and cargo/shipwreck. This established the material for the next section—state succession applied to underwater cultural heritage—where the chapter explored two controversial terms, namely, state of origin and identifiable owner. In this regard, it has been established that the indigenous communities should be taken on consideration for claims of their cultural treasures. In the last section, the chapter addressed the issue of the return of cultural treasures applied to colonised countries. Although the issue is resolved mostly by cultural diplomacy, meaning any kind of cultural exchange and co-operation between states, there are still some legal vacuums that complicate the question. The importance of cultural heritage arises not only because of its national interest, but also because it is a universal, collective and individual one.

It seems that the land debate is settled in legal terms, but underwater cultural heritage offers a whole new perspective full of controversy. *Nationless shipwrecks*, as applied to those from countries which have changed shape and consideration due to state succession, are still a source of legal complication. However, the postcolonial debate in archaeology and heritage studies is essential to provide the recognition of the past, since heritage provides the material that enables one to connect with the past (De Jong and Rowlands, 2008; Ferris et al., 2014). The focus on the lived experience of colonised and coloniser is having a large influence on contemporary archaeological theory and practice. It is through heritage that we define ourselves and recognise others. Cultural diversity is the common heritage of humanity and it is through heritage discourses of restitution, restoration and material preservation that colonised communities can turn into processes of reconciliation and the maintenance of cultural diversity. In nationless shipwrecks this discourse is interrupted by the system of salvage law that does not recognises the value of the wreck as an object of heritage but as property.

Shipwrecks and cargo ownership is a complex issue that has still not been resolved in the legal instruments protecting underwater cultural heritage. Although ancient shipwrecks belong to the nation in whose territorial water it lies, regardless of its origin, elsewhere, international admiralty law recognises certain rights to salvors over the shipwreck and it is where the conflicts arise. However, these rights to salvors over the shipwreck are based on an 'ownership' tradition over the wreck rather than on the approach of awarding the heritage which a value of heritage. Heritage is a concept intrinsically linked to the concept of identity and an object of underwater cultural heritage can become an evocative symbol of identification that acts as a trigger for emotions and narratives, creating a link between the community and the object. All the common criteria for the significance of the heritage stated in the Sofia Charter (1996) of ICOMOS and the 2001 UNESCO Convention (UNESCO, 2001): rare aspects, yield information, demonstrating principal characteristics of a class, high degree of achievement, association to a cultural group or the life or works of persons, are based on values. However, the tradition of salvage legislation insists in the concept of wreck ownership and bypasses the value of the wreck as heritage. However, the issue is not only the salvage of these objects but the posterior distribution of the cargo between nations with a possible link or the return of some objects to their territory of origin. The issue will still be complicated as long as the identity sensitivity will be the reason for claiming a cultural object.

This chapter has examined the concept of identity applied to colonised countries. However, identity is an intrinsic value which all underwater cultural heritage has. The issue of the South China Seas re-visit this concept: underwater cultural heritage is used for States and policy makers to manipulate and create a history that the community can be part of.

Notes

1 Reproduced from Perez-Alvaro, E. (2018). Nationless shipwrecks: state succession applied to underwater cultural heritage. In Berg, S. S. and Fiedler, E. *Cultural Heritage: Perspectives, Challenges and Future Directions*. Nova Science. Copyright © 2018, published by Nova Science. All rights reserved.

2 *Kingdom of Spain Reply to Claimant Republic of Peru Response to Spain's Motion to dismiss or for Summary Judgment*, 26 January 2009, p. 8.
3 United Nations. Department of Economic and Social Affairs. Division for Social Policy and Development. Secretariat of the Permanent Forum on Indigenous Issues. Workshop on Data Collection and Disaggregation for Indigenous Peoples. (New York, 19–21 January 2004). Available at: https://www.un.org/development/desa/dspd/ (accessed 3 December 2016).
4 Vienna Convention on Succession of States in respect of Treaties of 23 August 1978.
5 See, for instance, the following Peace Treaties:
Venezuela:
http://embajadadevenezuela.es/ (accessed 9 November 2017).
http://proteo2.sre.gob.mx/tratados/ARCHIVOS/ESPANA-PAZ%20Y%20AMISTAD.pdf (accessed 5 December 2016).
6 Intergovernmental Committee for Promoting the Return of Cultural Property to its Countries of Origin or its Restitution in case of Illicit Appropriation (ICPRCP). Available at: http://portal.unesco.org/culture/en/ev.php-URL_ID=35283&URL_DO=DO_TOPIC&URL_SECTION=201.html (accessed 8 January 2017).

Bibliography

Alarcon, J. M. (2015). Hundido con el oro de la 'Santa Cruzada'. *El Mundo, Cronica*. 13 December 2015.
Aznar-Gómez, M. J. (2010). Treasure hunters, sunken state vessels and the 2001 UNESCO convention on the protection of underwater cultural heritage. *International Journal of Marine and Coastal Law* 25(2): 209–236.
BBC (2015). ¿A quién le pertenecen los tesoros del galeón San José hallado en Colombia? [online]. *BBC, Mundo*. 7 December 2015. Available at: www.bbc.com/mundo/noticias/2015/12/151207_colombia_galeon_san_jose_patrimonio_subacuatico_colombia_amv (3 November 2017).
Boesten, E. (2002). *Archaeological and/or Historic Valuable Shipwreck in International Waters: Public International Law and What It Offers*. The Hague: Asser Press.
Chechi, A. (2008). The return of cultural objects removed in times of colonial domination and international law: the case of the Venus of Cyrene. *Italian Yearbook of International Law* 18(1): 159–181.
Chechi, A. (2014). *The Settlement of International Cultural Heritage Disputes*. Oxford: Oxford University Press.
De Jong, F. and Rowlands, M. (2008). Postconflict heritage. *Journal of Material Culture: Special Issue on Postconflict Heritage* 13(2): 500–518.
Derout, A. (1993). *La protection des biens culturels en droit communautaire*. Rennes: Editions Apogée.
Dromgoole, S. (2013). *Underwater Cultural Heritage and International Law*. (Vol. 101). Cambridge: Cambridge University Press.
Drye, W. (2015). Battle begins over world's richest shipwreck. [online]. *National Geographic*. 18 December 2015. Available at: http://news.nationalgeographic.com/2015/12/151218-san-jose-shipwreck-treasure-colombia-archaeology/.
Ferris, N., Harrison, R. and Wilcox, M. V. (eds.) (2014). *Rethinking Colonial Pasts through Archaeology*. Oxford: Oxford University Press.

Flores, F. (2003). Latin America: self-determination, minorities, indigenous people, stability of borders and problems of secession. In Dahlitz, J. (ed.), *Secession and International Law: Conflict Avoidance–Regional Appraisals*. New York: United Nations Publications: 227–242.

Greenfield, J. (1996). *The Return of Cultural Treasures*. Cambridge: Cambridge University Press.

Higgins, R. (2003). Self-determination and secession. In Dahlitz, J. (ed.), *Secession and International Law: Conflict Avoidance–Regional Appraisals*. New York: United Nations Publications: 21–38.

Jakubowski, A. (2014). Territoriality and state succession in cultural heritage. *International Journal of Cultural Property* 21(4): 375–396.

Jakubowski, A. (2015). *State Succession in Cultural Property*. Oxford: Oxford University Press.

Maarleveld, T. J. (2009). Drama, place and verifiable link: underwater cultural heritage, present experience and contention. In Turgeon, L. (ed.), *Spirit of Place: Between Tangible and Intangible Heritage*. Québec: Presses de l'Université Laval: 97–108.

Menon, P. K. (1991). *The Succession of States in Respect to Treaties, State Property, Archives, and Debts*. The Hague: Edwin Mellen Press.

Mur, R. (2015). Aparece el barco del Tesoro mas buscado del Caribe. *La Vanguardia*. 6 December 2015.

O'Connell, D. P. (1956). *The Law of State Succession*. Cambridge: Cambridge University Press.

O'Keefe, P. J. (2002). *Shipwrecked Heritage: A Commentary on the UNESCO Convention on Underwater Cultural Heritage*. Leicester: Institute of Art and Law.

Perez-Alvaro, E. (2014). Shipwrecks as watery graves: cultural attitudes, legal approach and ethical implications. In Jaste Ruiz, J. and Bou Franch, V. (eds.), *Derecho del Mar y Sostenibilidad Ambiental en el Mediterráneo*. Valencia: Tirant Lo-Blanch: 137–148.

Renfrew, C. and Bahn, P. (2008). *Archaeology: Theories, Methods and Practice*. London: Thames & Hudson.

Scovazzi, T. (2002). Convention on the protection of underwater cultural heritage. *Environmental Policy and Law* 32(3–4): 152–157.

Shearing, H. (2016). War at sea over £12bn in sunken Spanish treasure. *Sunday Times*. 19 June 2016. Available at: www.thetimes.co.uk/article/war-at-sea-over-12bn-in-sunken-spanish-treasure-kwjspbkgh.

Sofia Charter (1996). Charter on the protection and management of underwater cultural heritage. *ICOMOS*. Available at: www.international.icomos.org/charters/underwater_e.pdf (15 December 2017).

Stamatoudi, I. A. (2011). *Cultural Property Law and Restitution: A Commentary to International Conventions and European Union Law*. Cheltenham: Edward Elgar.

Stapley-Brown, V. (2016). More than 500 cultural objects returned to Ecuador. [online]. *The Art Newspaper*. Available at: http://theartnewspaper.com/news/news/more-than-500-cultural-objects-returned-to-ecuador/ (1 January 2019).

Triay, C. Z. (2014). Who is entitled to a shipwreck located in international waters? A contest for the spoils between salvors, the original owners, legitimate heirs, state governments and the historic preservationists. Doctoral dissertation, University of Cape Town.

UNCLOS (1982). United Nations Convention on the Law of the Sea. UN Doc. A/CONF. 62/122.

UNESCO (1954). Convention for the Protection of Cultural Property in the Event of Armed Conflict (3 August 2017).

UNESCO (1970). Convention on the Means on Prohibiting and Preventing the Illicit Import, Export and Transfer of Ownership of Cultural Property. Available at: www.unesco.org/new/en/culture/themes/illicit-trafficking-of-cultural-property/1970-convention/ (3 August 2017).

UNESCO (2001). Convention on the Protection of the Underwater Cultural Heritage. Available at: www.unesco.org/new/en/culture/themes/underwater-cultural-heritage/2001-convention/official-text/ (3 August 2017).

Vigni, P. (2012). Historic shipwrecks and the limits of the flag state exclusive rights. In Borelli, S. and Lenzerini, F. (eds.), *Cultural Heritage, Cultural Rights, Cultural Diversity: New Developments in International Law* (Vol. 4). Leiden: Martinus Nijhoff: 279–299.

Watters, D. R. (1983). The law of the sea treaty and underwater cultural resources. *American Antiquity* 48(4): 808–816.

Werner, D. (2013). Piracy in the courtroom: how to salvage $500 million in sunken treasure without making a cent. *University of Miami Law Review* 67(105): 1005–1038.

9 Human rights
Migrant shipwrecks

In history, there have been large movements of people for many reasons, such as climate change, conquest, slavery, demographic growth, or the formation of new states. This migration has either been forced or voluntary. Most of those movements have crossed continents and some of them have crossed the sea. Some of the vessels used for these movements have sunk, and there is still news today of sunken boats that have dead migrants on board. In fact, the trade of refugees is considered to be the modern-day slave trade. Population movements before 1945 were mainly, although not only, due to colonialism, slavery, and war refugees. These three movements are still happening: colonialism in the shape of domination and the exploitation of native people or of genocide (Castle and Miller, 2003), slavery in its modern form of women and children sexual exploitation, and war refugees, which is a problem that the world is facing more than ever.

For the benefit of the argument, this chapter will look at refugees' travels by boat as a continuation of the slavery middle passage. Although this approach may seem too ambitious, the abusive treatment of refugees in overcrowded dinghies, the human degradation on the journeys, the race and ethnicity of the victims, and the interconnection of the modern trade with the world economy are the main reasons for this inevitable comparison. There are, however, many other reasons, such as the high mortality of these population movements due to illness and shipwrecks (Bravo, 2007), the sea travel of the migrants to find a new country, and the human and legal neglect of the immigrants if they do reach land. Some of these refugees are part of a network of illegal smuggling or are forced to work once they arrive on land. In fact, 'the Coolie Trade' was, and seems to still be today, a type of slave trade Chinese to the American continent disguised as immigration movements. At the end of the 19th century, 300 Chinese were suffocated on board a ship from China to Peru when transported in slave-like conditions (Menefee, 2003) and in the same conditions in September 1991, American authorities intercepted a vessel carrying illegal Chinese immigrants (Menefee, 2000). If not intercepted, the immigrants would arrive to a life controlled by the Chinese tongs and 'snakeheads' who have sponsored their immigration, working for minimum wage and being threatened continuously to pay their debts (Menefee, 2000). According to the Global Slavery Index[1] in 2016, an estimated 24.9 million men, women, and children were living in modern slavery in Asia and the Pacific. The Asia and the Pacific region had the highest number of victims across all forms of modern slavery, accounting for 73 percent of victims of forced sexual exploitation, 68 percent of those forced to work by state authorities, 64 percent of those in forced labour exploitation, and 42 percent of all those in forced marriages. With some of the victims fleeing their countries the history of old and modern slavery and migration movements get blurred. However, slavery in the trans-Atlantic slave trade was legally recognised and it was, in somehow, controlled. However, trafficker-owners of the modern system dominate their victim by asserting physical control and threatening violence or even death, as well as asserting psychological control through passport and immigrant supervision, or threatening deportation or substitution with other victims.

What is more important for the development of this chapter is the travel by sea that both slaves and refugees have had to endure in order to reach the new land. Although most of those vessels and sunken boats do not have an especial cultural, historical or archaeological importance to be preserved as underwater cultural heritage, the process of recognising it as heritage is a memory-making activity that may serve as an example for the future, as it is today slave shipwrecks. As a consequence, this chapter explores not only slave and refugee shipwrecks that have been underwater for more than 100 years, but also vessels that still sink today. This will create a bridge that will let us explore the history of these human movements by sea, examining the ethics behind this human trafficking and its place within the underwater cultural heritage preservation debate, also examining the slaves and refugees' belongings on board of the vessels carrying them. To conclude, this study will analyse the responsibility that the international community has, not only with the refugees that reach land—out of our scope—but with the human remains after those boats have sunk.

Introduction

Forced population movements have always happened. In fact, as early as 740 BC, ten legendary tribes were expelled from the land of ancient Israel by Assyrian rulers. Even before that, there were possibly displacements due to climate changes. After that, there has been innumerable human movements of people who have left their land, by force or by choice, because of persecution, economic reasons, wars, hope of a better life, or who had been forced into slavery or sexual exploitation (Chalabi, 2013).

This chapter will be focusing on the displacement of people travelling by sea. The first of those documented forced displacements by sea happened after the Edict of Fontainebleu, 1685, when Louis XIV of France persecuted the Protestant Huguenots. Around 200,000 people fled their homes, a quarter of them moved to England by boat. Some years after, in 1881, after the assassination of Tsar Alexander II, more than two million Jews escaped to the UK, the United States, and the rest of Europe after a wave of anti-Jewish sentiment in Russia (Chalabi, 2013). Refugees were fleeing in order to save themselves, but others were deliberately targeted or 'transferred' by the state, as in the case of the slave trade. Between 1500 and 1860, European ships transported captive Africans from Europe to the Americas on what has been called the 'middle passage'. It has been suggested that more than 11 million slaves were carried, 9.6 million of which survived the middle passage (Webster, 2007). This slave trade was a driving force of the Industrial Revolution, as it resulted in both colonial expansion and investments in navigational technology (Fisher, 2007). In 1806, Britain abolished the slave trade. Before that, Denmark had been the first country to abolish it and had enacted an edict to this effect in 1803 (Webster, 2008a). From the 1400s until 1888, when Brazil ended its slave trade (the last country to do so), 9.5 million Africans were shipped from Africa (Bravo, 2007). The slaves were destined for all kind of labour, such as farming, candle making, ship-building, or furniture making.

Although this Atlantic Slave Trade was abolished in the 19th Century, there was another maritime slave trade operating out of Africa: the 'Red Sea and Indian Ocean Slave Trade', which survived well into the 20th Century (Menefee, 2003). In fact, slaves from Ethiopia and the Sudan have been shipped as late as 1960. In the late 19th and early 20th centuries a new kind of slavery arose: white women slavery. Women from Europe and the United States became sex workers as a result of economic, social, and cultural vulnerabilities. This has been called 'migratory prostitution', as organised networks targeted women to work in South America, the Middle East, and Asia (Bravo, 2007).

In the twentieth century, refugees were still leaving their countries. In 1972, more than 90,000 Asians were expelled from Uganda; half of them fled to the UK and some of them to Canada. Furthermore, the Balkans conflict forced 2.7 million to flee, and thousands of them travelled to the United States (Chalabi, 2013). History's refugees continue. Since 2011, thousands of Syrians have become refugees travelling by boat to Europe. An estimated 11 million Syrians have fled their homes, and about one million have requested asylum in Europe (United Nations High Commissioner for Refugees, 2016). Most of them use dinghies and plastic boats to cross the seas. Additionally, in the late 1980s, there was a growing number of victims being enslaved by modern-day traffickers: children sold by their parents, men, woman, and children were subjected to sexual or other exploitation schemes that offered employment abroad. It has been calculated that 27 million individuals are held in some form of involuntary servitude, and that the trade in humans is a $5 to $7 billion industry (Bravo, 2007). Many of these forced displacements have happened and still happen across the seas. Figure 9.1 shows an artwork by Syrian artist Issam Kourbaj Fitz, an installation of 1,000 miniature boats made from recycled bicycle mudguards, jam-packed

Figure 9.1 'Dark Water, Burning World 4' by Issam Kourbaj Fitz. Reproduced with permission of the author. Permission to reuse must be obtained from the rights holder.

with upright spent matches. The image serves to this chapter as a reflection about escaping Syrians, forced to flee their homeland in packed dinghies that may become shipwrecks at some point of their journey.

Issue

In the past, slave ships needed to be prepared for a slave voyage, which was expensive and complex (Slavery Museum, 2013). The middle passage has been calculated as taking 63 days (Eltis et al., 1999), and the full voyage could be completed in a year. However, a pure slave ship was not all that was required for a slaving venture. Ships travelling from Europe would be laden with trade goods to be exchanged for African slaves. The ship would look like a merchant ship, except for the open gratings or ventilation holes. They would also carry water casks, shackles, and handcuffs. From Africa, through the Atlantic and the Middle Passage, the ship would be transformed to accommodate human cargo by building a 'house', which was a temporary shelter erected on the main deck for the slaves while the ship was ready to sail, as well as the slave decks, which were where the African captives would stay during the voyage, in crowded, unsanitary, almost airless conditions (Webster, 2008a). Slaves could be men, women or children, who, after being captured, were shackled together and transported in dehumanising conditions (Slavery Museum, 2013). Some of them died before being loaded (Slavery Museum, 2013). The alterations to the ship were carried out in Africa and dismantled upon arrival in the Americas: the slave ships would then be transformed to carry colonial products when they returned from the Americas to Europe (Webster, 2007). In fact, slave wreckage sites are not very helpful to specifically understand the issue of slave trading, since the most important timber fittings of slave ships (*barricado*) were unlikely to survive, as they were built to be temporary. In addition, at each part of this triangular route, the ship would be transformed to accommodate the various cargo that would be loaded onto it, including the slaves. As a result, the ship would change depending on the leg of the trip.

Despite the importance of the subject, the number of excavated shipwrecks that are related to slavery is undeniably small (Webster, 2008a). However, there are some wrecks that have been researched; some of them have even been excavated, but none of them have been found with human remains of slaves on board. The *Henrietta Marie* was a London-based slaver, lost off Florida in 1700, and discovered accidentally by a commercial salvage company, Treasure Salvors Inc, in 1972. The artefacts recovered have helped to create an idea of the practices of the slave trade, since it is the most complete slave ship discovered and has been fully identified and investigated (Fisher, 2007). These artefacts include shackles and elephant ivory for trading. It sunk during the course of the slave trade, but no slaves were on board (Fisher, 2007). The *Fredensborg* was a ship that belonged to the Danish West-India Guinea Company and sank in 1768 in southern Norway. Every life on board was saved. The imprints of shackles have been found (Webster, 2008b). Another slave ship was the *James Matthews* a Portuguese-owned slaver, captured by the Royal Navy after the suppression of slave shipping, registered in London for trading purposes and grounded in a storm close to the coast of Western Australia. It was well preserved with more than 800 artefacts recovered, although none related to its slave-trading past. The *Adelaide* ran aground after leaving slaves in Haiti. Human remains were found, but none from slaves (Webster, 2008b). Finally, the *Guerrero*, still not found, was in transit to Cuba with more than 500 slaves on board (Eltis et al., 1999). Of those 500, 41 perished on board.

The typology of slave shipwrecks was the consequence of a full voyage with different goals. In any case, the slaves were an economic resource for the sellers, so it seems logical to assume that those sellers would have a special interest in having the slaves delivered, and having the ship arrive safely at its destination. However, in the case of refugee ships today, the immigrants pay to travel, and it is logic to think that the smugglers who organise these trips do not gain or lose anything if the ship does not arrive at its destination. To save costs, it can be assumed that the smugglers use cheap and basic watercraft, such as migrants' boats, which are mainly rubber boats or dinghies. In fact, increasing amounts of shipwrecks happening off the coasts of European countries are due to the use of overcrowded, small, and poor-quality plastic or rubber boats. The Smithsonian National Museum of American History shows how also in the 19th century, immigrants arrived in the United States in waves. On the opposite to today's conditions, immigrants were crossing the Atlantic and Pacific by steamships. Although steamship companies had designed first-class accommodation for high society passengers, immigrants were also allowed to travel by steamship. In fact, the immigrant trade was their main source of income. Immigrants would travel with their belongings, some of them in trunks, and in most cases, they would have guaranteed citizenship on arrival. However, immigrants were this welcome in the country until 1882 when competition for jobs increased and the Congress signed the first federal law to restrict immigration on a racial or ethnic basis.[2] These and other laws created the illegal immigration.

Some have argued that today's victim-slaves or refugees play an active role in their own victimisation, as they pay for their own transport. As a consequence, transporting the 'merchandise' is easier and cheaper than it was during trans-Atlantic slavery. In addition, the loss of this 'merchandise' has no consequence on their traders. During the trans-Atlantic slave trade, the trader would pay for the voyages, the maintaining and operating of the ship, the employment and feeding of a crew of sailors, the native procurers, the feeding and maintenance of the merchandise, as well as risking a loss from revolts and high mortality rates. The greatest expense for traders in modern trafficking, however, is just the corruption costs.

State of knowledge

Although Denmark was the first country to abolish the slave trade in 1803, slavery operating out of Africa was not abolished until the end of the 20th century; in fact, some would say that it has not yet been completely eradicated. However, it does seem that, after World War I, there were steps towards an official change on slavery. The 1919 Convention of St. Germain-en-Laye stated that parties would 'endeavour to secure the complete suppression of slavery in all its forms and of the slave-trade by land and sea' (St. Germain-en-Laye Convention, 1919).

The law of the sea also dealt with slave trade. In 1982, the United Nations Convention on the Law of the Sea (UNCLOS, 1982) tried to regulate the issue in two articles, 99 and 110:

Article 99. Prohibition of the transport of slaves
Every State shall take effective measures to prevent and punish the transport of slaves in ships authorized to fly its flag and to prevent the unlawful use of its flag for that purpose. Any slave taking refuge on board any ship, whatever its flag, shall *ipso facto* be free.

Slave ships would fly the flags of the nation trading them. Under the law of the flag, a ship has the nationality of the country whose flag it is entitled to fly, which is called the flag state. UNCLOS recognises that the flag state has exclusive jurisdiction over its vessels on the high seas, as well as responsibilities, such as ensuring that its ships comply with domestic and international regulations (Bennett, 2012). In the case of slave ships, their flag state was well assigned, and the ownership and research of the shipwreck can be understood as their flag state's responsibility.

The case of refugees' ships may prove to be more difficult. Most of the time, refugees do not travel with passports or identity papers, becoming deprived of full personhood. This is also a strategy for them to not be returned to their country of origin, since with no proof of identity, they cannot be returned anywhere. In fact, the Convention Relating to the Status of Stateless Persons (1954) states:

> *Article 1. Definition of the term 'stateless person'*
> 1. For the purpose of this Convention, the term 'stateless person' means a person who is not considered as a national by any State under the operation of its law.

> *Article 12. Personal status*
> 1. The personal status of a stateless person shall be governed by the law of the country of his domicile or, if he has no domicile, by the law of the country of his residence.

Furthermore, the dinghies or plastic boats do not fly under any flag. They are ships with no nationality at all; stateless and flagless. This means that no state can exercise control over them or provide them with protection: they may be stateless because they have lost their nationality or because they have never registered with any state, which is the case of the dinghies. Loewenfeld (1941) has compared a stateless person, such as a refugee, to a vessel on the open sea that is sailing under no flag. The question of which legal authority stateless refugees and vessels belong to, has still not been solved.

UNCLOS does not recognise stateless vessels as a universal crime. However, their status is still undefined, and consequently, the refugees' dinghies have no protection and are not the responsibility of any state. This complicates their ownership once they have sunk. However, although UNCLOS does not explicitly recognise that other states can exercise control over the flagless ship, Article 110 states that other vessels have the right to visit them:

> *Article 110. Right of visit*
> 1. Except where acts of interference derive from powers conferred by treaty, a warship which encounters on the high seas a foreign ship, other than a ship entitled to complete immunity in accordance with articles 95 and 96, is not justified in boarding it unless there is reasonable ground for suspecting that: [...]

(b) the ship is engaged in the slave trade; [...]
(d) the ship is without nationality; [...]

As a consequence, other boats can board ships without nationality but does not mean that refugee boats are illegal just because they do not navigate under a flag. However, they are inside a legal vacuum that complicates their protection, both while navigating and after they have sunk.

The 2001 UNESCO Convention for the Protection of the Underwater Cultural Heritage does not refer to 'flagless shipwrecks' (UNESCO, 2001). However, it states in Article 6.2:

> The Parties to such bilateral, regional or other multilateral agreements may invite States with a verifiable link, especially a cultural, historical or archaeological link, to the underwater cultural heritage concerned to join such agreements.

According to this article, even flagless shipwrecks could be under the protection of the 2001 UNESCO Convention. The state in whose waters the flagless shipwreck lies may invite a state with a cultural, historical, or archaeological link to the discovery. In the case of refugee shipwrecks, that link could be the nationality of those on board, or the port of origin. These shipwrecks would be the responsibility of the State in whose waters lie but could find an agreement with a country with a link for their memorialisation, as it will be studied in the proposal of this chapter.

Ethical dilemmas: human rights

Migration shipwrecks present several ethical human rights dilemmas. Slavery and refugees directly appeal to human rights conventions and agreements. Ships and shipwrecks are also affected by them.

Human remains

According to Eltis et al. (1999), the Transatlantic Trade Database has revealed that 800 vessels transporting slaves were lost at sea, 183 of which were lost while slaving or after embarkation. However, none of the wrecks that were discovered were carrying slaves when they sunk.

When claiming shipwrecks containing human remains, the main problem is one that effects shipwrecks in general: the issue of mobility. While on land, the limits of nations' boundaries offer security and protection. However, the case of the voyage into slavery was a specific and shared experience in the lives of both slaves and European crews, which is an interesting case study for us (Webster, 2008a). The possible solution for the preservation and respect of their remains that this chapter proposes is appealing to the states of the European crew, in order to research and protect both the shipwrecks and the human remains of the slaves. In the case of refugee shipwrecks, this may be more complicated. As said, the sunken boats are not of any archaeological, cultural or historical value, and so their study, analysis, and excavation may not be worth it. In most cases the shipwreck will not even exist, since the material of the dinghies is so perishable. The human remains, however, may still exist after the shipwreck, or they may be washed ashore. The respect given to those remains depends only on the waters where the shipwrecks lie, or the coasts where the human remains are washed to. As an example, Europe and Africa are separated by 7.7 nautical miles at the Gibraltar strait's narrowest point. That means that those waters are either Spain's territorial waters or Morocco's. Refugees often cross this strait, with hundreds of shipwrecks occurring every year. The issue is whether these countries, which may not be either responsible or contribute to these displacements, should ensure the respect and the preservation of the human remains of refugees on board of these shipwrecks and which lie in their waters.

Most bodies are lost at sea but many are washed ashore. Some others are recovered (Hernandez and Stylianou, 2016). Of the ones that are washed ashore or recovered, the identification process may be difficult, and in some cases, no one is able to identify the bodies. In Turkey, Greece, and Italy, the bodies are photographed, examined, and a DNA sample is taken. However, in the Greek islands, because of a lack of laboratories, migrants are often buried without being registered (Hernandez and Stylianou, 2016). Once the information is gathered, it goes into a folder with a case number assigned to it. That number will become that migrant's new ID on their grave. Those shipwrecks and their sites ashore could be declared submerged cemeteries.

Refugee shipwrecks rescue and disembark

Dealing with refugees travelling by sea is an issue that has been occurring for many years. The rescue of distressed refugees who have suffered a shipwreck and their consequent claims for asylum are under the framework of different international agreements, such as the 1982 Convention (UNCLOS, 1982), the International Convention for the Safety of Life at Sea (SOLAS), the International Convention on Search and Rescue at Sea (SAR Convention) and the Refugee Convention, which is the main legal structure dealing with the treatment of refugees (Barnes, 2004).

The first ethical dilemma that it may be found when dealing with refugee shipwrecks is the duty to rescue them, which is one of the most ancient aspects of the laws of the sea. However, complications arise because there is no provision for the disembarkation of rescued persons. Article 98 (1) of the 1982 UNCLOS Convention reads:

1. Every State shall require the master of a ship flying its flag, in so far as he can do so without serious danger to the ship, the crew or the passengers:

(a) to render assistance to any person found at sea in danger of being lost;
(b) to proceed with all possible speed to the rescue of persons in distress, if informed of their need of assistance, in so far as such action may reasonably be expected of him; [...]

However, although this obligation may have been implemented into domestic law, according to Barnes (2004), it has not been universally implemented. As a consequence, the moral reasons for assisting are often weighted by commercial reasons for refusing that assistance. In addition, it is custom for rescued persons to disembark at the next port of call, although there is not a rule for doing so. However, the next port of call may deny the disembarkation of the immigrants, which would become a problem for the rescue vessel.

Although these are the rules for the Exclusive Economic Zone and the high seas, there are not such obligations for the territorial sea, and although Barnes (2004) regards it as implicit, it remains at the discretion of the coastal state. In this regard, there are two further complications: the *right of innocent passage* and the *right of entry* into the port, which both challenge human rights obligations. According to the 1982 UNCLOS Convention, the right of innocent passage means that ships of all states enjoy the right of innocent passage through the territorial sea. However, this passage has to be continuous and expeditious, only anchoring if necessary by *force majeure* or to provide assistance to persons, ships, or aircraft in danger or distress (Article 18). However, the discussion arises in relation to the words 'innocent passage', which mean that:

Article 19.
1. Passage is innocent so long as it is not prejudicial to the peace, good order or security of the coastal State. [...]
2. Passage of a foreign ship shall be considered to be prejudicial to the peace, good order or security of the coastal State if in the territorial sea it engages in any of the following activities:
    (g) the loading or unloading of any commodity, currency or person contrary to the customs, fiscal, immigration or sanitary laws and regulations of the coastal State;

This means that bringing refugees to the coasts of a coastal state may be seen as a threat to the security of that state, or that the persons may be contrary to the immigration laws of the coastal state. As a consequence, the coastal state retains the authority to decide whether to accept refugees that have been rescued. If permission is denied, the ship will be loaded with the refugees, who will not have permission to disembark.

This brings us to the second complication: rights of entry into the port. Ports are internal waters, so they are under the sovereignty of the coastal state. Right of entry is a privilege. The only exception is the entry of vessels in distress for humanitarian reasons where entry into the port is the only course of action that might prevent an inevitable loss of life, or for urgent situations beyond the mariners control (Barnes, 2004). It can be argued that entry into the port of a coastal state of a ship carrying refugees is the only course of action preventing an inevitable loss of life. Although there may be refugees who are in very bad health, the coastal state may argue that this is not an inevitable loss of life, so the ship might have to look for another state to disembark.

However, these maritime regulations are challenged by human rights laws that state that all persons in distress at sea benefit from fundamental human rights, regardless of the geographic location, nationality, and status. Article 33.1 of the Refugee Convention 1951 reads:

> No Contracting State shall expel or return ('refouler') a refugee in any manner whatsoever to the frontiers of territories where his life or freedom would be threatened on account of his race, religion, nationality, membership of a particular social group or political opinion.

Consequently, the coastal state will be more inclined to forbid the disembarkation of people from migrant boats, in order to prevent rights of asylum and since the return of a refugee gets more complicated once the refugees are on land. However, although persons rescued by a ship come under jurisdiction of the vessel's flag-state, there is no obligation to grant them asylum, which seems contrary to this article (Barnes, 2004).

However, the 1951 Convention Relating to the Status of Refugees states:

> *Article 31. Refugees unlawfully in the country of refuge*
> 1. The Contracting States shall not impose penalties, on account of their illegal entry or presence, on refugees who, coming directly from a territory where their life or freedom was threatened in the sense of article 1, enter or are present in their territory without authorization, provided they present themselves without delay to the authorities and show good cause for their illegal entry or presence.

Also,

> *Article 32. Expulsion*
> 1. The Contracting States shall not expel a refugee lawfully in their territory save on grounds of national security or public order.

This controversy became a real case when, on the 10th of June 2018, Italy and Malta banned the landing of 629 immigrants rescued from Libya's maritime sea by the NGO's vessel Aquarius (EFE, 2018). After two days with no permission to dock in any country, the ship was offered port by the Spanish government, creating a growing undercurrent of tension among the Spanish society. The government has guaranteed refugee status to all migrants.

Neither the coastal state nor the flag-state have obligation to grant migrants asylum. However, if the migrants disembark, the state will be under obligation to not return them. As a consequence, coastal states that refuse to admit the refugees place flag states under pressure. National vessels will then think twice about rescuing refugees' shipwrecks, which leads us to the main ethical challenge: it is more appealing for a vessel, since there are more incentives, to rescue maritime property than to assist those in distress at sea, which leads to complications with States.

Cultural heritage on board the shipwrecks

This chapter has focused on the slaves and migrants, their shipwrecks, and their human remains. However, it has been documented (Agha, 2015) that refugees carry personal items with them after leaving their countries. These objects are usually symbols, or part of the identity of their country, such as necklaces, rosaries, Syrian flags, Palestinian charms, silver and wooden bracelets, clothes, flash drives with photos, or personal documents (Goldhill, 2015). When there is a shipwreck with dead bodies, these objects can either float, become attached to the body, or sink. However, if there is a chance to recover these objects, there is the opportunity to reconstruct the story of that person; identifying the body and burying them with a name, not only a number. As explained, a shipwreck is a window into a moment frozen in time. By analysing the evidence that has been found, it is possible to construct the true picture of the ship and the shipwreck. Items of clothing and personal objects can bring us into contact with people who died on board. If those objects of modern shipwrecks are kept, preserved, and analysed as cultural heritage, they will tell stories that could not be obtained otherwise.

Proposal: grave memorialization and survivor camps

Although this chapter has focused on current refugees' shipwrecks, migration by sea and shipwrecks have always happened. However, the issue has completely been forgotten in cultural heritage history. When drafting the 2001 UNESCO Convention it was discussed the possibility of including an article for protecting slave shipwrecks especially defended by African countries. However, there was not an agreement among the States and the article was finally not incorporated in the Convention The fact is that both slave and refugee shipwrecks have barely been investigated (Webster, 2008b; McGhee, 1997): archaeologists have rarely attempted to locate these wrecks, maybe for the perception of the subject as 'difficult' and preferably avoided since the history of naval battles, treasure, and sunken cities are more appealing (Webster, 2008b). Also, historic wrecks are often discovered by professional salvage companies whose targets are 'treasure ships', and who are not interested in the ship, but more in the economically valuable artefacts: the discovery of the slave shipwreck, *the Henrietta Marie,* raises the ethical issue of the wreck of a slave ship being discovered and claimed by a private company. It also renews, once more, the debate over collaboration between archaeologists and private companies.

It is out of the scope of this chapter to propose solutions to the current problem of rescuing refugees and returning them to their country. However, if this chapter can propose ideas for the shipwreck status of these refugees' dinghies and boats or the protection of the human remains of those who died on board, the underwater cultural heritage can set an example for helping to solve the problems of the 'real world'. It has often been critiqued that the protection of cultural heritage is not important compared to bigger problems in society, such as war, hunger, or crime. However, cultural heritage, and in this specific case, underwater cultural heritage, can contribute new perspectives for the real world.

First proposal: grave memorialisation

There is a nationalistic stance from countries to preserve only their war graves. However, very often, wars leave shared graves. One example of this is the wars that happened in territories of countries that did not participate in those wars. Those countries were just spectators but suffered the war and the loss of lives equally or more to those who fight them. One example is Chuuk. Japan, after declaring war on the United States in 1941, quickly completed the building of a military base in Chuuk. During the war, most Chuukese were forced to leave their homes to accommodate the Japanese military. The environment and historic sites were modified, and the military confiscated local foods. The bombing destroyed local crops and made it difficult to fish. Chuukese were forced into slave labour, with starvation and malnutrition becoming common (Jeffery, 2004): the shipwrecks and sunken cultural heritage are being recognised as sacred cultural sites associated with events of outstanding universal significance of World War II. The Chuukese's human remains and cultural history have never been recognised. Although Pacific Islanders do not need to see these sites listed in any convention (Jeffery, 2004), they need to be recognised as part of their cultural identity and respected as sacred sites. If refugees' bodies have become just a number on their grave—as explained in the case of some islands in Greece—instead of a name (Kovras and Robins, 2016) declaring them as war victims, a memorial or a symbol of recognition would give them the dignity that their families, relatives or communities are looking for. Refugees are usually running away from wars, injustices and threats and as a consequence they should be recognized as casualties of these wars and treated with the same honours as soldiers fighting those wars. However, families of dead migrants face legal, bureaucratic, and practical challenges that they have to face on their own because the deaths are at the border, not inside the limits of a frontier. This adds a strong emotional component (Kovras and Robins, 2016), as the deaths in the water border is, for the families, a difficult psychological trauma. In the same way, slave shipwrecks with human remains of slaves on board would also require a memorial, some kind of recognition for their communities to have that part of their past acknowledged.

States have been evading responsibility to refugees, adopting a passive stance, accepting them alive in some occasions, but doing nothing to recognise their bodies. Even if accepting refugees in a country can threaten security, the recognition of their trips, dangers, deaths, and burials as sacred places is not a threat; it should be seen as adequate diplomacy. States have recognised the magnitude of the slave trade and have publicly acknowledged it, through memorials, museums (e.g. the International Slavery Museum in Liverpool), and abolition acts. 'The story of transatlantic slavery is a fundamental and tragic human story that must be told, retold and never forgotten' (Slavery Museum, 2013). However, the difficulty arises when some want to forget the event rather than remember it, or when nothing has been learnt from the event.

Second proposal: shipwreck survivor camps

Shipwreck survivor camps have been a largely neglected part of maritime archaeology. However, as Gibbs (2003) recalls, shipwreck survivor camps have been a recurrent theme in our iconography, as in *Robinson Crusoe* where the protagonist spent 28 years in an island after a shipwreck. These survivor camps are places where those who made it off a wrecked vessel gathered after the wreck event. These camps show the development of authority structures, social organisations, psychological traumas and difficult dynamics (Gibbs, 2003). The occupation of these camps could last from a few hours to many months, depending on the appearance of rescuers. These camps were linked to the cultural attributes of the ship, and the adaptation of the survivors would depend on a range of variables, including: the health of those who survived the disaster, their skills understanding the challenges, the remaining floating cargo from their ship, their location and proximity to the wreck, the nature of the environment, whether food and water resources were available, the possibility of accessing shelters and structures, the development of a rescue strategy (either waiting, walk away from the site, send a boat for help, repairing the vessel or establishing a new settlement), and the contact with the locals of the new land (Gibbs, 2003). In any case, these camps are an invaluable source of information.

This example of these shipwreck settlements could be translated as the modern refugee camps. Some refugees which are rescued from a shipwreck are allocated in these reception centres that become new settlements for them; for some it is a place to stay while their request of asylum is being approved, but for others, it is a possible permanent situation, which is best that what they left back at home. As shipwreck survivor camps are a field of study inside the underwater cultural heritage realm, refugee camps will also be in the future: new cultures, new cultural heritage, and new history is written in these places, and they are all consequence of a maritime journey.

Conclusions

The discussion surrounding modern refugee shipwrecks is primarily focused on smugglers, rescues, or ideological and structural aspects of border policies (Kovras and Robins, 2016). This chapter has tried to apply cultural heritage protocols to an issue that does not seem to have a solution. Slavery is compared to forced migration because of the abusive treatment of both slaves and migrants, the race of the victims, and the connection of their trade with the world economy (Bravo, 2007). This analogy has been relevant for our consideration of human rights on the management of underwater cultural heritage.

Refugee shipwrecks are numerous, causing large numbers of causalities because of the poor conditions of the boats. Although states have fought, in theory, against any kind of slavery or inhuman treatment, the reality is that there has not even been a political process to recognise the dead bodies that were on board the shipwrecks, or to bring the idea of death as being sacred to the families of the dead migrants. And illegal immigration will continue happening. Although states do not have consistent human rights diplomacies because of national security and economic concerns, there may be something they can do to comply with human rights obligations. Sometimes, simply the respect of something as sacred as the death can alleviate the situation. The refugees' situation affects the society from which she or he originates, including their community, family and friends. As it has been seen, the laws in the case of migrants travelling by sea are based on maritime legislation, rather than human rights laws, which is why the discourse around refugee shipwrecks has mainly focused on two main points: the threat to the receiving countries and the humanitarian concerns by the international community. It may be time to look at past situations in relation to the modern problem, such as the slave trade, in order to find new solutions that can balance the state's necessity and the state's humanity.

Article 1A (2) of the 1951 Convention Relating to the Status of Refugees defines a refugee as a person who:

> owing to well-founded fear of being persecuted for reasons of race, religion, nationality, membership of a particular social group or political opinion, is outside the country of his nationality and is unable or, owing to such fear, is unwilling to avail himself of the protection of that country; or who, not having a nationality and being outside the country

of his former habitual residence as a result of such events, is unable or, owing to such fear, is unwilling to return to it.

In comparison with slaves, which were or are under the control of another person, the refugee seems not to lose control of ownership of self. However, this chapter has demonstrated that, in most cases, the refugee does not control his trip, his destiny, or his decisions. Smugglers, states of reception, and sometimes mafia on arrival control their lives. The main difference with the slave trade is that, in theory, the victim re-joins society as a 'free' person (Bravo, 2007).

For States, the fear of refugees is a domestic political issue that views border control as central to security (Maley, 2015). The issue can be eradicated from the root (the countries that refugees leave), from the journey (returning rescued refugees from shipwrecks to their countries of origin, which may be a problem if they have no identification documents), or at the end (returning the refugees once they have reached the new state). NGO diplomacy for human rights is a characteristic of contemporary international relations (Forsythe, 2015). In the case of refugee shipwrecks, the NGO's boats continuously rescue refugees on board of dinghies or boats, putting pressure on the vicinity countries to admit the refugees, who, on some occasions, arrive in hundreds. Wealthy, developed countries have more capacity to control the movement of refugees than poor countries, who will have limited capacity to withstand large flows (Maley, 2015): wealthy countries can deny visas and make asylum claims unsuccessful. However, the international community has the right and duty to intervene, and the denial of the acceptance of an NGO's vessel loaded with refugees in complicated health conditions seems to be a complicated action for international diplomacy. For some, the refugees' situation is the consequence of the contemporary global economy (Bravo, 2007), where people are smuggled, and refugees are depicted as criminals. With the slave trade, states would adopt an active role because the slave trade was legal in its time. With the refugee crisis, the states adopt a passive role. The result is the same: the permission to trade with human lives.

The ethical issues of human rights is a complicated topic for the management of underwater cultural heritage. It is a concept that is linked to conflict and cooperation which always clash with States strategies. But it is also a concept that is part of the management of this heritage, as this book studies in other chapters such as uses—which user has rights over the heritage, or nationless shipwrecks—how colonised countries can exercise their rights over their cultural heritage.

Notes

1 The Global Slavery Index. Available at: www.globalslaveryindex.org/2018/findings/regional-analysis/asia-and-the-pacific/.
2 American History on the Water. Available at: http://americanhistory.si.edu/onthewater/exhibition/5_2.html.

Bibliography

Agha, S. (2015). We asked refugees: what did you bring with you? [online]. *Mercy Corps Online*. 15 June 2015. Available at: www.mercycorps.org.uk/photoessays/ jordan-syria/we-asked-refugees-what-did-you-bring-you.

Barnes, R. (2004). Refugee law at sea. *The International and Comparative Law Quarterly* 53(1): 47–77.

Bennett, A. (2012). That sinking feeling: stateless ships, universal jurisdiction, and the drug trafficking vessel interdiction act. *Yale Journal International Law* 37(2): 433.

Bravo, K. E. (2007). Exploring the analogy between modern trafficking in humans and the trans-Atlantic slave trade. *Boston University International Law Journal* 25(2): 207–295.

Chalabi, M. (2013). What happened to history's refugees? [online]. *The Guardian: Data Blog*. 25 July 2013. Available at: www.theguardian.com/news/ datablog/interactive/2013/jul/25/what-happened-history-refugees.

Convention Relating to the Status of Refugees (1951). Article 1A. Available at: www. unhcr.org/uk/1951-refugee-convention.html (3 May 2018).

Convention Relating to the Status of Stateless Persons (1954). Articles 1 and 12. Available at: www.unhcr.org/.../1954-Convention-relating-to-the-Status-of-Stateless-Persons_ENG (4 May 2018).

EFE (2018). Italia y Malta impiden el desembarco de 629 inmigrantes rescatados en el mar. *El Mundo Online*. Available at: www.elmundo.es/internacional/2018/06/ 10/5b1d55f2468aeb8d1c8b458a.html.

Eltis, D., Behrendt, S. D., Richardson, D. and Klein H. S. (1999). *The Trans-Atlantic Slave Trade Database on CD-Rom (TSTD)*. Cambridge: Cambridge University Press.

Fisher, M. (2007). A slave ship speaks: the wreck of the Henrietta Marie. *A Prospectus for the Exhibition Tour*. Key West, FL: Mel Fisher Maritime Heritage Society.

Forsythe, D. P. (2015). Human rights. In Cooper, A.F., Heine, J. and Thakur, R. (eds.), *The Oxford Handbook of Modern Diplomacy*. Oxford: Oxford University Press: 658–672.

Gibbs, M. (2003). The archaeology of crisis: shipwreck survivor camps in Australasia. *Historical Archaeology* 37(1): 128–145.

Goldhill, O. (2015). What Syrian refugees carry in their bags as they leave their lives behind. [online]. *Quartz Online*. 6 September 2015. Available at: https:// qz.com/496220/photos-what-syrian-refugees-carry-in-their-bags-as-they-leave-their-lives-behind/.

Hernandez, V. and Stylianou, N. (2016). Buried without a name: the untold story of Europe's drowned migrants. [online]. *BBC News Online*. 10 March 2016. Available at: www.bbc.co.uk/news/resources/idt-91f3683c-5e3c-4a2e-92eb-7d7f6a024c02.

Jeffery, B. (2004). World War II underwater cultural heritage sites in Truk Lagoon: considering a case for World Heritage Listing. *International Journal of Nautical Archaeology* 33(1): 106–121.

Kovras, I. and Robins, S. (2016). Death as the border: managing missing migrants and unidentified bodies at the EU's Mediterranean frontier. *Political Geography* 55: 40–49.

Loewenfeld, E. (1941). Status of stateless persons. *Transactions of the Grotius Society* 27: 59–112.

Maley, W. (2015). Refugee diplomacy. In Cooper, A. F., Heine, J. and Thakur, R. (eds.), *The Oxford Handbook of Modern Diplomacy*. Oxford: Oxford University Press.

McGhee, F. (1997). Toward a postcolonial nautical archaeology. Master's thesis, University of Texas.

Menefee, S. P. (2000). The maritime slave trade: a 21st century problem. *ILSA Journal International & Comparative Law* 7(2): 495–509.

Menefee, S. P. (2003). The smuggling of refugees by sea: a modern day maritime slave trade. *Regent Journal International Law* 2(1): 1.

Slavery Museum (2013). *Transatlantic Slavery: An Introduction*. Liverpool: Liverpool University Press.

St. Germain-en-Laye Convention (1919). Preamble. Available at: https://iea.uoregon.edu/treaty-text/1919-congoriverentxt (8 May 2018).

UNCLOS (1982). United Nations Convention on the Law of the Sea. Available at: www.un.org/depts/los/convention_agreements/texts/unclos/unclos_e.pdf (3 May 2018).

UNESCO (2001). Convention on the Protection of the Underwater Cultural Heritage. Paris, 2 November 2001. Available at: http://unesdoc.unesco.org/images/0012/001260/126065e.pdf (3 May 2018).

United Nations High Commissioner for Refugees (2016). Force displacement in 2016. Available at: www.un.org/en/development/desa/population/.../coordination/.../14_UNHCR_nd.pdf (4 May 2018).

Webster, J. (2007). Ringed with the wrecks of slave ships: the Atlantic slave trade. *British Archaeology* 94(May/June 2007).

Webster, J. (2008a). Historical archaeology and the slave ship. *International Journal of Historical Archaeology* 12(1): 1–5.

Webster, J. (2008b). Slave ships and maritime archaeology: an overview. *International Journal of Historical Archaeology* 12(1): 6–19.

10 Politics

The South China Sea[1]

Heritage is always political: sites are transformed into transactional commodities which serve national and international interests which can either be extremely hurtful or extremely positive (Aplin, 2002; McDowell, 2008). Consequently, heritage not only becomes tangible objects and places, but extends to the intangible heritage of social practices, collective memories, and a sense of identity. This chapter demonstrates how interlinked the concepts of politics, identity and history are in relation to underwater cultural heritage. In fact, and according to Meskell (2016), the circuits around heritage include both national and international economic, legal, military, and political negotiations. Heritage, and in this case, underwater cultural heritage, becomes an agent for territory, sovereignty and security, and international corporate agreements.

Identity is fundamental to politics and is resultantly highly manipulated by governments in power. Humans attach names, myths, and effective value to things that become cultural resources (Lipe, 1984) and every state develops its own policy concerning heritage, based on what is worth preserving (Viejo-Rose, 2011; Carman, 1996). Flecker (2002) argued that underwater archaeology differs from terrestrial archaeology in that the former is involved in politics and ethics and states that shipwreck policy is formulated with money in mind. However, there are also examples of terrestrial heritage used for political claims (Meskell, 2016): the inclusion of specific places on the World Heritage List is one example, as this chapter will later explain. And it is also worth considering that data from marine exploration, including underwater archaeology, affects national defence sensitivity because it may uncover military security information, safety issues, environmental concerns, cultural evidence, or food security clues. Because of this, nations will want to protect their maritime territory, to avoid foreign inclusion and to safeguard their data. The ethics that the South China Sea conflict brings will highlight the way in which politics uses the past—both officially and unofficially—in order to exercise the power to control international affairs. Heritage is being instrumentalised and, although the discussion in the heritage realm has been focused to its use as a national tool, its use for further and more ambitious goals intertwines it with international politics and violence.

Introduction

The South China Sea has long been a contested seascape, manifested today in disputed claims over islands, their resulting maritime zones and maritime boundaries between a range of South East Asian nations, including Vietnam, Malaysia, Taiwan, Brunei and the Philippines, but principally China (Morton and Blackmore, 2001). In this battle for territory China has unsheathed what it hopes will be new weapons to buttress its claims: maritime archaeology and underwater cultural heritage. Essentially, China appears to be relying on maritime archaeology to adduce evidence that supports its territorial claims. That China, or rather, vessels of Chinese origin as well as Chinese peoples have visited, inhabited, used and exploited the islands and waters of the South China Sea is not generally disputed—though specific claims might be—the extent to which these may support claims of sovereignty over territory or right in respect of maritime zone in international law is ethically questionable.

This chapter questions the use of maritime archaeology and underwater cultural heritage as an evidentiary advantage in China's quest for sovereignty or rights in the South China Sea. In doing so, the history of the South China Sea is briefly reviewed with an emphasis on the role of maritime archaeology that had adduced evidence of this history. The Chinese attitude to its heritage, and in particular its underwater cultural heritage is explored, with an emphasis on the regulatory system that applies to underwater cultural heritage at sea. The chapter will also explore additional steps that China may be taking for its goals, such as the rejection of others' maritime archaeology or the inclusion of disputed sea territory in the World Heritage List. Against this background, the current role of maritime archaeology and underwater cultural heritage disputes is critically addressed, highlighting the use of this heritage as a resource for commercial contracts, regional defence and use of military installations. The example of the South China Sea only seems a case to discuss the role of heritage in international diplomacy, geopolitical manoeuvring and national interests.

Issue

The South China Sea is said to be the birthplace of the world's most ancient maritime culture (Hoagland, 1999). The Chinese civilisation arose inland, far from the mouth of the river Huang Ho around 1523–1027 B.C. By 214 B.C. it has expanded to reach the South China Sea, and the Nanhai maritime trade route between China and south-east Asia appears to have begun. However, the trade was not consolidated until the tenth century AD after the rise of Annam—Vietnam—and the Indianised states—Indo-China and Indonesia. Those civilisations turned to the Chinese for their commercial, cultural and political growth. The South China Sea become the second Silk Route of Asian East-West trade in commodities and ideas (Gungwu, 1958) where China had the maritime hegemony. This early trade with China was facilitated by other nations, both in South East Asia and those from Arabia and India.

While this history is recorded in various historical texts, it is the arch-aeological evidence of shipwrecks and their cargoes that reveal much about these early maritime cultures of the South China Sea. The subsequent western age of discovery and colonisation has also left a rich legacy of shipwrecks of Portugal, Netherlands, Spain and England in the South China Sea over a period of more than 450 years (Adams, 2013). The South China Sea has a wealth of underwater cultural heritage since it hosts some of the busiest maritime routes of ancient times, several battlefields and some of the oldest heritage on earth which represents the close interaction, activities, and accu-mulation of maritime history of various civilisations over generations. The Battle of Yamen in 1279, for example, is reported to have resulted in the sinking of over 2,000 warships (Gruber, 2008). It also provides information on the economic and cultural link between neighbouring countries.

Due to this great concentration of valuable wrecks, early investigations of South China Sea shipwrecks were undertaken under the mantle of sal-vage law, with commercial rather than archaeological aims. The discovery and salvage of the *Geldermalsen,* however, initiated a review of these activ-ities by many of the States of the South China Sea. The *Geldermalsen*, a Dutch East Indiaman, sank after striking a reef in the South China Sea in January 1952 on its return *journey* to Holland, having loaded a cargo of tea, spices, lacquerware, porcelain and gold at Canton (Miller, 1992). In 1985, salvor Michael Hatcher discovered the wreck in an undisclosed loca-tion, believed to be either within the exclusive economic zone of Indonesia (O'Keefe, 2002) or on the continental shelf of China (Zhao, 1992). When the salvage operation was completed, the salvors used dynamite to destroy the last traces of the wreck in order to ensure that the location of the wreck could not be ascertained (Zhao, 1992). The salvors recovered 160,000 pieces of export quality porcelain, 126 gold ingots, two bronze cannons, but few other artefacts. Accounts of the salvage describe the operation as 'strip-mining', where no account was taken of the archaeological value of the site and artefacts of little economic value was ignored or destroyed (Hatcher et al., 1987). The recovered porcelain was subsequently auctioned by Christie's Amsterdam, raising approximately $10–15 million (Pitchford, 2008: 74). Controversially, purchases of the artefacts at auction included a number of museums, including the British Museum. This was not the first wreck salvaged by Hatcher, who had for example, previously found a 1640 Chinese junk, from which 23,000 pieces of porcelain were recovered.

The fate of these wrecks, particularly the *Geldermalsen*, have been used extensively to illustrate the manner in which valuable archaeological and historical information is lost whilst the economic value of the wreck is maximised. Importantly, it also illustrates the difficulty faced by developing nations in preserving and regulating activities in their waters which are some distance from their shorelines. Flecker (2002) argues that while hundreds of shipwrecks have been found in the South China Sea, only 35 from earlier than the seventeenth century have been investigated and documented with sufficient rigour to provide a date and origin (Flecker, 2015). Nevertheless, these do illustrate the great variety of vessels that have sailed these seas. Of the 35, seven are of a type used through South East Asia and span the thousand years from the fourth century AD until the thirteenth century; two are of Arab origin from the ninth century while 15 are from the period between the fourteenth and sixteenth century and of a hybrid South East Asian and Chinese construction that then centred around Siam—today's Thailand. Eleven are Chinese junks dating from the late twelfth or early thirteenth century onwards (Flecker, 2015). It is particularly these vessels that the Chinese government has a particular interest in.

Following the concerns caused by the salvage of the *Geldermalsen* (Zhao, 1992), maritime archaeology in China is said to have begun then in 1987 with the establishment of the Centre for Underwater Archaeology in what is now the National Museum of China. In the same year, the discovery of the Nanhai-01 wreck off the coast of Guangdong province led in 2007, to its recovery and placement in a specially constructed museum; a significant undertaking that equals and arguably surpasses the recoveries of the *Vasa* and *Mary Rose*. These intervening years have seen considerable development ion State support maritime archaeology. In 2009, the State Administration of Cultural heritage (SACH) established the China Centre of Underwater Cultural Heritage Protection (CCUHP), which has worked with other departments, such as the Ministry of Foreign Affairs, Ministry of Transport and State Oceanic Administration, to develop a national policy and 'Protection team' to implement it. Since then, it has undertaken a range of activities. It has revised its policies on underwater cultural heritage and apparently 2,000 ships have been discovered by Chinese archaeologists, although this figure may be based on extrapolation from documentary sources rather than from archaeological survey (Hoagland, 1999). More recently, the National Underwater Cultural Heritage Protection South China Sea Base was established to centralise all South China Sea cultural heritage investigations, training, and research under one national-level organisation (Erickson and Bond, 2015). More controversially, a work station is planned to be constructed on Yongxing (Woody) Island, an island within the Paracels Islands, over which considerable dispute exists.

The broader South China Sea disputes arise from a complex historical, economic and geopolitical matrix (Catley and Keliat, 1997). It is beyond the remit of this chapter to address the disputed claims in any detail, but an overview is necessary to position the current Chinese approach to maritime archaeology and underwater cultural heritage.

State of knowledge

The geographical nature of the South China Sea is complex, with numerous islands, reefs, drying shoals and landmasses that are significantly indented and irregular. It is bordered by a number of states, all of which have claims to some of the islands and maritime zones of the South China Sea. While difficult to categorise, the disputes can be generally grouped into disputes over island territory and disputes over maritime territory; though these are intrinsically connected as islands give rise to rights over the waters that surround the islands. These claims to islands and waters can only be understood against the backdrop of the United Nations Convention on the Law of the Sea (UNCLOS, 1982), often regarded as the constitution of the oceans, concluded in 1982 and coming into force for States Parties in 1994.[2]

Against this backdrop of UNCLOS, and within the context of its claims to various maritime zones in the South China Sea, China adopted, in 1989 the Regulations Concerning the Management and Protection of Underwater Cultural Relics (Regulation, 1989). This legal regime applies to all cultural relics of any origin of historic, artistic and scientific value underwater but it does not cover 'objects that have remained underwater since 1911 and have nothing to do with important historical events, revolutionary movements or renowned personages'. Moreover, 'ownership' of all underwater cultural heritage within the Chinese internal waters and territorial sea is vested in the State (Fu, 2003). While the right to manage archaeological sites within the territorial seas is international practice, it is unusual for a State to claim ownership over foreign relics. In the contiguous zone, while State ownership of foreign vessels is not claimed, the regulation of activities directed at such heritage is subject to this legal regime (Fu, 2003). Beyond the contiguous zone, the legal regime does not provide the right to exercise jurisdiction with respect of underwater cultural heritage (Fu, 2006). This, however, is reflected in the fact that the Chinese regime claims jurisdiction over that which lies on foreign state's continental shelf (and exclusive economic zone), if the vessel 'originating from China' (Regulation, 1989. What this term means is not defined. According to Fu (2003) it could mean one of two things: if it means 'having the nationality of China', it would be more acceptable by the coastal states; however, if it means 'sailing to or from China' or 'historically or culturally connected to China' would be difficult to be accepted by a coastal State. This is extended to underwater cultural heritage in the Area, such that China claims such heritage 'only if' it originated from China.

It may seem that this regulation has been drafted towards protecting Chinese underwater cultural heritage in every possible zone even if under those premises it relinquishes ownership or jurisdiction over foreign vessels located in China's contiguous zone, continental shelf and Exclusive Economic Zone. China prefers to protect their own cultural heritage than claim jurisdiction over others. This approach follows China's current nationalistic approach to preservation of cultural heritage. Yet, it is not consistent with the approach taken many other States and is inconsistent with the 2001 UNESCO Convention of the Protection of the Underwater Cultural Heritage (UNESCO, 2001) in a great many respect. It is also arguably in breach of Article 303 of UNCLOS in that Article 303(1) provides that 'States have the duty to protect objects of an archaeological and historical nature found at sea and shall co-operate for this purpose'. While this is a vague and very general provision, it does require, as an imperative, State cooperation. China's claims on irrefutable ownership over their cultural heritage in foreign country's maritime zones outside its territorial sea and on the Area do not invite or opens the possibility of State cooperation.

This Chinese approach to underwater cultural heritage concentrates exclusively on Chinese heritage to the exclusion, and detriment, of other heritage in the South China Sea. More importantly, this exclusive focus naturally favours the search for and investigation of Chinese heritage, constituting evidence for its South China Sea claims, whilst excluding that which might favour other States' claims. However, these claims have been set out in the context of the maritime zones set out in UNCLOS and the jurisdictional regime appears to be generated solely by UNCLOS. In the context of the claims that arise in the South China Sea dispute, this is of some import. Not surprisingly, it is the islands of the South China Sea that are at the heart of the disputes; four groups of islands in particular. The Spratly Islands (Nansha) consist of more than 140 islets, reefs, shoals and sandbanks spread over 410,000 square kilometres, though arguably less than 40 comply with the UNCLOS definition of an island (Beckman, 2010: 48). The entire Spratly Islands are claimed by China, Taiwan and Vietnam, with some parts of it claimed by Philippines as part of its Kalayaan Island Group. Since one reef lies within 220nm of Brunei Darussalam, it also has a potential claim (Beckman, 2010: 48). The Parcel Islands (Xisa) consist of 35 islets, reefs, shoals and sandbanks over 15,000 square kilometres and are also claimed by China, Taiwan and Vietnam. Scarborough Shoal (Huangyan), a large atoll with a lagoon of 150 square kilometres, is claimed by China, Philippines and Taiwan. The Pratas Islands (Dongsha) are disputed between China and Taiwan, as is Macclesfield Bank (Zongsha), though this is a large atoll that is submerged even at low tide (Beckman, 2010: 50).

The claim to the islands of the South China Sea are thus less to do with the islands themselves and more to do with the maritime zones that these islands then generate in accordance with UNCLOS (See Hu, 2010). However, while UNCLOS addresses State's sovereignty, rights and duties over maritime spaces, including those off islands, it does not address issue of territorial sovereignty nor does it address how disputes over claims of sovereignty are to be resolved (Amer, 2014). Disputing parties are left to other rules of international law to determine issues of territorial sovereignty and the resolution of disputes in that regard. In June 2015 the United States pushed to get all claimants in the South China Sea to stop building projects (Tiezzi, 2015). However, China claims that its island construction does not affect freedom of navigation and overflight and only involves civilian purposes such a maritime search and rescue.

It is in relation to the claim of sovereignty over the islands as land territory that historic issues, and underwater cultural heritage, play a part—the archaeological evidence used as evidence to support claims of sovereignty may itself be contested (Bonnet, 2015). Title to territory may be acquired by States either by prescription or occupation. Occupation is a method of acquiring territory that does not belong to anyone, said to be *terra nullius* (Shaw, 2014: 363). It most often arises in the context of islands. Occupation requires that the state prove that it has the intention and will to act as sovereign and have a continuous and peaceful display of such sovereignty. Prescription is a mode of establishing title to territory which was not *terra nullius* and which was obtained in circumstances where it was either unlawful at the time or where the legality cannot be demonstrated (Shaw, 2014: 364). It is, in other words, a mode of acquiring title by adverse possession, that is in circumstances where there is the exercise of *de facto* sovereignty for a very long period over territory subject to sovereignty of another (Shearer, 1994: 153) or by immemorial possession, being

> a long continued possession, where no original source of proprietary right can be shown to exist, or where possession in the first instance being wrongful, the legitimate proprietor has neglected to assert his right, or has been unable to do so.
>
> > (Hall and Higgins, 1917: Section 36;
> > Jennings, 1963: 21)

Prescription or occupation requires an element variously described as 'peaceful and continuous display of authority' (Brownlie and Crawford, 2012: 139), 'continuous exercise of authority', 'continuous display of sovereignty', 'effective control' (Blum, 2012: 102), 'effective possession'[3] or 'effectivités'. In that occupation (or prescription) requires that the state prove not only that that it has the intention and will to act as sovereign and has in fact done so continuously and peacefully, historical evidence is significant. Indeed, the longer the duration of possession or occupation, the more substantial the justification for a continuous display of authority (Hill, 1945: 156). Herein possibly lies the use of underwater cultural heritage to support such territorial claims. It appears that the essential assertion is that China was the first to discover, name, explore and exploit the islands of the South China Sea and thus have sovereignty over these islands that then gives rise to the maritime territories. The claim of sovereignty to the islands in the South China Sea—that gives rise to significant maritime claims—is complicated by the fact that great disagreement exists as to whether many of the geographical features in question meet the UNCLOS definition of an island. These uncertainties have led to a scramble for possession of the islands of the South China Sea, as well as the construction of numerous artificial islands and the extension of low tide elevations on drying rocks to appear as islands (Page and Barnes, 2015). In fact, by 1999, nearly 1650 troops of five claimants governments had occupied at least forty-six of fifty-one land formations in the Spratly archipelago (Gao, 1994; Lin, 1997).

It is unlikely that any of these will give rise to continental shelf or EEZ claims around that feature, and at best, might give rise to a territorial sea. The Spratly islands, for example, were historically regarded as 'labyrinth of detached shoals' that were such a hazard to navigation as to be avoided if at all possible (Schofield, 2013: 19. See also Anderson and Van Logchem, 2014). The largest island in the group, Itu Aba is a mere 1.4km long and 370 m wide. As such, whether this is capable of sustaining human habitation and thus meeting the definition of Article 121 of UNCLOS was addressed in the South China Sea Arbitration, as were other features within this group.[4] Importantly, in concluding that Itu Aba, Thitu, West York, Spratly Island, South-West Cay, and North-East Cay are not capable of sustaining an economic life of their own within the meaning of Article 121(3), the Tribunal did have recourse to the historical record, especially in relation to the fisherman that had used the feature at least since the 1860s and other extractive industries that had used the features resources.[5] As such, historical and archaeological evidence certainly can play a role in these claims.

While these, for the most part, are claims to the islands themselves as land territory, China has, it is argued, a more ambitious claim. In 1947, China produced a map with eleven dotted lines, in a U shape, that essentially enclosed the South China Sea and the islands groups in dispute.[6] This was adopted, albeit with two of the lines erased, by the People's Republic of China. This nine-dash line is extensive and, for example, encircles both the Spratly and Parcel islands. Moreover, it overlaps with Exclusive Economic Zone claims of a number of States. It is not, however, entirely clear what this none-dotted line actually is intended to claim. The narrowest claim is to the islands enclosed within the nine-dotted lines, while the broadest claim is to all the waters enclosed therein as territorial seas on the basis that these waters have, historically, been Chinese waters. This claim would render the South China Sea a 'Chinese Lake' (Joyner, 1999: 77). Were China to assert this claim, it would have a significant effect on all the states bordering the South China Sea. In the 2016 South China Sea Arbitration, brought by the Philippines, China refused to recognise the jurisdiction of the Tribunal and took no part in the arbitration.[7] China did not therefore clarify its claim in respect of the nine-dash line.[8] As such, the Tribunal formulated China's claim, beyond those relating to sovereignty to the islands themselves, as a claim to 'relevant rights in the South China Sea, formed in the long historical course'.[9]

Overlaying the disputes is a number of other UNCLOS related issues. The manner of deployment of baselines from which all the maritime zones measured it set out in UNCLOS, with some degree of discretion given to the coastal States. However, disagreement has arisen in relation to some of these deployments, including those of Vietnam, China, and Taiwan (Beckman, 2010: 59). Furthermore, a number of the States bordering the South China Sea have not resolved their maritime delimitations provided for in UNCLOS. These are delimitations that indicate where neighbouring States' respective territorial seas, exclusive economic zones and continental shelves start and end or, for the Philippines and Indonesia, where their archipelagic waters start and end. Four of the principal coastal claimants (Cambodia, Indonesia, Malaysia and Thailand) rely on the median-line principle for offshore boundary delineation provided for in UNCLOS, but China and Vietnam have, given these on-going disputes, not specified the extent of their claims (Park, 1978). The extent of a number of States' continental shelves is also disputed (Beckman, 2010: 65–69). The status of the islands in the South China Sea naturally impacts greatly on these claims, but these are claims made consistent with UNCLOS, and it is the status of the islands, and possibly the greater claims implicated by the nine-dotted line claim, that underpins these maritime disputes.

In addition, the notion of historic title or historic rights have also arisen in relation to the law of the sea in this case. Importantly, though, it is conceptually distinct to the 'historical' evidence that might support a territorial claim to islands, as discussed above, though the same evidence might serve both purposes. Historic title or historic rights in UNCLOS addresses issues that might be said to arise from China's nine-dotted line claim to its maritime domain distinct from that which arises from its sovereignty over any island.[10] And although underwater cultural heritage is being used by China to support these historic rights, the international community seems to far to recognise them.

Ethical dilemmas: politics

China is a country with a 5,000-year long history and as a consequence it possesses a wealth of cultural heritage, although this heritage was not always treasured (Gruber, 2008). However, the Communist government, realised that cultural heritage is a political tool telling stories about the past and present, subjected to interpretation and negotiation. As China started with its nation-building task, it started to stress the constructive aspects of nationalism through cultural heritage. As Falkenhausen noted, 'a nationalist interpretive framework, emphasizing the antiquity, uniqueness, purity, and importance of Chinese civilization is basic to the pursuit of history and archaeology in China' (Falkenhausen, 1995). More recently, China's concern with its cultural heritage has included that no longer in China itself, especially that which left China through war and during periods of foreign domination. This is particularly the case, for example, with respect to Chinese cultural heritage in institutions such as the British Museum (Mail Online, 2013). When British Prime Minister David Cameron visited China in December 2013, he was inundated with demands for the restitution of cultural objects taken from China (Zhong, 2015). China has also asserted right to heritage in private hands, most notably when it unsuccessfully tried to stop the auction of two bronze statues taken from Beijing's Summer Palace by Anglo-French troops during the First Opium War (1856–1860) to China (Wong and Erlanger, 2013).

China has recently been described as being in a 'cultural heritage preservation fever' (Harrell, 2013), which extends beyond the Chinese government to its citizens, who are engaging in art and antiquities collecting in greater numbers. It is estimated that by 1999 consumers from Asia, particularly China, represents a quarter of Sotheby's auction house business (Hoagland, 1999).

Heritage is nowadays a constructive factor in unifying the Chinese nation. This use of cultural heritage to support claims of sovereignty are naturally linked with ideas of nationality, identity and place in the international family of nations. The theory that 'national identity' can be shaped through a few selected points of heritage and supporting mythologies has been largely studied: during a period of deciding what to preserve, efforts are made to shape public memory through the form of memorials, sites, references and public rituals (Viejo-Rose, 2011). As a consequence, cultural heritage is intrinsically political and symbolic: the heritage can be manipulated by rulers to remember history in a different way. In fact, and according to Pitchford (2008) governments, museums and other attractions and the law are political and powerful resources for the construction of national identities: it is the mobilisation of the past in the interest of national pride, unity and reform. China is in a process of nation-building making an immense effort to save everything from rituals to shipwrecks.

While China clearly want to protect its heritage this commitment to maritime archaeology is open to interpretation and been subject to some criticism. This is not surprising given that the Director of China's Centre of Underwater Cultural Heritage, Liu Shuguang, has declared that '[w]e want to find more evidence that can prove Chinese people went there and lived there, historical evidence that can help prove China is the sovereign owner of the South China Sea' (Page, 2013). China quite explicitly then is seeking to reinforce its maritime claims in the South China Sea by demonstrating an ancient Chinese presence that reinforces the idea of maritime supremacy through finds of porcelain, coins and underwater remains. Underwater archaeology is the tool to bolster claims of historical occupation and control in the South China Sea (Hoagland, 1999; Flecker 2015). The claims themselves are not new. In 1976, the Peking Review declared (Peking Review (1976) in Park (1978: 10):

> More than 2,000 years ago, Chinese people were already sailing on the turbulent waves of the South China Sea, as recorded in ancient Chinese literature. By the time of the Western and Easter Han dynasties (206 BC-220 AD) the South China Sea had become an important navigation route for China. As navigation steadily developed, long years of sailing the seas enabled the Chinese people to become the first discoverers and the masters of the south China Islands. Surveyed and named time and again and worked and administered without a break, theses valuable islands became an inalienable part of our beautiful motherland.

Active maritime archaeological activity has therefore been directed at these disputed areas. In 2007, for example, excavations were undertaken in Huaguangjao (discovery reef) in the Paracel Islands, an area disputed between China and Vietnam. Since at least 2013, China has also been conducting investigations in the disputed Spratly Islands. In 2014, China launched a state-of-the-art maritime archaeology vessel, Kaogu-01 (Erickson and Bond, 2015). Its first deployment was to investigate the Dongkengtuo wreck 48km off the coast. Importantly, it was deployed in disputed waters. The second deployment of Kaogu-01 was to Shanhu (Prattle) Island in the Paracels group, to investigate the site of the naval battle between China and South Vietnam in 1974 over the sovereignty of those islands. Vietnam still contests China's claim of these islands. As the Chinese vice minister of culture recognised: 'marine archaeology is an exercise that demonstrates national sovereignty' (Page, 2013).

Although China has used every available tool to support its claims over the islands—from legal strategies to use of force—there has been two further main courses of action that China is undertaking in relation to the underwater cultural heritage to support its claims, and which are ethically questionable:

Rejection of other's maritime archaeology

While China has undertaken these activities in the disputed zones it has exerted in superior might to prevent others from doing so, considering all excavations, other than official Chinese investigations, as unauthorised and illegal. In 2013, for example, a joint expedition between noted maritime archaeologist Franck Goddio and the National Museum of the Philippines in Scarborough Shoal off the coast of the Philippines, was expelled from the area by force (Page, 2013). Of concern, was the view of the China Centre of Underwater Cultural Heritage head Liu Shuguang, who argued that the intent of the expedition was '[t]o drag away this shipwreck. Because this was material evidence that Chinese people first found the Scarborough Shoal, they wanted to destroy evidence that was beneficial to China' (Page, 2013). Under the Chinese regime, any archaeological exploration or excavation in waters under Chinese jurisdiction have to be authorised. China has, using its significant maritime forces, enforced these laws within these zones. As such, all excavations, other than official Chinese investigations, are 'unauthorised' and 'illegal'.

The Maritime Silk Route

In 2014 UNESCO designated a new World Heritage Site: 'the Silk Road: the Routes Network of Chang'an-Tianshan Corridor'. This World Heritage Site is a 5,000 km section of the extensive Silk Roads network through China, Kyrgyzstan and Kazakhstan (UNESCO, 1972). China also wants to develop a 'Silk Road on the Sea', but the difficult with this is that the route would go through disputed waters and around the Paracel and Spratly Islands. With this aim China is excavating archaeological sites around these islands, which would justify China's sovereign claims to these features which would then both assist, and be bolstered by, a World Heritage listing. If the Maritime Silk Route would be listed as a World Heritage Site and China would be the only state party, they would have the duty of protect the territory, which would help on the ownership claims over the islands. The Convention only notes the cultural aspects of the heritage, but not the sovereignty of the territory. However, Article 11.3 of the 1972 International UNESCO Convention concerning the Protection of the World Cultural and Natural Heritage (UNESCO, 1972) stipulates:

> The inclusion of a property in the World Heritage List requires the consent of the State concerned. The inclusion of a property situated in a territory, sovereignty or jurisdiction over which is claimed by more than one State shall in no way prejudice the rights of the parties to the dispute.

Clearly controversy would arise if Vietnam and Philippines are regarded as States concerned and how the inclusion of ports in disputed islands would prejudice the rights of all States claiming soverignty and maritime rights in the South China Sea. This issue will be explored in the next section.

Proposal: diplomacy

In its introduction, the 2001 UNESCO Convention states that [...]

> cooperation among States, international organizations, scientific institutions, professional organizations, archaeologists, divers, other interested parties and the public at large is essential for the protection of underwater cultural heritage,

Article 19 also highlights cooperation and information-sharing and encourages state parties to collaborate in the investigation, excavation, documentation, conservation, study, and presentation of heritage. Rule 8 of the Annex insists again on international cooperation for effective exchange or use of archaeologists and other relevant professionals. These principles have been recognised by the community as the best protection and management of underwater cultural heritage. However, as already mentioned, China has not ratified the 2001 UNESCO Convention. In addition, and according to its inclusive legal regulations, it seems that not only does China refuse to cooperate, it also rejects others' maritime underwater cultural heritage.

However, China has pursued a new strategy to support its territorial claims and has traced a 'Silk Road on the Sea': a route that has been designed to go through disputed waters. Its listing as a World Heritage Site would seem to be like accepting China's ownership claims of these disputed waters, even if the 1972 UNESCO Convention states that the inclusion of property on claimed territory does not prejudice the rights of the parties. However, this approach has been used before by other countries and seems to involve much more than just the protection of a cultural site.

According to Wallerstein (2012), when a site is found on disputed territory, two potential scenarios are created. The first is that the state claims sovereignty over the territory at the site location and has effective control over the territory. The second is that the state that has a claim on the territory on which the site is found does not have effective control over that territory. Both applications could be considered by UNESCO since the Convention does not state otherwise. Since the aim of the Convention is to preserve and protect sites of universal value, politics should not be an obstacle. In fact, the discourse behind the inclusion of heritage in the List is that the site will not only belong to its country, but 'to the world'. However, accepting certain claims of rights over disputed territory seems beyond the scope of UNESCO.

There was a case in which an application made by Jordan in 1981 to include the Old City of Jerusalem and its walls in the List found the position of Israel, which had effective control of the territory (Wallerstein, 2012). The quandary would be if Vietnam and the Philippines were opposed to China's claim for inclusion in the list and how UNESCO would respond to that.

However, the clearest example of this controversy concluded on June 2011 when Thailand announced its withdrawal from the World Heritage Convention because UNESCO was reviewing Cambodia's application to include the Preah Vihear Temple—in disputed territory—in the World Heritage List. This case seemed to be larger than just the inclusion of heritage for its preservation. In fact, Meskell (2016) uncovered the diplomatic cables released by WikiLeaks in 2010 in relation to the Preah Vihear Temple and showed its inscription on the UNESCO World Heritage List as connected with national political intrigues, international border wars, bilateral negotiations surrounding gas and steel contracts, and military alignments. In fact, it seems like its inclusion has become irrelevant, but it is still highly valuable in state-to-state negotiations and exchanges of social capital (Meskell, 2016). The dispute left 85 casualties dead (18 Cambodians and 67 Thais) and more than 200 wounded on the two sides. Despite this tragedy happening in the public realm, the cables uncovered benefits of this inclusion: firstly, the inscription of the temple would resolve maritime claim disputes between both countries, and, secondly, it would increase US investors in Cambodia, such as Boeing, Nike, McDonalds, Pizza Hut, and Marlboro (Meskell, 2016). If Cambodia retained its temple, Thailand might enhance its underwater assets and the United States might negotiate for contracts.

This example shows that, even if it is well known that heritage is linked with politics, there are complex political transactions surrounding it that seem removed from logic, such as foreign interests, soft and hard power, and military calculation. Heritage is a term that is being used by various actors for reaching political goals. Declaring an object or a place as 'heritage' already involves exclusion or inclusion and the reactions of other actors. In addition, this preservation seems to be an obligation. The inclusion of a 'Silk Road on the Sea', through disputed waters, is just another example of the use of heritage as a transaction.

This chapter recognises the need to acknowledge the political interests behind each inclusion of a site as heritage. Management and preservation of underwater cultural heritage could be an 'excuse' to find common ground in political disputes. Part of a country's strategy for power is diplomacy. Diplomacy deals with the interface of conflict and peace-making and is about conducting relationships by, and among, international actors. However, there is currently a military, financial, political, and moral rebalancing in the world's power structure (Perez-Alvaro and Forrest, 2018), with an emerging reality of the power shift from the Atlantic to Asia and the Pacific, and specifically China. States try to rebalance their position without risking their international relationships. Underwater cultural heritage is just another excuse for states to claim their position in international ranking. Recognising its use as a political weapon will help heritage stakeholders and policy makers to protect it, not only for the benefit of a nation, but for the benefit of mankind.

Conclusions

The South China Sea historically was one of the busiest trading routes in the world and as a result it has a wealth of historic underwater cultural heritage. China is using this heritage, and the conduct of maritime archaeology, to bolster its territorial and maritime claims. While linked, these are being used differently. The search for, investigation of and possible recovery of underwater cultural heritage is taking place in waters over which there are sovereignty and control disputes. The very act of undertaking these activities appears to be used in support of the claims of sovereignty and control. So, for example, that the particular wreck being investigated might not be a 'Chinese' wreck is beside the point. The fact that it is being conducted by Chinese government entities is used to support China's right to undertake any activities in those waters. Should the wreck being investigated be a 'Chinese wreck', then the wreck, as underwater cultural heritage (including all that was on or in the wreck), is then used to support a broader claim to those waters—one apparently based on some form of historical title. These activities are clearly part of the broader South China Sea strategy and relevant Government officials have made this quite explicit (Erickson and Bond, 2015). This is juxtaposed with the limited maritime archaeology that has been undertaken prior to China's invigorated maritime archaeology programme, and the historical evidence that exists from source other than maritime archaeology. This then, is used as a basis for controlling maritime archaeology in this maritime territory, and from these maritime archaeological activities, revealing underwater cultural heritage that supports the very claim to the maritime territory that is presumed to exist in the first place. These complexities are exacerbated by China's more general approach to all Chinese cultural heritage and its role in modern China as a catalyst of nation-building. China's approach to the South China Sea, and particularly its maritime archaeological activity and is attitude to the underwater cultural heritage continues to colour its disputed claims in these waters—to the detriment of the archaeological record. However, this is just one example more of the use of heritage for political strategies. Although China is emphasising the protection of its underwater cultural heritage, its government has not expressed any intention on ratifying the 2001 UNESCO Convention, one of this reason being that it encourages States Parties to undertake underwater archaeological cooperation, technology transfer and information-sharing, precepts which do not seem suitable for China's interest. The use of underwater cultural heritage for political aims indicates two things: underwater cultural heritage is important enough to be preserved, and it is a new weapon for territorial, as well as political, aims. Political or religious regimes erasing images of another regime, religion, or nation are common, such as the destruction of images during the French Revolution or the destruction of the Bamiyan Buddhas by the Taliban regime. The process of destroying or removing objects, practices or—as in the case of the islands in the South China Sea—places is not only a destructive process, but a process of the creation of a new collective memory (Harrison, 2012). It is also a powerful symbol of the piece of heritage being taken or destroyed. In addition, the politics of the past and the present are woven into these processes.

Interpretation of heritage involves rewriting history. According to Graham (2016), if heritage is the contemporary use of the past and if its meanings are defined in the present, then we create the heritage that we require and manage it for a range of purposes defined by the needs and demands of our present societies. Underwater cultural heritage, for its proximity to the law of the sea, is being caught up in its principles and statutes and is becoming a powerful symbol for those who try to gain a space within the international political arena. Once an archaeological submerged place moves into the political arena, it becomes a symbol of something else. Therefore, underwater cultural heritage has become an essential tool for strategies in international recognition, self-determination, and defiance. As a consequence, politics is a concept interlinked to underwater cultural heritage in all aspects: management of underwater cultural heritage involve mostly political decisions for its valuation. Some of these decisions are taken for the interests of a country, and some for the interest of some communities. Therefore, politics is a concept essential in other chapters of this book: treasure hunting, money laundering, uses of the heritage, valuation of the heritage, they are all topics involved with political decisions.

Notes

1 Reproduced from Perez-Alvaro, E. and Forrest, C. (2018). Maritime archaeology and underwater cultural heritage in the disputed South China Sea. *International Journal of Cultural Property.* Copyright © 2018, published by Cambridge University Press. All rights reserved.
2 Tommy T. B. Koh, 1982. 'A Constitution for the Oceans' (statement by President Koh at the final session of the Conference at Montego Bay, 6 and 11 December 1982) reprinted in United nations, *The Law of the Sea: United Nations Convention on the Law of the Sea* (1983) E.83.V.5.
3 *The Minquiers and Ecrehos Case (France/United Kingdom)* [1953] ICJ Rep 47.
4 *Republic of the Philippines v. People's Republic of China*, PCA Case No. 2013–19 (12 July 2016), paras
5 *Republic of the Philippines v. People's Republic of China*, PCA Case No. 2013–19 (12 July 2016), para 597–614.
6 This map itself appears to have been based on a 1914 map. See Jinming and Dexia (2003): 287.
7 *Republic of the Philippines v. People's Republic of China*, PCA Case No. 2013–19 (12 July 2016), paras 116–144.
8 *Republic of the Philippines v. People's Republic of China*, PCA Case No. 2013–19 (12 July 2016), para 180.
9 *Republic of the Philippines v. People's Republic of China*, PCA Case No. 2013–19 (12 July 2016), para 206.
10 *Republic of the Philippines v. People's Republic of China*, PCA Case No. 2013–19 (12 July 2016), para 272.

Bibliography

Adams, J. (2013). The role of underwater archaeology in framing and facilitating the Chinese national strategic agenda. In Blumenfield, T. and Silverman, H. (eds.), *Cultural Heritage Politics in China*. New York: Springer: 261–282.

Amer, R. (2014). China, Vietnam, and the South China Sea: disputes and dispute management. *Ocean Development & International Law* 45(1): 17–40.

Anderson, D. and Van Logchem, Y. (2014). Rights and obligations in areas of overlapping maritime claims. In Jayakumar, S., Koh, T. and Beckman, R. (eds.), *The South China Sea Disputes and Law of the Sea*. Cheltenham: Edward Elgar.

Aplin, G. (2002). *Heritage Identification, Conservation and Management*. Oxford: Oxford University Press.

Beckman, R. (2010). South China Sea: how China could clarify its claims. RSIS Commentary 116.

Blum, Y. Z. (2012). *Historic Titles in International Law*. London: Springer.

Bonnet, F. (2015). Archaeology and Patriotism: Long Term Chinese Strategies in the South China Sea. Southeast Asia Sea Conference, Ateneo Law Center, Makati, 27 March 2015.

Brownlie, I. and Crawford, J. (2012). *Brownlie's Principles of Public International Law*. Oxford: Oxford University Press.

Carman, J. (1996). *Valuing Ancient Things: Archaeology and Law*. London: Leicester University Press: 67–96.

Catley, B. and Keliat, M. (1997). *Spratlys: The Dispute in the South China Sea*. Cheltenham: Ashgate: 9–17.

Erickson, A. S. and Bond, K. (2015). Archaeology and the South China Sea. *The Diplomat*. Available at: http://thediplomat.com/2015/07/archaeology-and-the-south-china-sea/ (5 February 2018).

Falkenhausen, L. (1995). The regionalist paradigm in Chinese archaeology. In Kohl, P. L. and Fawcett, C. (eds.), *Nationalism, Politics, and the Practice of Archaeology*. Cambridge: Cambridge University Press: 198–217.

Flecker, M. (2002). The ethics, politics and realities of maritime archaeology in Southeast Asia. *The International Journal of Nautical Archaeology* 21(1): 12–24.

Flecker, M. (2015). Archaeology could wreck China's sea claims. [online]. *Today*. 5 May 2015. Available at: www.todayonline.com/world/asia/archaeology-could-wreck-chinas-sea-claims (6 February 2018).

Fu, K. (2003). Chinese perspective on the UNESCO Convention on the Protection of the Underwater Cultural Heritage. *International Journal of Marine and Coastal Law* 18(1): 109–126.

Fu, K. (2006). China (including Taiwan). In Dromgoole, S. (ed.), *The Protection of the Underwater Cultural Heritage: National Perspectives in Light of the UNESCO Convention 2001*. Leiden: Martinus Nijhoff: 17–41.

Gao, Z. (1994). The South China sea: from conflict to cooperation? *Ocean Development & International Law* 25(3): 345–359.

Graham, B. (2016). Heritage as knowledge: capital or culture? *Urban Studies* 39(5–6): 1003–1017.

Gruber, S. (2008). *Protecting China's Cultural Heritage Sites in Times of Rapid Change: Current Developments, Practice and Law*. Legal Studies Research Paper No. 08/93. University of Sydney, Sydney Law School.

Gungwu, W. (1958). The Nanhai trade: a study of the early history of Chinese trade in the South China Sea. *Journal of the Malayan Branch of the Royal Asiatic Society* 31(2(182)): 1–135.

Hall, W. E. and Higgins, A. P. (1917). *A Treatise on International Law*. Oxford: Clarendon Press.

Harrell, S. (2013). China's tangled web of heritage. In Blumenfield, T. and Silverman, H. (eds.), *Cultural Heritage Politics in China*. New York: Springer: 285–293.

Harrison, R. (2012). *Heritage: Critical Approaches*. London: Routledge.

Hatcher, M., Thorncroft, A. and De Rham, M. (1987). *The Nanking Cargo*. London: Hamish Hamilton: 166.

Hill, N. L. (1945). *Claims to Territory in International Law and Relations*. New York: Oxford University Press.

Hoagland, P. (1999). China. In Dromgoole, S. (ed.), *Legal Protection of the Underwater Cultural Heritage: National and International Perspectives*. The Hague: Kluwer Law International: 35–36.

Hu, N. A. (2010). South China Sea: troubled waters or a sea of opportunity? *Ocean Development & International Law* 41(3): 203–213.

Jennings, R. Y. (1963). *The Acquisition of Territory in International Law*. Manchester: Manchester University Press.

Jinming, L. and Dexia, L. (2003). The dotted line on the Chinese map of the South China Sea: a note. *Ocean Development & International Law* 34(3–4): 287–295.

Joyner, C. C. (1999). The Spratly Islands dispute in the South China Sea: problems, policies, and prospects for diplomatic accommodation. *Investigating Confidence-Building Measures in the Asia-Pacific Region: Stimson Center Report* 28: 53–108.

Lin, C. (1997). Taiwan's South China Sea policy. *Asian Survey* 37(4): 323–339.

Lipe, W. D. (1984). Value and meaning in cultural resources. In H. Cleere (ed.), *Approaches to the Archaeological Heritage*. Cambridge: Cambridge University Press: 1–11.

Mail Online (2013). 'Give us back our treasure': Chinese demand Cameron returns priceless artefacts looted during 19th century Boxer Rebellion. [online]. *Daily Mail*. 4 December 2013. Available at: www.dailymail.co.uk/news/article-2518111/China-demand-David-Cameron-return-Boxer-Rebellion-artefacts.html (1 March 2018).

McDowell, S. (2008). Heritage, memory and identity. In Graham, B. and Howard, P. (eds.), *The Ashgate Research Companion to Heritage and Identity*. Cornwall: Ashgate: 37–54.

Meskell, L. (2016). World heritage and WikiLeaks: territory, trade, and temples on the Thai-Cambodian border. *Current Anthropology* 57(1): 72–95.

Miller, G. L. (1992). The second destruction of the *Geldermalsen*. *Historical Archaeology* 26(4): 124–131.

Morton, B. and Blackmore, G. (2001). South China Sea. *Marine Pollution Bulletin* 42(12): 1236–1263.

O'Keefe, P. J. (2002). Negotiating the future of the underwater cultural heritage. In Brodie, N. and Tubb, K. W. (ed.), *Illicit Antiquities: The Theft of Culture and the Extinction of Archaeology*. London: Routledge: 137–161.

Page, J. (2013). Chinese territorial strife hits archaeology. [online]. *Wall Street Journal*. 2 December 2013. Available at www.wsj.com/articles/SB10001424052702304470504579164873258159410 (2 April 2018).

Page, J. and Barnes, J. E. (2015). China expands island construction in disputed South China Sea. [online]. *Wall Street Journal*. 18 February 2015. Available at: www.wsj.com/articles/china-expands-island-construction-in-disputed-south-china-sea-1424290852.

Park, C. (1978). The South China Sea disputes: who owns the islands and the natural resources? *Ocean Development & International Law* 5(1): 27–59

Perez-Alvaro, E. and Forrest, C. (2018). Maritime archaeology and underwater cultural heritage in the disputed South China Sea. *International Journal of Cultural Property* 25(03): 375–401.

Pitchford, S. (2008). *Identity Tourism: Imaging and Imagining the Nation* (Vol. 10). Bingley: Emerald Group.

Regulation (1989). Regulations Concerning the Management and Protection of Underwater Cultural Relics, China on 20 October 1989. Available at: www.china.org.cn/english/zhuanti/3represents/76269.htm (21 December 2017).

Schofield, C. (2013). What's at stake in the South China Sea? Geographical and geopolitical considerations. In Beckman, R., Townsend-Gault, I., Schofield, C. and Davenport, T. (eds.), *Beyond Territorial Disputes in the South China Sea*. Cheltenham: Edward Elgar.

Shaw, M. N. (2014). *International Law* (7th edn). Cambridge: Cambridge University Press.

Shearer, I. A. (ed.) (1994). *Starke's International Law* (11th edn). London: Butterworths.

Tiezzi, S. (2015). Why China is stopping its South China Sea Island-building (for now). [online]. *The Diplomat*. 16 June 2015. Available at: https://thediplomat.com/2015/06/why-china-is-stopping-its-south-china-sea-island-building-for-now/ (3 January 2018).

UNCLOS (1982). United Nations Convention on the Law of the Sea. Available at: www.un.org/depts/los/convention_agreements/convention_overview_conven tion.htm (3 May 2018).

UNESCO (1972). Convention Concerning the Protection of the World Cultural and Natural Heritage. Paris, 16 November 1972. Available at: http://whc.unesco.org/ en/conventiontext/ (3 May 2018).

UNESCO (2001). Convention on the Protection of the Underwater Cultural Heritage. Paris, 2 November 2001. Available at: http://unesdoc.unesco.org/images/0012/ 001260/126065e.pdf (3 May 2018).

Viejo-Rose, D. (2011). *Reconstructing Spain: Cultural Heritage and Memory after Civil War*. Sussex: Sussex Academic Press.

Wallerstein, S. (2012). Who can apply to add sites situated in disputed territory to the World Heritage List? [online]. *Blog of the European Journal of International Law*. 17 September 2012. Available at: www.ejiltalk.org/category/international-tribunals/unesco/ (5 February 2018).

Wong, E. and Erlanger, S. (2013). Frenchman will return to China prized bronze artifacts looted in 19th century. [online]. *New York Times*. 27 April 2013. Available at: www.nytimes.com/2013/04/27/world/europe/frenchman-will-return-to-china-prized-bronze-artifacts-looted-in-19th-century.html?_r=0 (6 February 2018).

Zhao, H. (1992). Recent developments in the legal protection of historic shipwrecks in China. *Ocean Development & International Law* 23(4): 305–333.

Zhong, H. (2015). Legal protection of Chinese relics: a justification for the return. *Art Antiquity and Law* 20(1): 47.

11 Other practices
Treasure hunters and money laundering

Some underwater cultural heritage, especially historic shipwrecks, not only have an archaeological, historical or artistic value but they can also have high economic value. The underwater cultural heritage is a hidden archaeological patrimony and an economic resource, not only for the associated states, but also for private companies. Due to the romantic notion of treasures at the bottom of oceans, underwater cultural heritage has been subjected to 'unprofessional' recovery that can spoil the objects without an adequate archaeological record being maintained. In addition, underwater cultural heritage objects are sold at a profit. This practice can result in money laundering and terrorist financing by international criminal enterprises because of its apparent legality.

The economic value of underwater cultural heritage has largely been discussed in the literature, specifically in relation to treasure hunters. Legal and illicit dealings of underwater cultural heritage revolves primarily around the way the object has been acquired and/or moved (Bowman, 2008); however, this an ambiguous issue since it is possible to identify three different categories of dealing with the acquired items. The first category is trading cultural objects from underwater sites that have been acquired through authorised excavations and commercial exploitation; this involves legal recoveries of cultural objects from heritage sites to be returned to the rightful owner or sold. These excavations may or may not be performed by archaeologists; however, the objects are returned to the rightful owner. This is the 'whitest' category of the three although there are two issues associated with this option. Firstly, although some countries may 'authorise' the excavations, UNESCO (2016) warns that legally permitted commercial exploitation is no less problematic than illegal pillaging, since it disregards scientific information, and artefacts are treated inappropriately as there is focus on reselling these items. Secondly, although the state where the items are discovered may be 'the rightful owner', some authorise the use of these cultural objects for its use in other industries, such as micro-chips businesses (UNESCO, 2016). Other states may reach a deal so the commercial salvors can keep and sell the 'trade objects' that are considered duplicates with no cultural significance, such as large volumes of coins or replicated items (Stemm, 2000). However, according to UNESCO (2016), these commercial companies often engage in fraud, tax-evasion and money laundering often inflating the valuable cargo to attract naïve investors, which creates further complications. The second category of illicit handling of cultural objects is grouped in a more 'grey area'. For example, objects whose documentation or provenience have been lost, such as items that were excavated prior to the establishment of patrimony laws in the country of origin, objects acquired under a colonial rule or objects recovered by amateurs, fishermen or divers before they were considered cultural and significant. The last category involves objects that have been looted, either in unauthorised excavations or that have been illegally removed. These are considered as 'black' cultural objects with no provenance. According to UNESCO (2016), pillaging is the theft of cultural objects from a heritage site in violation of the law. This is a common phenomenon including sport diving activities where the objects are kept as souvenirs and specialised treasure hunting companies.

This chapter will examine these three categories, particularly the 'white' and 'black' underwater cultural heritage markets that are often confused in literature: some companies 'legally' exploit the underwater cultural heritage and some 'illegally' pillage it. As a consequence, the chapter will deal with the economic utilisation of this heritage and the issue of using it for illegal purposes.

Introduction

Archaeologists are against treasure hunters and commercial salvors in excavations mainly because the last ones are more preoccupied in identifying specific objects of high economic value and they get frustrated if they discover other vessels along the way (Maarleveld, 2011: 922). Maarleveld (2011) also posited other problems, such as the urge for identifying the material to avoid economic losses, dispersing the collection with a short description in an auction or the donations of artefacts to those who have supported them in their endeavours. As Gould (2011) states, treasure hunters sell off valuable items and transfer the burden of conservation of ordinary materials to museums, braking up the principle of association (where archaeological material should remain together). For Coroneos (2006: 120), the main issue relates to timing; the more time spent on a site, the less profit gained. As a consequence, the study of archaeological sites may be non-existent or minimal.

Throckmorton (1998) calculated that the most inefficient treasure hunt cost US$500,000 for 16 days at sea, and most investors are satisfied if they are included as part of the adventure because it is exciting. Treasure hunters and commercial salvors plunder wrecks for valuables, but Dromgoole (2004) estimated that a wreck needs to be worth more than US$10 million to be commercially attractive for salvage. Currently, approximately four vessels of this value have been recovered. And although some cargos can be worth US $500 million (Villegas-Zamora, 2008: 22) this economic value is only calculated when the archaeological standards are compromised by the demands of the market under a quick profit and imperative auction houses trigger the demand. For instance, the economic importance of the recent discovery of the vessel, *Nuestra Senora de las Mercedes*, the Spanish frigate loaded with over US$500 million worth of gold and silver coins is a landmark in archaeology, both terrestrial and underwater (Aznar-Gómez, 2010). However, UNESCO (2016) claimed that with the announcement of the discovery, Odyssey Marine Exploration, the salvage company involved in the excavation, increased its shares value by more than US$200 million although according to UNESCO (2016) some of the coins found were damaged as they did not receive the appropriate conservation treatment, therefore, the actual value of the cargo did not exceed US$13 million. However, according to Aznar- Gómez (2004: 79), 'scattered around the Spanish coastline lies more gold and silver than in the vaults of the Bank of Spain'. This is because many of the sunken galleons were laden with a fortune of gold, silver and other precious materials plundered from colonies between the 16th and 19th centuries (Bass, 2005). In fact, it has been calculated that sunken treasure worth US$1 billion is lying in the Mediterranean Sea; however, the real value will probably never be known (Dromgoole, 2004). Elsewhere in the world, there are more sunken treasures in the Atlantic, Caribbean and Pacific, estimated to be worth millions; however, it is impossible to know how many wrecks exist at the bottom of oceans (Dromgoole, 2004). Throckmorton (1998: 81) calculated that only one in 20 salvage companies have any chance of making money. Furthermore, Kleeberg (2013) examined the profitability of six commercial salvage ventures: *Nuestra Señora de Atocha, Nuestra Señora de la Pura y Limpia Concepción, Whydah Galley, HMS De Braak, SS Central America* and *SS Brother Jonathan,* and concluded all lost money in their excavations. Ocean salvaging is an expensive and dangerous operation and the value of the artefacts that are found cannot cover these expenses, especially because the most commonly found sellable artefacts are silver coins that actively corrode in saltwater, and coin collectors will only pay high premiums if there are in exquisite condition (Kleeberg, 2013).

Throckmorton (1998) revealed that the salvage boom has cost Florida State millions because of the associated legal cases of the artefacts. He claimed that today's treasure hunters are promoted on Wall Street and the Vancouver Stock Exchange, and their investors include some of the wealthiest people in the world. However, the salvage industry only benefits promoters and lawyers, according to Throckmorton (1998). In fact, Kleeberg (2013) affirmed that commercial salvage of historic shipwrecks is an unprofitable investment, where the investors respond to the cult of the entrepreneur, celebrity and wealth. Kleeberg (2013) stated that people invest in these ventures because they are poorly informed, they expect to buy a piece of an 'adventure' and as the initial investment in these ventures are usually quite low, they are easily trapped.

Issue

For some authors, museums attract tourists and economies supported by the tourism industry do not need to have an agreement with salvor companies (Carman, 2002). However, in poorer countries, the combination of commercial salvage and archaeology is a model difficult to overcome (Flecker, 2002). For instance, in Southeast Asia, governments cannot afford excavating shipwrecks and displaying the items, therefore, commercial companies are necessary to provide the funding (Flecker, 2002). For instance, in Indonesia's archipelago, it is believed there are more historic shipwrecks than in any other country worldwide (Flecker, 2002). For this reason, a policy was developed by which groups could salvage historical shipwrecks in Indonesian waters and 50% of the salvaged cargo would be handed over to the government. As Flecker (2002) affirmed, the country lacks trained personnel and as the industry is profitable, fishermen look for new archaeological sites now, even though they are not trained and do not follow archaeological standards (Kaiser, 1993). However, Indonesia has recently imposed a moratorium on salvage contracts and it is revising their policy. According to Flecker (2002), a significant amount of historical information is being lost daily throughout Asia and deals with private companies are the only solution for these countries. However, Throckmorton (1998) defended that if a poor country that uses salvage for funding, builds museums to display the artefacts instead, this would attract tourists and its economic gain would be stronger, albeit slow. Bass (2005: 27) stated:

> archaeologists face the constant threat of the looting of historic wrecks by treasure hunters for personal gain rather than for the benefit of humankind. [...] No countries have ever benefited as much from treasure hunting as from true archaeology, which results in museums that attract thousands, even millions, of visitors.

From UNESCO, efforts are made to train people as archaeologists with projects such as the *Training Manual for the UNESCO Foundation Course on the Protection and Management of Underwater Cultural Heritage in Asia and the Pacific* (Manders and Underwood, 2012).

One of the biggest problems for the commercialisation of underwater cultural heritage is the legislative gaps that exist. As previously mentioned, the protection of underwater cultural heritage is a combination of both international and domestic laws. However, there are two outdated precepts in international sea laws that conflict with the protection of the underwater cultural heritage: the law of finds and the salvage law. These conflicts exist as maritime laws were initially drafted with salvaging in mind, i.e. things from the past with a present-day value, and they disregard the broader and more current issue of heritage value. With regards to the law of finds, if the ship-wreck is owned by someone, the salvor is entitled to compensation; however, not the title. If someone finds and gains title to the vessel, it is assumed that is was abandoned by its owner; this relates to the common law doctrine of 'finders, keepers'. If the property, i.e. the vessel, is abandoned, the owner has relinquished the title voluntarily, or the title has been lost, then the salvor is entitled to the property; however, abandonment must be proven (Elia, 2000). Salvage is an old concept of maritime laws that rewards the salvor when recovering objects from the bottom of the sea. One core principle is that the salvor acts not in his or her own interest, but in the interest of the owner of the vessel, under dangerous circumstances (Juvelier, 2016). The law of sal-vage is considered part of customary international law and there are three elements required for a successful claim of salvage: 'marine peril', volun-tary service and success in the operation. Conflicts with 'treasure hunters' arise mostly because the recovery of goods at sea are considered 'at peril' i.e. usually in danger of being lost by sinking. Treasure hunters apply this maritime principle to ancient shipwrecks and property, and this is considered inherently 'at risk'. However, as mentioned previously, shipwrecks are better protected by the sludge at the bottom of the sea, therefore, such a 'risk' does not exist. This is a legal provision developed to deal with emergencies, such as in instances where a vessel can only be saved if it is rescued within the few precious hours after it sinks, rather than in the event where the ship sank long before. This law has been compared in relation to underwater cultural heri-tage with an order that you did not ask for but you have to pay: since you did not ask for that order, you did not established any terms or conditions, but you still have to pay for it. That is the comparison with recovery by commer-cial companies: they 'rescue' your shipwreck, a shipwreck that you did not order to rescue and as a consequence a rescue whose terms and conditions were not agreed, but you still have to 'pay'—or compensate—for the order.

The law of salvage was drafted under the 1989 Salvage Convention that had already included an article that applied to underwater cultural heritage indirectly:

> *Article 30. Reservations*
> 1. Any State may, at the time of signature, ratification, acceptance, approval or accession, reserve the right not to apply the provisions of this Convention: [...]
> (d) when the property involved is maritime cultural property of prehistoric, archaeological or historic interest and is situated on the sea-bed.

However, the 1982 United Nations Convention on the Law of the Sea (UNCLOS, 1982) complicated the issue when one of its only articles referred to archaeological and historical objects found at sea:

Article 303. Archaeological and historical objects found at sea

1. States have the duty to protect objects of an archaeological and historical nature found at sea and shall cooperate for this purpose.
2. In order to control traffic in such objects, the coastal State may, in applying article 33, presume that their removal from the sea-bed in the zone referred to in that article without its approval would result in an infringement within its territory or territorial sea of the laws and regulations referred to in that article.

Including this exception:

3. Nothing in this article affects the rights of identifiable owners, the law of salvage or other rules of admiralty, or laws and practices with respect to cultural exchanges.

As a consequence, salvage law is still considered an issue when applied to underwater cultural heritage. According to Forrest (2003), archaeologists believe that the application of law of salvage has three main consequences for underwater cultural heritage: (1) the granting of ownership of artefacts to salvors *in lieu* of a salvage award, (2) the splitting up of a collection, and (3) the excavation techniques required to minimise commercial costs and maximise the salvage award. Forrest (2003) also highlighted:

[S]alvage law is at odds with the preservation of underwater cultural heritage. This does not mean that underwater cultural heritage does not, or should not, embody an economic value only that salvage law as the means of realizing that economic value; is inappropriate because it causes an imbalance between the realization of the economic and archaeological values of the underwater cultural heritage.

The 2001 UNESCO Convention condemned the law of salvage by stating some exceptions:

Article 4 — Any activity relating to underwater cultural heritage to which this Convention applies shall not be subject to the law of salvage or law of finds, unless it:

(a) is authorized by the competent authorities, and
(b) is in full conformity with this Convention, and
(c) ensures that any recovery of the underwater cultural heritage achieves its maximum protection.

This salvage clause was written as a compromise between civil law countries who rejected the application of the law of salvage and common laws in countries that supported salvaging (Juvelier, 2016). The salvage law is also challenged in the Convention through its non-commercialisation clause:

> Rule 2. The commercial exploitation of underwater cultural heritage for trade or speculation or its irretrievable dispersal is fundamentally incompatible with the protection and proper management of underwater cultural heritage. Underwater cultural heritage shall not be traded, sold, bought or bartered as commercial goods.
>
> This Rule cannot be interpreted as preventing:
>
> (a) the provision of professional archaeological services or necessary services incidental thereto whose nature and purpose are in full conformity with this Convention and are subject to the authorization of the competent authorities; [...]

Although this clause allows certain commercial actors to access underwater cultural heritage, it requires state supervision and control over salvors, treasure hunters and contractors (Juvelier, 2016).

Another main point of conflict between archaeologists and private companies relates not only to the methodology of recovery but also to the commercialisation of the objects (Elia, 2000). Underwater archaeologists claim that artefacts from shipwrecks should never be sold or be part of private collections, and that dispersal of collection does not allow scientific studies. Treasure salvors argue that other cultural items, such as paintings, can be privately owned, used economically and should not be differ from underwater items. In addition, the economic benefit can also be obtained from media rights or the exhibitions of those objects. This does not damage the heritage (Fletcher-Tomenius and Forrest, 2000). And although, according to Kingsley (2001) the *Hoi An* and *Tek Sing* shipwrecks were both excavated by private companies to 'scientific' standards with the results being published, the objects found in the excavations were auctioned as treasures and this was denounced by archaeologists as the sale of 'primary research data' (Kingsley, 2003). The main cause of debate between archaeologists and commercial salvors is the meaning of the word 'treasure' applied to shipwrecks; this directly implies that the heritage has an economic value. The problem is that technology develops faster than the appreciation of objects. For Villegas-Zamora (2008: 18), the romantic idea of shipwrecks has affected others in addition to treasure hunters. For instance, Pickford's (1994) book, 'The Atlas of Shipwrecks and Treasure' established that materials on shipwrecks are treasures rather than information data. However, according to Throckmorton (1998: 82), materials with no records that have not been intelligently excavated have no value. The *Nanking*, an almost intact shipwreck was purposefully damaged using dynamite to access the Chinese blue and white porcelain onboard (Throckmorton, 1998: 82). Gould (2011) states that to increase the price of coins and material, treasure hunters create 'sea stories' about the shipwreck to create an historical association to attract buyers. In the case of the Egyptian tombs, for instance, although the material was salvaged, the historical value survived because the tombs remained intact, as opposed to shipwrecks that are often destroyed without retaining the information by either commercial salvors or pillagers. It is worth highlighting the case of the *Atocha*, excavated by Mel Fisher, who focus the propeller wash of his boat directly down at the sea-bed. In shallow waters, this allowed to blow away timbers and left gold and silver bars intact and exposed (Gould, 2011). A further issue related to looting activities is that it also desecrates grave sites (UNESCO, 2016).

State of knowledge

There are approximately 100–200 shipwrecks around the world that contain worthy fortunes and when they are discovered and recovered, treasure hunters will not have interest in the rest of the shipwrecks. In fact, and according to Coroneos (2006, p. 112), Australia fought and won the battle with treasure hunters in the 1970s so Australian archaeologists do not seem to have to fight against treasure hunters anymore since it seems difficult that more shipwrecks with cargo worth millions of dollars are going to be discovered within Australian waters (Coroneos, 2006: 112). As Kingsley (2001) claimed, underwater archaeology is an expensive business; it has different hazardous moral mazes, such as the significant costs associated with the excavation and the cargo that is languished in museum storage. Kingsley (2001) calculated that every month of underwater excavation requires one year of conservation, registration and research. Kingsley (2001) also stated that commercial salvors and pillagers are two different issues; however, according to Wreckwatch (2011), treasure hunting is redundant and commercial marine archaeology has emerged. In this regard, maritime commercial archaeological companies are common in Europe and America. Construction or development of ports and harbours require previous analysis and research for archaeological materials. Excavations are executed by archaeologists but paid for by construction companies. The archaeological process needs to be fast since the construction companies are paying the cost. As a consequence, underwater archaeologists argue that commercial recovery does not result in good archaeology; every day of research on an excavation, the more money the construction company loses. Therefore, construction companies prefer a quick survey or no survey at all to reduce costs. However, and according to Kingsley (2003), these private companies are the ones that are developing underwater archaeology; for instance, he maintained that deep-water excavation is possible thanks to Odyssey Marine Exploration, the first company to work on deep-water shipwrecks and that is working to incorporate new methods and standards for the future of deep-water excavations. In this regard, and according to Fletcher-Tomenius and Forrest (2000), some companies, like *ProSea*, are promoting responsible and professional recovery of deep-sea historic wrecks. For them, salvage is applicable but the International Convention on Salvage (1989) should not apply, where the salvor has the right to keep the artefacts rescued. *ProSea* has also created its own convention including statements suggesting that the state has preferential rights to purchase the salvaged artefacts.

UNESCO (2016) has listed some cases of commercial exploitation of underwater cultural heritage such as *the Cirebon Wreck* (Indonesia): in 2003, local Indonesian fishermen caught Chinese ceramics in their nets in the Northern Java Sea, off Cirebon in Indonesia. These ceramics belonged to a shipwreck that had sunk at the turn of the first millennium. In 2004, the wreck was commercially exploited by a private Belgian company with assistance from a Belgian museum and 500,000 pieces of cargo were collected, although half were thrown back in the sea as the objects were not considered valuable. The largest part of the artefact collection that was left behind were sold on the international market in 2013. Another example is *the Belitung Wreck* (Indonesia) which was commercially exploited and destroyed in 1998. The Indonesian government issued some licences to have the objects exported. However, the fund share given to Indonesia, despite a legal dispute, was minimal. The artefacts that would have constituted a museum collection were sold and dispersed and there is nothing left of the shipwreck. Some ancient Portuguese wrecks (Mozambique) were also exploited by a commercial enterprise off Ilha de Mozambique. Many of the precious historic artefacts and testimonies of early seafaring were sold and the objects were melted for the production of micro-chips. The *San José Wreck* (Panama) was a Spanish galleon that sank in the archipelago of Las Perlas in the 17th century. Treasure hunters working on the San José caused significant damage to the seabed using propeller-wash deflectors to recover the artefacts lying in the area, without any research questions addressed. Although these shipwrecks were 'legally' excavated, with permission sought from the coastal states, they have been badly damaged and the information that they offered has been destroyed. As a consequence, these commercial salvors achieved the same level of damage as pillagers. Not only were archaeological methods not observed in most cases but also the sale of the artefacts benefited only a few people or parties and not everyone. Therefore, this is why UNESCO (2016) stated that legally permitted commercial exploitation is as damaging as illegal pillaging.

Ethical dilemmas: other practices

The issue of commercial exploitation of underwater cultural heritage seems to be broader than the loss of historical information and the sale of cultural objects. UNESCO (2016) stated that large treasure hunting companies often operate in illegal side activities, permitting investors to avoid paying taxes by investing in their companies or help in money laundering through trafficking ancient artefacts, displayed and marketed in 'shipwreck fairs' (Gould, 2011). In fact, the sale of cultural heritage used for money laundering and terrorist financing is continuously increasing. This market, because of its confidentiality, portability and price volatility, is extremely profitable (Giroud and Lechtman, 2015). In fact, sometimes the quantity of artefacts is so large that it threats lowering the market prices due to the increase in supply. As a consequence, companies throw these cultural objects back into the ocean for destruction (UNESCO, 2016). Other times, the commercial salvors overestimate the value of cargo to attract investment. These investors expect a big return that never usually eventuates, particularly as most commercial salvage operations are not profitable (UNESCO, 2016). However, the objects are often sold on the black/illegal market and are used to increase share values and investments or for money laundering.

Money laundering refers to the cleaning of dirty money generated by criminal activity (Lilley, 2009). Money laundering in relation to cultural objects uses a broad range of techniques, such as the use of fake money for the purchase of cultural objects, or at auctions (Giroud and Lechtman, 2015). It is necessary for smuggled artefacts to appear legitimate, therefore, provenances can be forged. All these techniques are easily applied to the sale of underwater cultural objects. It has been revealed that the sale of cultural heritage profits from mark-ups of 50 to 1000 times compared to the price paid to the excavator; therefore, paying an excavator US$1,000 for an item translates to the sale of that item for US$1 million by the collector in the same year (Nemeth, 2007). However, the issue extends beyond money laundering; according to McIntee (2016), artefact smuggling is related to the drugs trade, and as a consequence, being suspected of smuggling artefacts will mean being suspected of drugs smuggling. In fact, in order to sell the cultural objects, they need to be licit and this usually involves organised criminal activities. For example, this could include a network of smugglers, some corrupt customs inspectors and others involved in different illegal activities (Bowman, 2008). According to Nemeth (2007), pre-existing smuggling routes for narcotics and weapons provide the same channels for the illicit export of cultural heritage. As a consequence, artefact smuggling is also associated with terrorism and buying arms by looting historical sites. McIntee (2016) highlighted that many of the smuggling networks, especially in the Middle East, are run by terrorist groups. In fact, financing terrorist groups with the sale of cultural objects, some from underwater sites, is a reality. According to Giroud and Lechtman (2015), the territories controlled by Islamic State in Iraq and the Levan are subjected to cultural looting; this has led to the UN Security Council adopting Resolution 2199 in February 2015 to address this issue.[1] In Resolution 2199, the Security Council underlines the obligations and steps required by Member States to prevent terrorist groups in Iraq and Syria from benefitting from engaging directly or indirectly in the looting and smuggling of cultural heritage items, among other things. Nemeth (2007) claimed that terrorist groups destabilise the political structure of the host nations, distracting the local security forces and allowing clandestine excavations. In addition, these groups employ cultural cleansing, i.e. destroying ethnically symbolic cultural heritage, to threaten national securities. However, in the case of the underwater cultural heritage, this cultural cleansing is not occurring, partly because of accessibility issues to the submerged archaeological sites.

This speculation on cultural heritage transforms it from a victim of armed conflict to the commodity of a major illicit market that has been calculated as comparable to the volume of weapons and narcotics trafficking (Nemeth, 2007). As a consequence, in times of peace, the multibillion-dollar illicit trade of cultural heritage still threats international security for being a source of political violence, and an intersection with trafficking in narcotics and weapons. Therefore, underwater cultural heritage is now an instrument of political violence.

Proposal: plan of action

Combating money laundering and terrorism financing is difficult since dealing with cultural objects is characterised by discretion, and most actors in this market do not fall under any special supervision. This issue challenges and impairs the fight against money laundering and financing of terrorism in relation to cultural heritage (Giroud and Lechtman, 2015).

In the specific case of underwater cultural heritage, some solutions, such as inventories of sites, satellite surveillance, control dives and cooperation between agencies may be of help. However, there is a need to have a detailed protocol to protect the extraction of the object for its sale and use for money laundering. This protocol should include, first, exposing underwater illicit archaeology: the looting of archaeological sites irreparably damages the archaeological record of the objects and impoverishes the states' culture to the extent that they cannot easily reconstruct their own history. International cooperation, as well as cooperation between agencies, such as divers, environmental organisations, fishermen or governments, is necessary to avoid the looting of underwater archaeological sites. Second, it is necessary reporting unprovenanced cultural heritage objects in auction houses and museums: high ethical standards for acquisitions should be set and museums and auction houses should avoid giving tacit support to the market of unprovenanced material through their acquisition activities. Edson (1997: 187) suggested every object subject to a possible acquisition should be carefully studied in order to know everything about the piece, such as previous ownership, where it was excavated, its history, condition and current legal status. If there is any doubt about the provenance of a piece, it should be communicated to the relevant authorities and not proceed with the acquisition or loan. Third, it is essential to highlight the ethics around this illicit trade: states provide incentives for research and play a vital role in education, outreach and art preservation of their cultural objects and they must take precautions when signing agreements with commercial salvors to ensure that the objects recovered from underwater cultural heritage sites are archaeologically excavated. The contracts should be terminated if some of the objects recovered are looted or illegally exported: documentary evidence is necessary to prove the ethical status of a cultural item. Fourth, discussing the review and possible combination of laws: disharmony in laws in relation to cultural heritage law and maritime law can be damaging to the interests of nations, museums, auction houses, individuals, and our collective cultural heritage. Fifth, exploring individual cases: not all countries have the same economic means to fight against money laundering or terrorist financing and not all objects are subjected to this kind of market. As a consequence, although there is a need for a common protocol of all underwater cultural objects, studying the object individually is key to retaining and protecting all objects. Sixth, relating historical knowledge to a present-day problem: a cultural object without a precise provenance is of limited historical significance for the current study of our past. Archaeologists turn to antiquities with increasing frequency, seeking the missing pieces of an ancient puzzle. Finally, being part of public opinion: the multilateral protection of underwater cultural heritage under current regulations does not work properly. Policy makers and cultural heritage stakeholders need to work together with the public to get results. If society is as aware of the danger of losing cultural heritage as it is of the pollution of the planet and endangered species, maybe people's mentality will change on how important preserving our past is. If the public is excluded from all the decisions, the heritage will continue to be damaged and wrongfully exploited for commercial purposes.

One of the advantages that commercial companies promote and exploit in order to get funding from investors is presenting underwater cultural heritage as an adventure under the sea. Perhaps this is a solution for archaeologists: to present their work under water as an adventure to raise funds not only from governments, but from private funders who are excited to pay for it. The inclusion of the public is essential for the protection of underwater cultural heritage and interest would grow if people felt they belonged to a common project.

Conclusions

Both legal and illegal recovery of underwater cultural heritage can cause damage in the archaeological context, but it is the sale of the artefacts the complicated issue. Over centuries, archaeology as a field of study has advanced from searching for treasure to searching for knowledge and the term salvage only relates to a world and lure of sunken treasures. As a consequence, salvage law and heritage law are directed by different values: in practice, salvage law is linked to commercial value and has historical precedence, therefore, prevailing. However, since an historic shipwreck in not in 'marine peril' and is not a conflict of interests with the owner, salvage law is inherently inapplicable. Even if the recovery of objects has been authorised, the sale of them creates a conflict between dealers, auction houses, collectors and museums, all of which support the cultural heritage market, and the archaeologists, source nations and others, who want to restrict such trade, is becoming more pronounced. In addition, the sale of objects is creating laundering money businesses and even terrorism financing. If governments follow the market of these objects, they will have a new angle in the fight against money laundering and international crime and underwater cultural heritage will benefit from this protection. As Fletcher-Tomenius and Forrest (2000) argued, although historic shipwrecks are an archaeological resource, they can also contain cargo capable of re-entering the stream of commerce, be of interest to biologists or they can be an obstacle for the oil and gas industry. Archaeologists—especially in the context of the then ongoing UNESCO Convention debate—enjoyed 'disproportionate attention in the debate' (Fletcher-Tomenius and Forrest, 2000: 1) as other groups also have interest in the resource, such as the treasure salvage companies and the sport diving community. Fletcher-Tomenius and Forrest (2000) claimed the archaeological community had too much influence in the political arena and legislation took a disproportionate account of the interests of this user group: as salvors have never acted as a group, they had no influence on the political decisions relating to underwater cultural heritage. Underwater heritage is now accessible to anyone who can afford it, since old submerged cultural sites are no longer protected by natural inaccessibility (Villegas-Zamora, 2008: 18). It may be true than treasure hunters, aided by the media and by high-profile marketing, offer public spectacles that the public wants (Gould, 2011). However, underwater archaeology, although a science, does not to be boring. Maybe it is time for archaeologist to offer spectacles based in science to the public so underwater cultural heritage can be not only understood, but also loved.

Fighting the commercial value of underwater cultural heritage is a difficult task, particularly if the economic value increases after an academic paper is published on the cargo (Colwell-Chanthaphonh et al., 2008). Treasure hunters, their auction houses and their customers disregard museum organisations, archaeological societies and the UNESCO Convention because these are bodies lacking enforcement powers. Fighting against the use of underwater cultural heritage in money laundering and terrorism financing is even more difficult. Money laundering can only be fought through cooperation between different countries and their organisations. The field of underwater cultural heritage is not a sphere foreign to international security: common laws, the sharing of information and cooperation between different disciplines are ways to ensure that help is reciprocated. Cultural heritage will benefit from more protection but also government's security and its fight against money laundering and terrorist financing will benefit from learning from other disciplines.

It is necessary to consider other practices on the management of underwater cultural heritage because the seas are a source with many actors. Taking decisions and not considering those other actors only brings complicated controversies. New alternatives have to be constantly sought.

Note

1   Resolution 2199 (2015) of the Council of Security of the United Nations dated 12 February 2015. Available at: www.un.org/sc/suborg/en/node/5248.

Bibliography

Aznar-Gómez, M. J. (2004). *La protección internacional del patrimonio cultural subacuático con especial referencia al caso de España*. Valencia: Tirant Lo Blanch.

Aznar-Gómez, M. J. (2010). Treasure hunters, sunken state vessels and the 2001 UNESCO Convention on the Protection of Underwater Cultural Heritage. *The International Journal of Marine and Coastal Law* 25(2): 209–236.

Bass, G. F. (2005). *Beneath the Seven Seas: Adventures with the Institute of Nautical Archaeology*. London: Thames and Hudson.

Bowman, B. A. (2008). Transnational crimes against culture: looting at archaeological sites and the 'grey' market in antiquities. *Journal of Contemporary Criminal Justice* 24(3): 225–242.

Carman, J. (2002). *Archaeology and Heritage: An Introduction*. London: Continuum Press.

Colwell-Chanthaphonh, C., Hollowell, J. and McGill, D. (2008). *Ethics in Action: Case Studies in Archaeological Dilemmas*. Washington, DC: Society for American Archaeology. The SAA Press.

Coroneos, C. (2006). The ethics and values of maritime archaeology. In Staniforth, M. and Nash, M. (eds.), *Maritime Archaeology: Australian Approaches*. New York: Springer: 111–122.

Dromgoole, S. (2004). Murky waters for government policy: the case of a 17th century British warship and 10 tonnes of gold coins. *Marine Policy* 28(3): 189–198.

Edson, G. (ed.) (1997). *Museum Ethics*. London: Routledge.

Elia, R. (2000). US protection of underwater cultural heritage beyond the territorial sea: problems and prospects. *International Journal of Nautical Archaeology* 29(1): 43–56.

Flecker, M. (2002). The ethics, politics, and realities of maritime archaeology in Southeast Asia. *The International Journal of Nautical Archaeology* 31(1): 12–24.

Fletcher-Tomenius, P. and Forrest, C. (2000). Historic wreck in international waters: conflict or consensus? *Marine Policy* 24(1): 1–10.

Forrest, C. (2003). Has the application of salvage law to underwater cultural heritage. *Journal of Maritime Law & Commerce* 34(2): 309–342.

Giroud, S. and Lechtman, D. (2015). Art, money laundering and terrorist financing: new developments in Swiss law: art, cultural institutions and heritage law. *International Bar Association Online*. Available at: www.ibanet.org/Article/Detail. aspx?ArticleUid=1955a8f5-bdaa-447d-9b57-a95309cf350a (16 June 2018).

Gould, R. A. (2011). *Archaeology and the Social History of Ships*. Cambridge: Cambridge University Press.

International Convention on Salvage (1989). International Maritime Organization. Available at: www.jus.uio.no/lm/imo.salvage.convention.1989/doc.html (19 June 2018).

Juvelier, B. (2016). Salvaging history: underwater cultural heritage and commercial salvage. *American University International Law Review* 32(5): 1023–1045.

Kaiser, T. (1993). The antiquities market. *Journal of Field Archaeology* 20(3): 347–355.

Kingsley, S. (2001). The unexcluded past: managing shipwreck archaeology. *Minerva* 12(1): 37–43.

Kingsley, S. (2003). Odyssey marine exploration and deep-sea shipwreck archaeology: the state of the art. *Minerva* 14: 33–37.

Kleeberg, J. M. (2013). A critique of the fundamentals of the 'commercial salvage' model of the excavation of historic shipwrecks: an examination of the profitability of six commercial salvage ventures. *Technical Briefs in Historical Archaeology* 7: 19–30.

Lilley, P. (2009). *Dirty Dealing: The Untold Truth about Global Money Laundering, International Crime and Terrorism*. London: Kogan Page.

Maarleveld, T. J. (2011). Ethics, underwater cultural heritage, and international law. In Catsambis, A., Ford, B. and Hamilton, D. L. (eds.), *The Oxford Handbook of Maritime Archaeology*. Oxford: Oxford University Press: 917–941.

Manders, M. and Underwood, C. (2012). *Training Manual for the UNESCO Foundation Course on the Protection and Management of Underwater Cultural Heritage in Asia and the Pacific*. Bangkok: UNESCO.

McIntee, D. (2016). *Fortune and Glory: A Treasure Hunter's Handbook*. Oxford: Osprey Publishing.

Nemeth, E. (2007). Cultural security: the evolving role of art in international security. *Terrorism and Political Violence* 19: 19–42. Routledge.

Pickford, N. (1994). *The Atlas of Shipwreck and Treasure*. London: Dorling Kindersley.

Stemm, G. (2000). Differentiation of Shipwreck Artifacts as a Resource Management Tool. Association of Dive Contractors/Maine Technology Society UI 2000 Conference, January 2000. Available at: www.shipwreck.net (23 June 2018).

Throckmorton, P. (1998). The world's worst investment: the economics of treasure hunting with real-life comparisons. In Babits, L. E. and van Tilburg, H. (eds.), *Maritime Archaeology: A Reader of Substantive and Theoretical Contributions*. The Springer Series in Underwater Archaeology. New York: Springer: 75–83.

UNCLOS (1982). United Nations Convention on the Law of the Sea. Available at: www.un.org/depts/los/convention_agreements/convention_overview_convention.htm (16 June 2018).

UNESCO (2016). *The Impact of Treasure Hunting on Submerged Archaeological Sites*. Paris: Secretariat of the UNESCO Convention on the Protection of the Underwater Cultural Heritage.

Villegas-Zamora, T. V. (2008). The impact of commercial exploitation on the preservation of underwater cultural heritage. *Museum International* 60(4): 18–30.

Wreckwatch (2011). The sunken past: shipwrecks lost in translation. [online]. *Wreckwatch*. 28 September 2011. Available at: http://wreckwatch.wordpress.com/2011/09/28/the-sunken-past-shipwrecks-lost-in-translation (23 June 2018).

Part III

Conclusions

12 Conclusions

This book has attempted to highlight ethical issues that challenge the management of underwater cultural heritage in particular and cultural heritage in general. The approach for this goal has been to raise nine cases that questions main pillars that have been taken for granted on cultural heritage policies: valuation, uses, preservation, sustainability, intangibility, identity, human rights, politics and other practices of heritage.

Decisions on management of underwater remains need to be made based on values of the material and most of these decisions are governed by ethics (Coroneos, 2006: 111). The complex ethics of land archaeology are now being faced by underwater archaeology. When talking about ethics, is not necessarily the case that looting an underwater cultural heritage site is wrong. Ethics, as it has been explored, can involve grey scale decisions. However, although ethics aspire to be universal and resolve dilemmas, most of them need to be evaluated on a case-by-case base. In underwater cultural heritage, legal efforts have been directed to fight against treasure hunters: commercial salvage aims to bring items to the surface as efficiently and fast as possible to maximise the return on sale. Salvage techniques can be too destructive for archaeological purposes and archaeological techniques too slow for the economy of commercial salvage. For instance, the already mentioned salvage law expects the circumstances of modern shipwreck where the name and ownership is known. So it struggles with historic wrecks whose name and ownership is unknown or uncertain. It will not fail with Classical or prehistoric wrecks which did not know ownership or 'flagging' by a nation-state of modern type. This is because salvage laws and heritage laws are directed by different values: theoretically, under heritage laws, underwater excavations must provide evidence of provenance and preservation *in situ*. In practice, salvage laws (linked to commercial value) have historical precedent and prevails. In fact, and although over centuries archaeology as a field of study has advanced from searching for treasure to searching for knowledge, salvage is still in a world of treasures: the lure of sunken treasures. At the heart of these problems is the issue of funding excavations: excavating a shipwreck is an expensive venture. In fact, Bass (2003) believes that treasure hunters make more money by enticing investors than by finding treasures.

However, for some authors, the main issue surrounding commercial salvage is not concerned with the rescue of the archaeological pieces but with the commercialisation of the objects that are rescued. For archaeologists, archaeological objects can offer information in the future when technological instruments may develop: destroying or selling them can deprive humanity of essential knowledge.

Negotiations between countries or between countries and private companies stand at a crossroads (O'Keefe, 1996). It is necessary that archaeologists and salvors discover a method to ensure a balance between commercial exploitation and heritage preservation. Nevertheless, some authors are opposed to an agreement between underwater archaeologists and salvage companies: Bass (2003) claims that in the same way that land archaeologists are not asked to cooperate with tom robbers, underwater archaeologists should not be asked to cooperate with salvage companies. In this regard, one of the main factors is the traditions that are so deeply rooted in cultural heritage management. New questions are barely asked and old precepts are barely challenged. The literature still fights against old enemies and does not visualise new ones. The cultural heritage management is anchored in old controversies: like medicine, archaeology needs continuously fresh debates on newly arising dilemmas. The community is relaying its history, its past and in some way its future in the hands of archaeologists (Coroneos, 2006: 112): how the cultural heritage is going to be managed and not manipulated will build the history of an individual, a community or a national. So archaeologists should serve those communities as much as a doctor or a teacher does, with the same ethics of responsibility and diligence: they need to adapt to new obstacles as part of their responsibilities. The results of these ethical reflections are written and unwritten codes and rules. However, new development and new interest complicates the matter (Maarleveld, 2011). If those legal instruments are not carefully drafted, there is a danger that more ethical controversies will be introduced into the debate. Society needs to understand that legal tools should not be eternally untouched: they need to be continually reviewed to catch up with the developments on the field.

Table 12.1 summarises some general terms that have been studied in this book. The conclusion is that the ethical challenges that underwater cultural heritage faces share common concerns. Multidisciplinary management is the best solution to find solutions for both preservation and enjoyment of underwater cultural heritage.

The first conclusion to highlight from this book is that although the 2001 UNESCO Convention for the Protection of the Underwater Cultural Heritage (UNESCO, 2001) set 100 years as the limit for the protection of the underwater cultural heritage, the reality is that some sites must be treated as being more significant than others. The definition, claiming a time number, not only excludes important sites but also includes not so important sites. The definition should be the basis for a valuation and appreciation of the

Table 12.1 Key terms for each case study

	Violin Titanic	Ancient lead	Climate change	In situ	Watery graves	Nationless shipwrecks	Migrant shipwrecks	South China Sea	Treasure hunters
Valuation	*	*	*	*	*	*	*	*	*
Uses	*	*		*				*	*
Intangible	*								
Politics			*		*	*	*	*	*
Identity					*	*	*	*	
Sustainability	*	*	*	*	*	*	*		*
Management		*	*	*		*	*	*	
Sociology						*	*	*	*
Human rights					*	*	*		
Tourism	*			*	*				
Mankind	*	*	*		*	*	*	*	*
History	*	*			*	*	*	*	*
Memory	*					*	*		*
Restitution	*	*			*	*			*
Colonialism		*	*	*	*	*	*	*	*
Context	*	*	*	*	*			*	*
Access	*	*		*	*				*
Pollution		*	*	*	*				
Cooperation	*				*	*	*	*	*
Diplomacy					*	*	*	*	*
Definition	*	*	*	*	*		*		

underwater cultural heritage and not according to a time limit. The law sometimes seems to decide upon what is and what is not heritage and what should or should not be protected: the violin of the *Titanic*, being a unique piece of heritage, is not protected under the 2001 UNESCO Convention; however, the 1,000 ingots of ancient lead with no particularities among them are protected.

Another conclusion is the fact that underwater cultural heritage management embraces a wide variety of groups—academics, tourism, education, coastal development and even private companies (Kingsley, 2011)—also rises controversy since excluding any of these groups from the management policies means that those groups will still carry out their business but in a controversial way. It is necessary to think about the general benefit, consider the own goals and be flexible with other points of view. For instance, according to Bederman (1999) the fishing industry has been the largest user and destroyer of wrecks as artificial reefs. However, fishing cannot be forbidden just for the benefit of the preservation of the underwater cultural heritage. Only rules for their coexistence can be established. A major controversy that has been common to all case studies has been the duality between individual and humanity. The violin of the *Titanic* chapter has highlighted the private property of the violin against the right to enjoy it by humanity. In the case of the ancient lead, however, there is a case of dispute between humanity against humanity: a knowledge benefit for humanity against knowledge also for the benefit of humanity. In the case of the human remains, the dilemma is the private interests of a family to recover the body against the public interest that a body can offer as a source of knowledge: heritage hold by private owners should be able to be enjoyed by the public. Climate change establishes a controversy between the preservation *in situ* that benefits knowledge sought by archaeologists as stewardships against their visibility of those sites available to humanity if they continue to be preserved *in situ*. Also migrant shipwrecks or nationless shipwrecks, the South China Sea or the issue of treasure hunters bring controversies between the individual benefit or the human right to enjoy the underwater cultural heritage.

Preservation for the future is an established precept, the reason being that we will have more tools that will help to analyse and research the heritage with more developed techniques. However, there will always be the possibility of having better techniques but no shipwrecks will endure forever. In addition, preserving for future generations implies deciding for future generations although it is impossible to know what future generations will want. It is time to protect for the present, trying to establish policies that can help other fields to develop. Sometimes it is impossible to protect the entire heritage as their proposed function. It is essential not to be trapped by melancholia and pragmatics and start being flexible. Creating a hierarchy of values will help us to evaluate the importance of the heritage to preserve. The past is a renewable resource since there will always be a past. There will also be a heritage to protect and as time passes, the amount of heritage will multiply, and we will be talking of 'accumulation' of heritage (Harrison, 2013). We have to learn how to lose part of the heritage since it may mean that the essential heritage that should be preserved is lost for being too abundant and that heritage will stop being appreciated for being 'especial' and will start being 'normal'.

Specific proposals

Some solutions have been proposed for each of the ethical controversies raised in this book (Table 12.2):

Valuation: the violin of the Titanic

After the discussion of the valuation of the violin, it was concluded that the violin, for the different values that it has been bestowed with (even the economic and 'prosthetic' ones) is now considered to be part of the heritage of the *Titanic*. However, it is currently in private hands and can therefore not be appreciated by everyone. In order to comply with this requirement, this study proposes two alternatives, which can be applied to any object of heritage under the same circumstances: if the violin is considered by the government, heritage managers or visitors to be public property, then it has to be recognised as such according to its importance, not by the time it has been underwater. It can also be recognised as an object of the collection from the *Titanic*, and as a consequence it cannot be separated from the main collection. It can also be transformed to be played, highlighting its value as a sound window, as a spreader of emotions. As a consequence, if one of these valuations is important enough to establish the violin as public property, then the government, under the right of expropriation, could force the owner to sell the violin in order to make it accessible to the public. However,

Table 12.2 Proposed solution for each of the case studies

Chapter	Proposal
3. Valuation: the violin of the *Titanic*	Change in the status
4. Uses: ancient lead for dark matter experiments	Animals' protocol
5. Preservation: climate change	Natural/cultural partnership
6. Sustainability: preservation *in situ*	Sustainable blue cultural heritage
7. Intangibility: watery graves	Intangible/invisible/absent
8. Identity: nationless shipwrecks	Agreements
9. Human rights: migrant shipwrecks	Grave memorialisation and survivor camps
10. Politics: the South China Sea	Diplomacy
11. Other practices: treasure hunters and money laundering	Plan of action

if this option seems excessive, then the government can also apply 'the right of first refusal' or 'the right of repurchase', which would make it the first and preferred buyer in the case of a new sale or it could have retrospective character and repeat the auction, with the government as the preferred buyer. However, if it is established that the violin is considered private property because of its economic value, the one that is paramount in its valuation, then the violin can still be of public benefit if a condition of public accessibility is established. In this sense, the owner would also benefit from this option because the violin, as a heritage item, could be included on the World Heritage lists, gaining prestige as a result. As a consequence, in a future sale, the violin would be revaluated as an object of World Heritage and its economic value would increase.

Uses: ancient lead for dark matter experiments

The case of using ancient lead for particle physics experiments opens a debate as to whether its use should be allowed if it is detrimental to underwater cultural heritage. This chapter has proposed establishing a protocol of intervention, which means that this study agrees with the utilisation of underwater cultural heritage for uses other than archaeological ones. Several reasons support this choice. For instance, the uses of underwater cultural heritage object for experiments on dark matter could be established under an agreement with archaeologists that does not contravene the 2001 UNESCO Convention, except in the integrity of material, keeping collections together and trading of objects. Preservation *in situ*, although it is not complied with, means that the phrasing of the article 'considered as the first option' does not prohibit its recovery. This study also suggests, however, that although some uses can be allowed, there should be a mandatory impact assessment of these activities. Firstly, the uses of these underwater cultural heritage objects will need to be carefully weighted. They will have to benefit humanity, they will have to disclose all information on experiments and they will have to be able to demonstrate that no other material can be used in place of the underwater cultural heritage material. In addition, there should be agreements that the material will be used according to strict scientific protocols. As a consequence, the protocols, although not preventing the loss of the material, would guarantee that the information gained from the lead would be beneficial to humanity as a whole.

Preservation: climate change

The main point of concern highlighted by this study has been the separation of the different heritage that composes the seas: the differentiation between natural and cultural heritage prejudices in the fight against the effects of climate change. The chapter proposes the inclusion of underwater cultural heritage alongside natural heritage preservation policies. This measure will offer a more specific protection to underwater cultural heritage that can be affected by climate change more in line with coral reef protection than, for instance, protection of archaeological sites located on land. Therefore, underwater cultural heritage would be protected under environmental standards, considering the oceans and shipwrecks to be indivisible. This step would allow a pooling of resources against the adverse effects of climate change. In addition, four steps have been proposed by this study: recognising loss—that although climate change will destroy some heritage sites, it will also create new heritage; starting the debate—only by triggering the challenge will solutions be found; creating a legal framework—since the 2001 convention does not mention climate change, countries will have difficulty incorporating international measures into their national policies; and finally, recognising underwater cultural heritage as a natural resource.

Sustainability: preservation in situ

Preservation of underwater cultural heritage and accessibility has to find the right balance in order to allow underwater cultural heritage to be preserved and appreciated by future generations. However, tourism has always been a difficult concept to balance with preservation and as a consequence, the concept of sustainability is essential in this debate, opening the door to the concept of 'blue cultural heritage': underwater cultural heritage sites can be places to visit and learn from. However, its accessibility depends upon the method of preservation. Some underwater cultural heritage can be recovered and exhibited in museums where it is accessible to all. However, this will not be possible in all cases. Some of it will have to be preserved *in situ* as a diving site or even as an underwater museum. Preservation *in situ*, as a consequence, is still considered to be the primary option, not only because underwater cultural heritage is best protected under water, but also because, as has already been mentioned in this study, not all shipwrecks can be recovered. The options that have already been suggested for the accessibility of underwater cultural heritage sites (such as underwater submarine parks or museums) would become a reality—which may face threats in the future but will, nevertheless, allow the public to enjoy and understand the underwater cultural heritage sites. This understanding will help to protect these sites for future generations.

Intangibility: watery graves

This study has attempted to highlight two main controversies arising from the management of human remains on underwater cultural heritage. The first one is the existence of those shipwrecks which were a scene of a humanitarian tragedy but that do not contain human remains. The second one is the consideration of those scenarios that, although the shipwrecks are of special scientific or educational interest, still have surviving relatives of the original crew; or are shipwrecks with passengers that are not included on the 'standard' countries' ownership. As a consequence, this study has proposed a new categorisation of these scenarios under three main labels: intangible heritage, absent heritage and invisible heritage. Under the first category, shipwrecks containing human remains would be considered as 'venerated sites' which are part of a community cultural space, and as a consequence would be considered intangible cultural heritage. The other two categories of the shipwrecks as absent and invisible heritage. The treatment of human remains on underwater cultural heritage sites as 'invisible heritage' would imply the consideration of shipwrecks as 'cemeteries' for those human remains that were once on there but have now disappeared. The shipwreck would then leave their 'footprints'—human remains that may have disappeared, but still need to be respected. A final option has been considered by this study, which is the treatment of human remains as 'absent heritage', which would imply that the shipwrecks are a 'frame' of what is no longer there. These human remains would be considered 'absent presence'. The consequence would be the memorialisation of those shipwrecks as 'containers' of sacred remains.

Identity: nationless shipwrecks

The return of cultural objects as a compensation element to colonised countries has been largely discussed in the literature. However, the issue is more complicated when considering newly created nations whose territories used to belong to other nations that still exist today. The debate on state succession and territorial provenance has complicated this issue further. However, the return of those objects is not the only solution for those countries that feel that these cultural objects are part of their 'roots'. Firstly, the acknowledgement of the objects provenance by the guardian country is a diplomatic movement that eases the tensions between the nations involved. However, other solutions such as permanent or temporary loans, common exhibitions or collective projects will share the cultural object between the interested countries, thereby avoiding exclusivity and making cultural heritage sites accessible to more people from different backgrounds and from different parts of the world.

Human rights: migrant shipwrecks

Human rights raise complicated issues in relation to the management of underwater cultural heritage, especially in relation to migrant and slave shipwrecks. This chapter has suggested two proposals to honour and remember the victims of those shipwrecks: grave memorialisation since declaring refugees as war victims will guarantee recognition, which is sometimes enough for their families or their communities. There is a strong emotional component in shipwrecks, and their memorialisation as proof of an active position by governments will help to heal traumas. Watery graves are, again, an emotional salve to an everyday trauma. The second proposal is treating shipwrecks as survivor camps: these camps are an essential source of information on a shipwreck where survivors have attempted to survive after the wreck event. This example of settlement can be thought of as being modern refugee camps where new cultures, new ways of life and new areas cultural heritage are born as a consequence of a maritime journey.

Politics: the South China Sea

Cooperation between countries and organisations is an essential precept for the management of underwater cultural heritage. However, complex political strategies often prioritise their own ambitions over common interests. This chapter suggests diplomacy as a tool to conduct relationships between international actors. Underwater cultural heritage can be used as an excuse for diplomatic goals. Countries trying to balance their position on the international stage could manage their underwater cultural heritage protecting what is theirs but understanding that is also a common, international heritage. Agreements between countries for protecting underwater cultural heritage in international waters, or underwater cultural heritage with links to different nations can alleviate tensions created by other nationalistic objectives. The chapter has highlighted China's strategy on controlling its maritime cultural heritage in order to control a broader maritime territory, which brings broader fishing areas, access to more mineral resources and capacity for creating more national security. Just by 'managing' their maritime cultural heritage, the benefits brought to the country will be difficult to achieve by other means. This management is manipulated in such a way that other countries cannot go against it; which reminds us, once again, of the importance of underwater cultural heritage not only for its archaeological value but also for its other numerous values—in this specific case as a diplomatic instrument.

Other practices: treasure hunters and money laundering

Treasure hunting and looting of underwater sites has been one of the main objectives for the international community to tackle. The main literature and legal instruments are again focused on fighting these businesses that are more focused on the retrieval of the archaeological objects themselves, than on acquiring archaeological data. In addition, the commercialisation of these objects is seen by the archaeological community as a major problem. However, the full implications of this commercialisation seem to be more complicated than the loss of the heritage. Money laundering and terrorism financing appear to be involved in the sale of underwater cultural heritage objects. And although these markets are difficult to control, managing the underwater cultural heritage could help to restrict these illegal businesses.

Exposing illicit underwater archaeology; reporting unprovenanced cultural heritage objects; judging the integrity of museums, private collectors and auction houses; understanding the ethics behind the illicit trade; discussing the combinations of laws, both those against money laundering and those protecting the cultural heritage; exploring individual cases; applying historical knowledge to the present-day problem; and making the public part of both the problems and solutions can help to combine efforts to tackle money laundering policy makers and to assist cultural heritage policy makers. Once again, global challenges can benefit from the establishment of thorough underwater cultural heritage management policies.

General proposals

Underwater cultural heritage is, as said, a vast resource and as a consequence we need to be selective for its protection. The decision has to be based on technical, political and legal decisions. For some authors (Aznar-Gómez, 2004), however, underwater heritage is still an abandoned form of heritage which is neglected and forgotten. This work has tried to demonstrate that underwater cultural heritage is also a threatened heritage, both socially and legally: although international legal instruments have been already devoted to the protection of underwater cultural heritage, international agreements are binding only upon governments but not on an individual or group if they are not incorporated into national law (Carman, 2013).

The definition of underwater cultural heritage by the limit of 100 years under the 2001 UNESCO Convention has been concluded by this book as one of the main damaging articles to all the case studies that this work has presented. Only a definition of underwater cultural heritage by significance through award of values guarantees that the main pieces of heritage will be preserved for the future of humanity. In view of these results, this study would like to propose two alternatives to the consideration of a shipwreck, an object or a site as part of underwater cultural heritage:

Seeing it in a bigger picture

A first solution for the definition of underwater cultural heritage would be its classification into four categories based on physical mobility: underwater cultural heritage can be both movable *and* immovable, but it is also an archaeological field as well as an object immersed in the sea: the vessels, the anchors or even whole shipwrecks must be considered as movable goods; after all, they can be and are moved, as the *Mary Rose* was. However, they could also be considered as an immovable object, especially if the hull cannot be lifted. In addition, the physical context of these items is crucial to their understanding (Bator, 1981: 65) and as a consequence underwater cultural heritage can also be considered as an archaeological field. Finally, for being an object that ultimately belongs to the sea (since oceans are the last place of destination of shipwrecks) they can also be considered as objects in the sea. The result of this classification is its protection from different legislation other than the 2001 UNESCO Convention (UNESCO, 2001). The UNESCO Conventions have to be combined in order to be suitable for all range of underwater cultural heritage sites. In this regard, six main Conventions stand as guidelines on the protection of heritage that could be applied to underwater cultural heritage, namely from the most recent one: the 2005 Convention on the Protection and Promotion of the Diversity of Cultural Expressions (UNESCO, 2005), the 2003 Convention for the Safeguarding of the Intangible Cultural Heritage (UNESCO, 2003), the 2001 UNESCO Convention on the Protection of the Underwater Cultural Heritage (UNESCO, 2001), the 1972 Convention concerning the Protection of the World Cultural and Natural Heritage (UNESCO, 1972), the 1970 Convention on the Means of Prohibiting and Preventing the Illicit Import, Export and Transfer of Ownership of Cultural Property (UNESCO, 1970) or the 1954 Convention for the Protection of Cultural Property in the Event of Armed Conflict (UNESCO, 1954). None of them have a sole article excluding other legal instruments for protection of the heritage, and, as a consequence, can be combined. International regulations also allow the placing of underwater cultural heritage in other heritage contexts, establishing comparisons and choosing the most appropriated situation for each circumstance since some of the issues that have arisen are related to the definition and classification that the legislation applies to each heritage. However, one of the main lessons learned from this study is that the law means what it says, and, what is more important, it does not mean what it does not say. Therefore, applying the legal instruments to underwater cultural heritage has to be managed in conformity with what the law *says* in order to avoid second interpretations and manipulations that can be as damaging to the heritage as the lack of legislation.

Seeing it as a process of yes or no questions

The second proposal is for consideration of a shipwreck, object or site as underwater cultural heritage according to a 'questionnaire' where at least one of the requirements has to be fulfilled. The process would be based on values classification. The first question would be: does the site contain human remains? If it does, three options can be contemplated depending on culture or relatives' choice: recovering them, leaving them or treating the shipwreck as a grave that will require preservation. In this last option, the shipwreck can be preserved as a cemetery—a mere watery grave—or as a memorial, enhancing its significance for society. If human remains are not contained on the shipwreck, a new question should be asked: does the site have heritage value? In this category we would include its value as a source of knowledge, as a unique element, as an element with historical, scientific, aesthetic significance or social significance, as an element in unique condition or as an element with interpretative potential. If any of these requirements is fulfilled, the shipwreck, site or object will need to be preserved and protected by law. However, if it is not, we will have to answer the next question: does the site have touristic value? Maybe the shipwreck, object or site is spectacular, and it could attract tourism or maybe it is known or famous because of the media or the film and has created an interest in society—as in the violin of the *Titanic*. And in these possible circumstances, it should be preserved. If none of these cases exist and tourism may not be an option for it, we should ask the last question: does the site have any other value? For instance, in the case of the shipwrecks, it may have a value as a natural reef that requires its preservation, so it does not alter the fauna and the natural equilibrium of the place. If none of these requirements is accomplished, the shipwreck, object or site should not be considered underwater cultural heritage in order not to fall into an accumulation of heritage which requires being selective. In this regard, if it is a shipwreck that is left outside this consideration for her 'insignificance', questions about her risk to navigation should be asked. If she is a risk, should she be lifted or destroyed? If it is not, it is time to evaluate if the shipwreck, object or site has other uses such as a source for other disciplines (i.e., ancient ingots). If that is the case, heritage makers need to learn to let go of the heritage if the right provisions are taken. If any of these requirements are accomplished, the shipwreck, site or object should be preserved. Its preservation will depend on various factors such as policymakers' decisions, culture or funding but four main outcomes can be explored: as a museum piece—inside or outside the water. Its main problem would be the maintenance. It could include monitoring or visiting policies such as scuba diving visits or museum entrance, as a watery grave (preserved for respect although it would face a problem of possible disturbance), as 'mere' underwater cultural heritage (to be treated as such but not practise any option towards it, just preserving its existence), as a 'new-labelled' heritage (intangible, absent, invisible or as part of natural heritage), as new concepts that have to be assimilated and explored, and other legal instruments may be applied.

This study is aware that this proposal is too ambitious and careful measures should be taken. However, the preservation of underwater cultural heritage needs a pro-active point of view, opening new possibilities and risk in order not to fall into a spiral of accumulation of heritage that will de-evaluate the one that really matters. In addition, this is a solution that would remove from the legislation its power of decision on definition of underwater cultural heritage, so it could carry out its true function: protection of what it has already defined as underwater cultural heritage.

'Immediate [...] problems are frequently linked with much larger ones' (Colwell-Chanthaphonh et al., 2008: 45). The study has outlined the procedures related to the formation, management and preservation of cultural heritage and has examined closely nine cases in which these issues have arisen. It has also considered the extent to which existent legislations are adequate to address any concerns regarding these controversies. This book concludes that although the law is a key mechanism for the protection of underwater cultural heritage that maintains accepted principles and ethics, the objective that the law targets—treasure hunters—is a relative minor risk compared with the legal threats that the law obviates. In addition, legal mechanisms fail to legislate on new values because the drafting process is slower than the breakthroughs in the field of cultural heritage studies. While the white and black matters are well defined and protected, the grey areas that the law does not specifically cover can be interpreted as leading to a loss of underwater cultural heritage. As a consequence, legislation should serve as a guideline on the protection instead of being a decisive instrument. Although non-legal studies in cultural heritage studies are not trained to discern the contradictions of legal instruments this book has been able to discuss those contradictions in relation to cultural heritage matters. International law cannot be ignored on cultural heritage studies but nor can it be the deciding instrument. Kingsley (2011: 225) claims that time will prove that the 2001 UNESCO Convention is restricted in scope and not the 'Holy Grail that heritage bodies believe': the 2001 Convention benefits of being a non-funded convention with an annex. Updating this annex should be seen as a real possibility: new actions to stop the damaging effects on underwater cultural heritage by an 'out-to-date' legislation should be taken.

Recommendations for future research

There are some areas of research in the topic that have been briefly explored but that are necessary to develop: other ethical dilemmas, such as the changes of 'ownership' of the countries, the birth of new cultural heritage or the dangers carried out by development works. These issues are worth being addressed in the future. They are topics that will have an impact on the preservation of cultural heritage sooner or later. As, already said, positing new cases is fundamental but complex and controversial (Tarlow, 2006). This work has also addressed when cultural heritage becomes cultural heritage but it has not addressed when it ceased to be so: researches into this dilemma deserve another book. The line that future research in the area should pursue is, as a consequence, directed to look for new solutions for that heritage that matters because of its 'valuation' and more importantly, letting go of that heritage which is not of much importance. It is time to step forward and accept that heritage may have other values for other people.

Final findings

This book has been written in order to provoke some discussion on values, significance of underwater cultural heritage and its legal protection. Three last considerations want to be highlighted. First is that one of the most striking conclusions that has been determined is that the economic value in heritage only exists when and if other values have been bestowed. It is the process of becoming heritage that makes it valuable for the profit market. As a consequence, it is necessary to understand that the economic value of an object of heritage exists because the heritage has been valued as such. However, it is an intrinsic value of heritage that it can be prioritised or not, depending on the steward or the community. Second, it has been resolved that the literature in the field fills their pages on what to preserve and why it is so important to preserve. However, the academic field has barely dared to talk about what not to preserve and why it is not worth protecting. Setting the precedents of neglecting some heritage will avoid an accumulation of heritage and the heritage that is decided to be preserved after it is bestowed with value will be more appreciated. It might be that a solution in this regard may be the comparison of different heritage in order to organise them into a hierarchy according to its importance. Finally, it is necessary to address new questions: underwater cultural heritage is still work in progress. This work in progress demands that each technical dilemma is looked at from the point of view of the ethical debate and then the legal instruments to protect the underwater cultural heritage should take the risk, present the dilemmas to the political agendas and find solutions.

Bibliography

Aznar-Gómez, M. J. (2004). *La protección internacional del patrimonio cultural subacuático con especial referencia al caso de España*. Valencia: Tirant Lo Blanch.
Bass, G. F. (2003). The ethics of shipwreck archaeology. In Zimmerman, L. J., Vitelli, J. D. and Hollowell-Zimmer, J. (eds.), *Ethical Issues in Archaeology*. Oxford: Alta Mira Press: 57–70.
Bator, P. M. (1981). *The International Trade in Art*. London: University of Chicago Press.
Bederman, D. J. (1999). The UNESCO Draft Convention on Underwater Cultural Heritage: A Critique and Counter-Proposal. *Journal of Maritime Law and Commerce* 30(2): 331–362.
Carman, J. (2013). Legislation in archaeology: overview and introduction. In Smith, C. (ed.), *Encyclopaedia of Global Archaeology*. New York: Springer: 4469–4485.
Colwell-Chanthaphonh, C., Hollowell, J. and McGill, D. (2008). *Ethics in Action: Case Studies in Archaeological Dilemmas*. Washington, DC: Society for American Archaeology, SAA Press.
Coroneos, C. (2006). The ethics and values of maritime archaeology. In Staniforth, M. and Nash, M. (eds.), *Maritime Archaeology: Australian Approaches*. New York: Springer: 111–122.
Harrison, R. (2013). *Heritage: Critical Approaches*. New York: Routledge.
Kingsley, S. (2011). Challenges of maritime archaeology: in too deep. In King, T. F. (ed.), *A Companion to Cultural Resource Management*. Chichester: Wiley-Blackwell: 223–244.
Maarleveld, T. J. (2011). Ethics, underwater cultural heritage, and international law. In Catsambis, A., Ford, B. and Hamilton, D. L. (eds.), *The Oxford Handbook of Maritime Archaeology*. Oxford: Oxford University Press: 917–941.

O'Keefe, P. (1996). Protecting the underwater cultural heritage: the international law association draft convention. *Marine Policy* 20(4): 297–307.

Tarlow, S. (2006). Archaeological ethics and the people of the past. In Scarre, C. and Scarre, G. (eds.), *The Ethics of Archaeology: Philosophical Perspectives on Archaeological Practice*. Cambridge: Cambridge University Press: 199–217.

UNESCO (1954). Convention for the Protection of Cultural Property in the Event of Armed Conflict with Regulations or the Execution of the Convention 1954, The Hague, 14 May 1954. Available at: http://portal.unesco.org/en/ev.php-URL_ID=13637&URL_DO=DO_TOPIC&URL_SECTION=201.html (4 September 2018).

UNESCO (1970). Convention on the Means of Prohibition and Preventing the Illicit Import, Export and Transfer of Ownership of Cultural Property 1970, Paris, 14 November 1970. Available at: http://portal.unesco.org/en/ev.php-URL_ID=13039&URL_DO=DO_TOPIC&URL_SECTION=201.html (4 September 2018).

UNESCO (1972). Convention concerning the Protection of the World Cultural and Natural Heritage, Paris, 16 November 1972. Available at: http://whc.unesco.org/en/conventiontext/. (4 September 2018)

UNESCO (2001). Convention on the Protection of the Underwater Cultural Heritage, Paris, 2 November 2001. Available at: http://unesdoc.unesco.org/images/0012/001260/126065e.pdf (4 September 2018).

UNESCO (2003). Convention for the Safeguarding of the Intangible Cultural Heritage 2003, Paris, 17 October 2003. Available at: http://portal.unesco.org/en/ev.php-URL_ID=17716&URL_DO=DO_TOPIC&URL_SECTION=201.html (4 September 2018).

UNESCO (2005). Convention on the Protection and Promotion of the Diversity of Cultural Expressions 2005, Paris, 20 October 2005. Available at: http://portal.unesco.org/en/ev.php-URL_ID=31038&URL_DO=DO_TOPIC&URL_SECTION=201.html (4 September 2018).

Afterword

The journey undertaken by our ship, *Heritage*, ends here.
She has become a shipwreck.
For many this may be a misfortune but for us,
a sunken ship is a new opportunity to manage and protect
underwater cultural heritage for the benefit of mankind.

Index

Made in United States
North Haven, CT
02 February 2024